THE BEST IS YET . . .

MORRIS L. ERNST

THE BEST
IS YET...

HARPER & BROTHERS
PUBLISHERS
New York · London

THE BEST IS YET . . .

Copyright, 1945, by Margaret S. Ernst
Printed in the United States of America

4-5

FIRST EDITION

C-U

To Aunt Sis—

WHO KNOWS WHAT LIFE IS ABOUT

CONTENTS

[vii]

THE BEST IS YET...

I HAVE been playing in a science laboratory for nearly twenty years. It's a small laboratory on Nantucket Island —a garden on one side of our home and the beach and water out to the cutter *Truant's* mooring on the other side. It's plenty big. Enough unsolved phenomena of nature perform for us each day to keep us in a constant questioning mood. We wonder about the left-handedness of birds, the clarity of sound underwater, the slow march of the magnetic pole toward what we call the North Pole, the rhythm of the tides and wind and weather. Aside from a barometer and a Kenyon Weathercaster, we have no scientific equipment. In fact, we frolic along in simple amazement amidst the imponderable *x*'s of nature. Imponderable at least to us. And when we confront our friends who have scientific training with questions about the schizophrenia of our nondreaming hound, or the migratory sex urge of eels, we are met with disdain and such varied solutions that we let them alone and go back once more to the encyclopedias in the Athenaeum Library, downtown Nantucket.

Keeping science notes has been fun. They are notes only in the sense of recording observations, asking questions and propounding usually improbable answers. Maybe in historic terms the most improbable answers are nearest the truth in the realms of natural science.

With thousands of words of notes I approached Cass Canfield of Harper & Brothers. For some odd reason— maybe because we live so much with authors and publishers —I have been infected with the author disease. Cass said he was amused, and as far as I could discover knew none of the answers to my queries but said it was no book.

[xi]

Once more he asked me to do an autobiography—a kind of country-city lawyer volume with behind-the-scenes law office tales. I explained why I couldn't do that kind of book. Clients might tell their stories from their side of the table. The episodes belong to them and them alone. I'm quite sure I would be unable, even if emotionally willing, to camouflage other people's secrets. The results would be stilted and far from the truth. Likewise, episodes—exciting at least to me on the periphery of our political life—are not my stories, my secrets to tell. In fact, the most precious parts of life cannot ever be related.

And then Cass, the incorrigible publisher, suggested I do a kind of free-wheeling series of pieces about sailing and censorship, carpentry and law, Joyce's *Ulysses* and Mayor Hague of Jersey City, Banking Board experiences and deafness—in short, a book about what has interested me. A gracious good fortune has given me innumerable opportunities to pitch for freedom on many fronts. I'm reminded that once in England years ago I thought of giving a party to some of the British authors whose works I have defended—Havelock Ellis, Marie Stopes, Radclyffe Hall, James Joyce—to name a few.

It's been a life of unbelievably lucky breaks. Maybe it's two lives—one in Nantucket with cruising and carpentry; the other in the most exciting of professions, the law, with its tangents of governmental service in insurance, banking, coal mining, and other fields.

I sent a draft of the manuscript to Connie, my daughter who was working on radio for OWI in London. While robots were driving her from her flat she wrote, "I'm returning your old Omar Khayyám. I know the stories so well that I think I made them up myself." My son Roger, first-class private in Civil Affairs, also in London, suggested changes in organization of the volume—a Maypole figure came to his mind, the pole being the fight for freedom of man's spirit. Joan, the youngest, out West riding horses in the Rockies, was most amused at the chapter about her deafness. Then my wife

Margaret—a real author—took up sledge hammers held only by etymologists.

Three other members of the household know much about me. For twenty years Kitty O'Connor has been sneaking too many onions into the hamburgers, while Josephine Houlihan fussed about my dragging sand through the living room at Nantucket. And Delia—our children's nurse, retired and now our annual visiting assistant gardener—Delia, whose grace is part of all of us, is too gentle to be critical. These seven are my immediate audience, my background, my old friends.

At first I called the book "It's Been Fun," but someone at Harper's innocently made a notation on the margin when halfway through—"So Far So Good." And that's the title.

Years ago Heywood Broun and Ruth Hale came to the office to see me about a situation which troubled them sorely. Ruth, an archfeminist then married to Heywood, choked a trifle and then asked me to do her a great personal favor. And before I could answer, she said, "I hate to ask favors. This is the first I have asked of anyone in years. But I can ask you because your cup is running over."

I still think it is my nicest compliment. And so far life has been good to me.

P.S.

After the book was in type I learned that gracious Charlie Towne had a volume ready for publication using the title— So Far So Good. So, good luck, Charlie.

A mad quick shift had to be made. I have always cherished these lines from Browning's "Rabbi Ben Ezra":

> Grow old along with me!
> The best is yet to be,
> The last of life, for which the first was made:

From this I chose The Best Is Yet . . . as the title. I adopt it without fingers crossed—knowing full well how unimportant titles are.

THE BEST IS YET . . .

CHAPTER I

CONNIE SENT ME A LETTER Russell Maloney, of the New Yorker, wrote her to England. Russell and a gang were playing that game where a group names a flower, a picture, a color, and a piece of music, and the player who has left the room tries to guess the person typified by these objects. It seems the guess was Gandhi, and the group had me in mind.

All of which proves the difficulty of description. But if I tried to pick the one word that summed up what I have done with the game of living, I'm sure the word would be "luck." Others no doubt would pick less kindly words, but I know it's luck. Aside from Joan's deafness, which has turned out to be a victory for her and a great education for all who know her, my life has been such a consistent chain of good fortune that long ago I stopped knocking on wood.

Typical of my kindly fate was the morning when I rode on top of the Fifth Avenue bus to the office. Invariably, I sat below. Seldom do I smoke before I get to the office. But one morning I lit a cigarette as I walked down the stoop. I hadn't finished by the time I got to the corner. I didn't throw the cigarette away, and went upstairs on the bus. A few blocks up the Avenue an acquaintance sat down next to me. I hadn't seen him for months, maybe as much as a year. We chatted. Would I come to his house and meet some of his industrial associates that evening? I would. There resulted a friendship, an exciting exploration, and a client relationship of high merit.

Let the experts who figure out mathematical probabilities

play with that one. It's like looking at a thousand Yale locks and, with a single key, picking out the lock to fit. It's like the chance of a monkey at a typewriter in time writing the dictionary. And so do I see my whole life as a series of lucky chances.

During college days I knew Herb Wolff and Laurie and Eddie Greenbaum, later to be my partners for life. No ordinary written partnership agreement has ever existed between us, for as lawyers we know that there are relationships in life which rest on values not enhanced by legal writings. After college I had to give up hope of practicing law. My generous father, with a rare intuition of the future growth of Manhattan, just guessed on too many key spots, spread his investments too thin and could not afford a daytime law education for me. As a result, I went into business.

Today it seems improbable but true that as treasurer of a shirt company I spent unexciting days at a factory on the Gowanus Canal in Brooklyn keeping books for the production of men's shirts at $4.50 a dozen. Ugly shirts—with colored cuffs and bosoms and white bodies. Shirts marketed by sitting in outer offices of retail stores as a beggar waiting to see and "get in" with the buyers. The name we took for the business was to assure success: USONA, the trick being that it stood for United States of North America. The company did well and I lost none of my $3,000 borrowed investment as a one-third owner. But in all truth, it did much better after I left to go into a job in the retail furniture installment business near Gates Avenue, Brooklyn. Here again I was a sort of bookkeeper and office manager, seldom buying but often helping on the floor selling to newlyweds who wanted to buy more on credit than they could afford. Installment selling in our economy, if fully appreciated, reveals a great deal about our mores. The great art is to find out how much the customer's salary really amounts to. Coming in to fit out his home, with his prospective bride on his arm, he is anxious to show off. Nothing is too good for his girl. It was delicate fun discovering the nature of his job without offending. We

[2]

couldn't say with directness: "What do you earn each week? If it's $20, you can afford only 10 per cent, or $2 a week for furnishing your home, and we can give you only a hundred weeks to pay off. That limits you to a $200 outfit. So please keep your bride's eyes away from that $18 lamp."

It was difficult to hold the purchase down in amount. And even if the purchase was limited, a furniture credit man is also at times the head of a marriage clinic. Many times a couple who had looked well adjusted while they were selecting beds and bureaus would telephone in a week for the store to take back all the goods. When they came in to explain the reason, it often developed that the furniture store was in the middle of a terrific family battle. The home was to be broken up over such a serious issue as where the serving table should stand in the dining room. Then a gift from the store of that lamp the lady had eyed would patch up the fight.

I learned much. I did well—earning big money for a youngster and always feeling that I was overpaid. But though learning, it wasn't my dish. Still I was boxed. Life had me in a corner. Married, living up on West End Avenue in Manhattan, two hours in the subway six days a week, with Saturday night at the store until midnight, was less than the kind of living I wanted. But one night, at the old St. Nicholas ice-skating rink, I met Herbert Carlebach, a classmate of high-school days. Herbert had a high hat before any other boy of my acquaintance (I never had one), he was socially popular and ambitious. He told me he was in Wall Street, but studying law at night. If he could do it, why shouldn't I make a try at it? I went home and the very next morning registered at New York Law School. Suppose I had not gone ice-skating?

Then for a year or more, on casual meetings with my future and present partners, I jestingly said, "Whenever you are finished clerking and ready to start a firm, give me a ring." They did so. Then and now, this luck seems little short of a roulette wheel's consistently hitting the same number. It has been one of my greatest good fortunes, although I've

[3]

been a terrible worry to them at times. They didn't always like my representation of causes which were less than popular and often at the time less than respectable. But they stood it with unbelievable generosity.

Margaret and I met by merest chance and under circumstances close to duress. I know that most meetings in life are chance, but this one had an odd twist—I could have missed a great hunk of joy by the slightest turn of the wheel.

And Nantucket, a rich portion of our lives, was first mentioned casually by Elsie and Howard Cullman. They had been there the previous summer. Margaret and I went up one dismal windy weekend in April, twenty years ago. Found no cottage to rent but left our name at a hotel. Someone might give up a reservation. And here we are with deep roots on this island.

It's no answer to say there might have been other partners, another Margaret and another island for full living. There might have been. But it's quite inconceivable that they could have been as tender, as satisfactory, as desirable as what I've had.

"Luck" is the word for it and I'm not at all superstitious. Some people have it and some haven't. Many good friends of ours have runs of bad luck, and I mean something more significant even than illness or death or financial setback.

Maybe luck is the sequel to suffering at some fortunate stage of life. Ten years ago Judge Brandeis asked me what people thought of Franklin Roosevelt in New York. I said that some few people thought he was too casual. The Judge looked at me and asked, "Have you ever suffered?" I said, "Sure." He asked, "How often?" "Three times," I answered glibly. The old judge said, "No one has suffered more than once. But if you recall your suffering, whether it was a death, or physical pain, or financial insecurity, you will recall that you were very casual to life during that period of pain. Money meant nothing to you. You were objective to all around you. And this great man Roosevelt was on his back for a year and didn't know whether he would ever get up to make another

[4]

speech. No wonder," said the Judge, "he could send a message to Congress on an agricultural bill saying in effect: 'This
is a good bill. I hope it works. If it doesn't, I'll let you
know.'"

When one has been near death as was F.D.R., a perspective is born, issues take on proper proportions, and values
carry within themselves a sound and satisfying relativity.

NANTUCKET AND NEW YORK: TWO ISLANDS

Four months in Nantucket for Maggie, with three months
for me every year for twenty years except for that one summer
trip through Italian back roads in a little Fiat in 1937. About
four years altogether of our lives on the island. It's easy to dig
in and plant roots in a small community. Roy True, the
Bowdoin carpenter, Cora Stevens of Petticoat Lane and bit-
terly anti-Roosevelt, Ann Harmon of the white crop of hair
next door, gracious Mrs. Walling at the ticket office, and a
hundred or more people whom I'm glad to see every spring.
As soon as we get to Nantucket we run around to see the
Seldens at their house Seldenshalf. Years ago when Charlie
was in London for the New York *Times* I spent the evening
with him when news of Dollfuss's death came over the wires
from Vienna.

The life up there is nearly opposite to the one I lead in
New York City. Busy all day with hands instead of tongues.
No guests except the ladies from Covington, Louisiana,
Margaret's mother and aunt, with once in a while Mabel
Souvaine or Edith Dreifus or Edna Ferber or crashing Rollin
Kirby. There are very few people we want to see in the
summer. We probably have too many people around all
winter, at least I do, what with three or four nights a week
from midnight on at the Algonquin or Sardi's or Jack &
Charlie's.

In the fall we come back to New York after a parting look
at the twenty-foot pines, which we planted as six-inch sprouts,
and a phrase of thanks for Edward Ludwig, the intelligent

architect who built our house as if he intended to live in his own creation, a rare trait for any architect.

New York, dirty, not sandy, the city where no one notices direction or speed of wind and where stars are scarcely seen. I love New York. I doubt if I could live elsewhere the year around, but I also know that no one really lives in New York, or at least in Manhattan. People sleep there. They work there. They go to movies there. But they have no roots or homes. Most New Yorkers move every two or three years. I'm quite sure that all three of our kids are thankful that they have lived all their lives in the century-old 11th Street house, with the giant Tree of Heaven in the back yard, and the Nantucket home, and with Jo and Kitty and Delia. Connie, and Roger and Joan have no recollection of other homes or cook or maid or nurse. We all love Delia. I guess she is wise not to take on another Roger or Joan for another fifteen years, with the emotional ties that would have to be created only to be once again disturbed and reduced.

New York is a desperate city for living. It's too big for anyone to belong to it. No one knows anything about its schools or police or street cleaning. There can be no "concern" in a city that size. It's unfortunate for the nation that this giant city is the bottleneck for our national culture. Every boy or girl with a fiddle, typewriter, paintbrush, or radio voice must travel through the narrow pipeline of New York to get a hearing. The domination of New York makes it difficult for indigenous art and culture to survive and grow to national dimensions west of the Hudson. Years ago I urged that radio licenses be distributed with a conscious preference in wave length and power to cities far away from New York.

New York, smaller than Philadelphia in 1787 at the time of the Constitutional Convention there, has grown in part because of artificial freight rates on railroads. The iron horses were driven by bankers in New York City and so it was easy to give preference to New York and, later, to Pittsburgh for the steel rails. "Pittsburgh plus" can't remain for long. Soon we will approach "Manhattan minus."

[6]

New York's debt and per capita tax burden are shocking. In our adoration of Gargantua we were led to believe that there would be savings and economies as cities grew bigger. The reverse is the case. Some time ago I analyzed the costs of running cities in proportion to size. The curve goes up sharply after cities reach 500,000 population. Think of the human waste when men must go 100 miles for drinking water, and children can't find parks within a few blocks of their homes.

In 1898, at the peak of our mania for billion dollar corporations, about the time when overbig U. S. Steel was launched, we were sold the gold brick of forming five boroughs into Greater New York. It was a dire mistake. We might well have combined police and water and one or two other services. But parks and schools and street cleaning, all would be better if separately run. I imagine that the only way to save the city from inevitable bankruptcy—the debt and budget go up nearly every year—will be to break it up again. Then once more the inhabitants of Brooklyn or Queens or other boroughs will have a concern with their own intimate governments. And only through intimate concern can there be elimination of waste, experimentation for improvement, and direct responsibility of officials to a people that watches over them. At the height of the blitz on London, a friend of Louis D. Brandeis once said to me, "Well, L.D.B. and his fight against bigness have saved London." The Jerry could not end the water, light and power services of London. They had never been centralized as had ours in New York City. In London, if you move from one part of the city to another you have to pay a new deposit for gas or light. Hence London was saved. Centralization for stock market purposes would have meant centralization as bombing objectives. In New York City—for reasons of speculation rather than reduction of costs to consumers—consolidations went so far that a dozen hits of bombs might have left us without water, light or power. Giants are awkward in war as well as in peace.

It would be fun helping a candidate such as General Bill

O'Dwyer in a campaign for mayor in 1945 on a Liberal-Democratic platform urging a commission to explore the breakup of New York into five cities. A too-big city ineluctably leads to a weak Mayor Hylan or a dictatorial Mayor LaGuardia.

CHAPTER II

RELIEF IN WOOD

IT'S RAINING HERE at Nantucket and it's a swell day for working in the shop. The shop in my life is probably sheer compensation for being a lawyer. At the lathe I feel quite creative. A block of maple starts spinning and even though I vaguely know what I want to make, the design is truly developed by free wheeling. It's not difficult, but full of disappointments, errors and corrections. While spinning, the wood always looks deceptively smooth. Each wood has different qualities and grains, and mixing the wood by lamination is always exciting. I've already finished a table service—berry bowls, salad plates, etc.—all made in different shapes and out of different woods. Lumber is satisfactory and alive compared to clay or marble or metals. Maybe that's because wood died so recently while stone and metal have been dead for millions of years.

"A poor workman blames his tools" is not mere cynicism, for I have learned again and again that sharp tools are the requisite for clean, clear results. And each tool contains within itself its own little tricks. Less than twenty years ago I didn't know one tool from another. In fact, I'd never done any carpentry work except for one year in the lower school at Horace Mann, and I don't recall what caused me to go so heavily into carpentry, unless it was Margaret's demands for

[8]

this and that around the place. The very first project was a doghouse for Pat the Spaniel, then a playhouse for the kids on the beach (which I shingled from the top down until I discovered that what I was doing was wrong), and then all five of us, with a few random guests, built the workshop—French doors, brick porch, shingled sides and all. And no carpenter touched it, and it has never leaked since, but some blood of Rex Stout, visiting us at the time of building, is on the westerly side. I remember that while working on the scale drawings I had to relearn square root in order to figure out the length of rafters after determining the pitch of the roof. And then the problem of how to put up the first set of rafters. The grocery boys from Ashley's kidded me and advised me to get a sky hook which from above could hold up the rafters while I nailed them in place.

Someday when we, Maggie and I, shrink our homing needs, I'd really like to design and build a little house where we can take care of everything and have everything within reach of the hand, standing in the center of the house.

It's all been a great joy, building much of our furniture for Nantucket and New York. Walnut tables and desks, maple beds, pine garden furniture, all our own odd design and really made to order to fit special needs. Roger and Joan, and, to a lesser extent, Connie, built their own bookcases and desks and benches from the time they were eight years old. When Joan was six, she went up to the peak of the roof of the shop and nailed in shingles. I'll confess I don't like peaks of roofs, since I am a little frightened by height.

The garden is not my dish—other than planting the pine seedlings, cutting the grass, and doing the heavy work. In my youth, I never did learn the names of all the flowers and I do believe a bald knowledge of the descriptive vocabulary is a necessary precursor to fussing in a garden. But Maggie, who knows all flora and fauna in English and Latin, has worn down her knees working at the beds. Each year in May, when we come up, it looks slow and late and brown. But by

July all is lush, with roses covering all the fences, and parts of the roofs. It's full of blue—the greatest garden color.

I imagine one of the secrets to outside joys is to watch the dimensions of projects. No garden should be so big as to require paid help. No boat should need a hired hand. For as soon as that outside nonamateur is doing some of the work, the owner starts to retire. The gardener begins by carrying heavy loam but soon does some weeding and ends up cutting the flowers for the dining-room table. He gets the fun. The theory of Too Big fits into all important parts of life—gardening, sailing, carpentry—as well as into business and cities and nations.

CHAPTER III

THE JUDGE'S LAMP

JUDGE BRANDEIS, OF COURSE, was the leading exponent of the thesis that bigness is a curse. Recently I was reminded of the lively discussions we often had, when Joan, Margaret and I set off for a two-day wartime cruise. From Nantucket we went to Hadley's Harbor, our favorite this side of Maine. Hadley's, opposite Woods Hole, is quiet, wooded and protected. Inside of Naushon Island, that peaceful playground of the Forbes family, there are roads for horses and buggies, and no cars. From Hadley's back through that five-knot current of the Hole we shot on to Stage Harbor, close by Chatham. For years we set sail direct for Stage Harbor, getting stuck once in a while on that outside shoal right in front of the old lighthouse. Twice the Coast Guard towed me off the same shifting sand bar. But Stage Harbor in those days meant Judge Brandeis. The old judge was the spiritual landfall of the cruise. An hour or so with him was a refresher for spirit and mind. Right up to his last summer he walked that little stretch down to the road to meet us. He wasn't much for crowds or even threes. By twos he shed his light and wisdom on that porch where lawbooks were stowed in packing boxes and the picture of his beloved Judge Cardozo was no product of a modern photographic studio but rather a newspaper-clipped snapshot stuck up with a thumbtack.

The last time I saw him at Chatham, an English couple were just leaving. The Judge had asked, "Would you English people rather die than be slaves?" To which the reply came easily and simply, "Surely, Judge, we would." The Judge quietly added, "Then you will live." And maybe that's the story of the spirit of England. For never should we forget that, while Russia was shipping oil to the Nazis, and while we —all but President Roosevelt and a very few of vision—were opposing fortification of Guam, after Hitler took the Sudeten; while Congress was passing the Draft Act by only one vote; while a picket line against preparedness tramped in front of the White House; at such a time when Russia and the United States were asleep or worse, the little British Isle held the world's fort of freedom. Seven hundred old crates, called planes, defended England with success, because free men can fly better than slaves. This period of the Battle of Britain is one of the miracles of our lifetime. And the old Judge knew what spirit meant in war and in peace, on the earth or in the stratosphere.

For years I had argued against his thesis of the Curse of Bigness. Pragmatically I became persuaded. When the title and mortgage companies were about to fail, I helped draft for Governor Lehman legislation to cope with the hundreds of thousands of holders of certificates in undivided mortgages. Later, when the companies with three billion dollars of mortgage obligations were taken over by the state, we acted as counsel to George Van Schaick, the Superintendent of Insurance, who had this stiff job on his hands. Stiff it was, with some of our biggest attorneys trying to make political capital out of the misery of millions of little investors. In fact, one outstanding criminal lawyer went on the radio to solicit business for a lawyer he had befriended. If an unknown lawyer had violated the legal conventions in this fashion the big shots at the Bar Association would no doubt have taken action, but success at the Bar often brings immunity from professional interference.

We handled a variety of these mortgage companies in our office, running from a tiny hundred-million-dollar one to a slim giant reaching a half billion dollars. But the biggest of all the companies dealt in telephone numbers—for the Bond and Mortgage Guarantee Company, with about twenty millions of assets, had guaranteed a billion dollars of investors —an astronomical relationship, if any.

In the unraveling of this mess I came to see most clearly that by and large corruption and mismanagement were in direct relationship to size, and that investors suffered losses in proportion to the size of the companies which had seduced them to invest. I talked it all over with the Judge many times. He was right. There is an optimum point to man's capacity to manage men and dollars. In a billion dollar company there are illusions of savings, but in the long run the giants all go broke. Look for the biggest American companies of the 1880's, 1890's, 1900's. Few, if any, exist today. The men on top of "too big" business have no intimacy or concern with their own businesses.

It was in 1939 that the Judge dropped me a brief line— always his letters were handwritten and beautifully written —suggesting that I do a book on the economic factors of excessive size in business and government and cities. He hoped I would explore the optimum point of efficiency of a coal company, a city, a savings bank, a steel factory, et cetera. I wrote back that, whereas I had written several books, alone or in collaboration, I was less than a publisher's favorite. With more than generous reviews I was nevertheless known, at least within my family, as Liggett's Friend. In a very few months after publication my writings were being sold as remainders on drugstore counters. I suggested that Stuart

Chase, who had the knack of writing mass economics, could do the job far better. I treasure the Judge's return request that I should do the book. I did it. I called it *Too Big*. I like it. Rather often I still get letters from students and teachers asking me to write further on the subject. *Too Big* got swell reviews, but all the attention that Robert Lamont, editor of Little, Brown, the publishers, put into the volume brought them no dividends.

I owe the great Judge much. He was a man of no aesthetic sense. His home, his furniture, his pictures were far from becoming or beautiful. In fact, the only thing beautiful about the Judge was the Judge himself.

On my desk at the office there stands the lamp which rested in front of his chair on the Supreme Court Bench in Washington from June, 1916, to February, 1939. He had told me he wanted me to have it. His family graciously wrote me that it was mine. I wrote to Mr. Thomas E. Waggaman, marshal of the Supreme Court, and asked if he would kindly ship it on. He replied in effect—"Sorry, I have no right to send the lamp; it is the property of the Court." But friendly research on the marshal's part showed that, whereas the lamp could not be given to me, or even sold to me, it could be exchanged for a lamp of equal value. Did I care to send a lamp of equal value down to the Court? Equal value! There was no dollar value for the ugly goose-necked lamp. It was a lawyer's Aladdin's lamp or Diogenes' lantern. For nearly twenty-three years the lamp had shed light on the Judge's wisdom. One of the other judges of that same court, hearing of the marshal's wise legal philosophy of exchange, wrote me a line: "Who says the law ain't wonderful?"

I have the lamp. I don't want any more possessions. In fact, with the kids off on their own, Maggie and I are going through the inevitable shrinking processes where homes are "too big" and possessions are increasingly a source of tyranny. But this old lamp I love. Not much of a mystic, I nevertheless touch it once in a while with my finger tips as if the spirit of Louis Dembitz Brandeis might be transmitted through brass and twinkling light. At least it can't hurt me to have a bright reminder of one of my very few important men friends.

THE CATASTROPHE OF SHOES FOR AMERICANS

Years ago Judge Brandeis told me the story of the catastrophe of shoes for Americans. It seems that a group of people had garnered together all the significant shoe machinery patents and business of the nation. This group of businessmen had vision. They decided to rent the machines rather than sell them. Thus they would permit small shoe-makers to go into business. They also agreed to service and fix up the machines if broken. Again a wise move because small shoemakers could not afford to hire, locally, highly skilled repairmen.

And still no important advance in the art of shoemaking appeared in our nation for many decades. This giant trust could sue out of business any pretender to power, any claimant to new patents. Moreover, holding the market under its foot, there seemed to be no need for further research. Why improve and advance the manufacture of shoes so long as no shoe factory could exist without the United's machinery? Stagnation through power and size! This in a land crying out about rugged individualism.

The same kind of story can be told in many other commodities. Not until Myron Taylor's regime in United States Steel did that giant company have a real research laboratory.

THE FANTASTIC EXPRESS COMPANY

But of all the improbable enterprises on the American scene I suggest for scrutiny the Railway Express Company. This enterprise is owned by about seventy railroads. It is co-operatively owned. It has a virtual monopoly. There is some competition on very small packages via the parcel post

[14]

of the United States Post Office, freight competition of the same railroads, and the growing new air express.

The express business is a natural. It's essential. It's still much quicker than fast freight and, above all other selling points, it picks up from the sender and delivers to the receiver. Door-to-door service is an important convenience.

But express, being owned by nearly all the railroads, is owned by nobody. It goes along on public momentum, or rather public necessity and need rather than on ingenuity. The railroads, suffering also from gargantuanism, agree among themselves on how packages handled by express should be turned over to railroads. Thus the service of carrying an express parcel on a train has no necessary relationship to the cheapest or the quickest route. It's all worked out on old formulas and agreements set up at the time when certain railways took over the monopoly of the express business.

Bad as that is, it isn't the worst feature of the business. These great railroads do not charge a single penny for carrying express parcels for their own Railway Express Company. There are no tariff schedules. The setup merely provides that the railroads get back from the express company whatever is left in the express company's cash drawer at the end of each year. Naturally the amounts paid to railroads shrink year by year, only to be boosted by a war. I haven't checked up on the figures since the war began, but the railroads have been paid at various times for their part of the service—that is, the actual carrying of the express parcels exclusive of the truck deliveries at each end—as much as fifty cents out of every dollar I paid when I sent a parcel, and as little as thirty cents.

Eventually the profits will evaporate entirely. And why not? What more absurd business arrangement than to say to an employee, I'll take for my part of the work whatever you have left over at the end of the year? I can imagine no more effective inducement to waste. What possible economic pressure is there for retrenchment—or, more important still, for ingenuity? The chances of new ideas and new blood in this business have been reduced to a minimum. So here we have in one company all the dangers and vices of a public monopoly, even though it is controlled by a government commission.

A series of regional express companies with interchange facilities, as with passenger railway tickets, might bring some relief. At least there would be comparative competition between the regional companies.

This is no chicken-feed business. It runs to more than $255 million a year. It carries over 165 million parcels annually. In practicing before the Interstate Commerce Commission on a matter affecting the Railway Express Company I jestingly offered to take a job with the company provided I got not a cent of salary. All I'd want would be an insignificant percentage of the savings, or profits, or increased business done. As a matter of fact, the railways could well afford to pay someone as a salary 10 per cent of all additional net income received by the railroads as their share of the express services rendered.

CHAPTER IV

SIGNIFICANT TRIVIA

JUST BACK IN OUR HARBOR after a cruise. There is no sweeter landfall than the water tank on Nantucket, visible on ultraclear days from the black can off Cape Poge. This trip in June was brief and typically Junish for these waters. It started with sunshine and then, after a night at Hadley's, the only craft in that nook, a blow came up. Off we went into the Hole the next morning. Seeing no flag warning near Nobska light, we foolishly relied on man rather than on nature. The gulls had gone inland, and the sun had risen above a bank of clouds after going down in a yellow sky. I guess I'll never learn to trust a gull more than a government. It's like people who believe there is something sacred in printed matter.

But deep inside I know that the trivia shown by nature are the best advices for man, if man is wise. Nothing is too minute to watch. Maybe a new Newton is needed to dramatize the law of antigravitation. The upsurge has a power far above the downpull. The blades of tough sand grass push up through the new macadam road laid down by Road Commissioner Tice. The power to smash an atom or propel a robot plane is negligible compared to the force within the little dry-looking seed as it crashes man-made hard rock. The synchronization of a glass globe, trembling agog and finally broken, because a singer strikes a pure note, has a mystic quality as yet unaccepted by man's daily consciousness. And yet we understand a falling airplane.

Maybe only in old age, for a person unfortunately never trained in the sciences of natural phenomena, do all trivia become significant. As years go by, new apperceptions develop. The pictures on my walls for years have been beautiful, but I must confess that now days go by without my really noticing or enjoying them. That crude, carved pirate's head, hewn out by an angry sailor maliciously chipping his hate of the mate, is noted by my eyes every day. The tightly written small books, Ethan Frome, Lost Lady and the like—if there be many such-like—increase in value compared to Gone With the Wind and all the heavy tomes. Each separate Spanish and Mexican dish and bowl is my favorite art collection.

A little cactus on our beach doorstep—maybe the farthest north cactus growing by its own choice on our eastern seaboard—has a distinction of its own. The last rosebud to disappear is as choice as the first just because she fights for life in late September though all her friends died long ago.

While in Lisbon waiting for a plane to England in November, 1943, I picked up a copy of the London Times. That great paper had sacrificed twenty per cent of its circulation during the paper ration era in order to keep up printing the Parliament debates and its famous letter page. On that page I read: "Swallows Dallying in the South." I thought: England is saved—for surely that's what the war is about in part: that men should even in wartime be able to know when the swallows dally in the south. I put that portion of the *Times* under the glass top of my office desk. I like it there.

Intimacies are made out of odd episodes that acquire significance, and weld people together. A mythical character, a taxi driver Joseph, has caused more wholesome laughter in our family than the wittiest writings of all literature. The origin of Joseph is forgotten—why he was born is unknown—but he exists with more flesh and blood than any popular funny man on the radio. He lives near by. He has had many wives and flocks of children. His nephews and nieces play terrible pranks. He is peculiarly fond of Joan—even to the point of her boredom. He tells many jokes and riddles—so low and punning that no one in our family would dare do more than repeat them as Joseph's product. He is everywhere, at any time Roger or I want him. The essence of his character is lack of consistency or pride. Joan tries to kill him at times. But Joseph lives forever.

Life, or at least the most delicious parts of it, are lived in the mind. But I, at least, live a better part of this make-up, make-believe world when I live it with others. Maybe the secret is taking trouble. Only rarely have I met people who wanted to take much trouble with relationships. Trouble isn't the right word. It connotes a little of the idea of bother, a chore, a nuisance. What I mean is something akin to nursing but without sickness or ailment. The Quaker's word "concern" is the key to what I mean. And it isn't taking your hat off in an elevator or sending bonbons or flowers on anniversaries. Although I do wish I had remembered my kids' birthdays and my wedding anniversaries instead of having Connie remind me to buy something for Maggie, on the eve of a celebration.

It's not easy to buy things. I'm afraid of clerks in stores and for years Margaret bought all my clothes. It always seemed cruel to look at a lot of ties and not buy some. I guess I'm a pushover for clerks, and for barbers who can mush my hair with anything, before I'll say "No, I don't want it." Then again, there is no possession that any of us wants, except maybe for the boat or the shop. The only present we would really like to get is a pass for Madison Square Garden for all events and I'd give Maggie my fight tickets for her to take a beau. General Reed Kilpatrick, head of the Garden, please take note if you read this.

Inconsistent as it may be, the Garden is our winter home—hockey three nights a week with affection for players, and joy in watching easy rhythms. Track meets with the great last stretch of a Cunningham and the inhuman ease of a Warmerdam, flying above fifteen feet as he rejects the pole. My gratitude to the Garden got me so far as to write a profile of General Kilpatrick who runs that tops of American halls, where all kinds of groups meet and where, at all too high prices, we vicarious athletes can cheer and identify ourselves with human beings who beat records of other human beings.

Every time Greg Rice came into that long last stretch I could run better the next day. Gertrude Ederle, as Heywood Broun pointed out, helped all women swimmers. The intangibles, the trivia, are the significant realities of daily living.

CHAPTER V

As A BOOKKEEPER by profession a third of a century ago, I've never lost the joy of reading statistics. The World Almanac is my bedside volume if I'm not reading Wells' and Huxley's *The Science of Life*, or some similar tome.

With an odd decimal method of thinking I've always been interested in taxes, budgets and revenue. My first writing, with Joseph J. Klein the accountant, was a slender volume for the New York Real Estate Board on the ordinarily dull subject of "Income Taxes in Relation to Real Property." In a society of tenants rather than owners, complicated social tax formulas are needed to draw legalistic lines between short-term leases and outright deeds.

Taxes are without a doubt the simplest leverage known to society for directing social impulses. Alexander Hamilton in his first great message as Secretary of the Treasury faced an agrarian society about to develop an industrial life. Hence he proposed taxes known as tariffs at ports of entry, to put a burden on purchases ordinarily made by farmers from overseas. This tariff-tax would protect the small factories just being established on the eastern seaboard. In turn he hoped that the industrial workers thus aided in jobs could afford to buy more food from the farmers. Here was a round-the-circle tax program inaugurated at the start of our nation to help equalize the farm and urban incomes. This I have felt is identical in reverse gear to Henry Wallace's program in aid of farm purchasing power created by a tax on city folk when they buy farm products. Thus in turn, the farmers' income being boosted, they would be able to buy more of the manu-factured goods produced in the cities.

As our co-operative undertakings shifted from a few canals and public fire engines to irrigation, roads, public schools and the myriad efforts for which separate individual enterprise was of less avail, increasing amounts of our national income were collected by taxes. Taxes are never just for revenue. They cannot fail to have direct impacts on farms or cities, or finance or industry, or labor.

And now we buy great portions of our services and com-forts from the state cheaper than we buy from a few private utilities—gas, light, power, water and telephone. On Nan-tucket—with the highest light rate in the land—a few private services cost as much as roads and health and schools and police and fire protection all together. Some years ago I wanted to buy an electric stove. The utility manager laughed at me. I must be crazy. When I suggested that a low rate would bring hundreds of orders for electric stoves and water heaters, he evinced no interest.

The great problem of taxes is to collect the needed money without putting brakes on private initiative and new enter-prise. Few politicians dare explain to labor that there is no revenue left to be collected from the upper-bracket income group. There are only 37,600 people with more than $50,000 annual income. If we took all their income above $50,000, we would collect only enough to run the war for a day or so. This doesn't mean that we should give relief to the lucky. For psychological reasons, against the background of an un-informed public, an argument can be made for taxing large incomes heavily in order to collect what we need from the small income group which has 96.6 per cent of the national income.

In 1894 our Congress favored an income tax but the Supreme Court was advised by Joseph Choate, the leading lawyer of his generation, that this was "communism." This was the first use of that word I find in our lawbooks. In 1913 the people by constitutional amendment made income taxes lawful. Then for a decade farmers were exempted by all kinds of indirect provisions. Only 1½ million people filed any returns. Now we are a nation of income tax payers.

Previously taxes were used to retard card playing, drinking and smoking. From now on, if we want to preserve small business and the individual profit motive we must shift our attack. We can put small units in a position to compete with giants by geometrically increasing taxes on mere size. On this theory chain store taxes were enacted.

Years ago I took one of our leading chain store merchants to visit with Judge Brandeis—the judge who first saw the advantages of taxes to preserve private initiative. My merchant friend was concerned over the court's upholding chain store taxes. I have told the story often and on the least provocation. But it's worth repeating. In my book *Too Big*, the story runs in part:

I went with the chain-store magnate to the Judge's home. We spent an hour or so talking about the philosophy of chain stores. The Judge showed an intimate knowledge of the details of chain-store operation. Gently he stated his position. Given a piece of soil such as we have in the United States, rich with grain, power, oil and coal, the only difference between poverty and riches lies in the development of the human mind. Imagination and initiative spell prosperity in the long run. Chains create neither. The men on top, geniuses as many of them are, cannot envisage the industrial tides of the nation. Their corporations are too vast even for acute men to comprehend. So the men on top do not get a chance fully to use their great talents. Their power is blinding. Often it confuses them. Few are able to resist the temptation of abusing power. Meanwhile, the mass of men down below never grow, never develop, never get a chance to use their abilities. A decent society cannot develop in such environs. Too great power for a few and a life as robots for the masses will spell increasing trouble for us all. Democracy means intimacy with facts, exchange of ideas between equals, and a chance for all men to express their talents, great or meager, free from oppressive power of others.

With a twinkle in his eye, the Judge turned and asked, "You

wouldn't allow one of your store managers to sell a loaf of bread or buy a can of peas except at the price you fix?"

"Of course I wouldn't," came the emphatic reply.

The Judge continued, "I dare say you could open up a grocery store opposite any one of your chain stores and in sixty days compete your chain store out of business."

Forgetting his mission for a split second, the millionaire chain man answered, "Why, Judge, I could do it in thirty."

The discussion went on for quite a time, and, to my surprise, the millionaire merchant started to talk about the possible sale of thousands of his shops to his clerks, and the conversion of clerks into shop owners. He had all the money he wanted. These store managers could buy their shops for $3,000 or $4,000. That's all there was to the inventories. They could pay $500 or so down, and the balance over two or three years. The bigger stores they couldn't finance either in purchase or in operation. But many stores might be sold to the present managers.

Here was a merchant prince playing with an idea which would affect profoundly our entire national economy in its deepest terms. I imagined the increased capacity which such a move would create in these thousands of new store owners. New blood would run in the bodies of those clerks. Every fortunate father knows the joy he experiences if he is able to give to his child a chance to make his way in an undertaking of his own. I envisaged thousands of towns buzzing with the excitement of the birth of new personalities. The blossoming of spring when the sap runs in the trees would be nothing compared to the coming of age of this crop of clerks. Some would not survive a hard winter, but the loss by a few would be more than compensated for by the inspiration of the many. The average man, who is the base of the democratic process, would have elbowroom once more.

But I was dreaming ahead of the talk. The chain man pondered and then asked, "Judge, if I sold these thousands of stores to my managers, of course the contract might provide that each of these stores buy coffee and crackers and canned fruits from our wholesale department?"

Quietly the Judge said, "Oh, no. Don't you see if these store owners have to buy from you they will continue to act like unthinking clerks. And, what is even worse, you won't for long give them the best possible coffee at the lowest possible price. You

[23]

won't stay on your toes. Who would, with an assured market of purchasers? And in time you will dry up."

Mr. Chain Man saw the point. "I guess you are right, Judge," he declared. "Competition is the spice of life." There was a pause. "But, Judge," he said, "the contract of sale might include some annual payment for the use of our name?"

"Of course," said the Judge. "That name has been developed by you and your capital and your effort. It has value. A fair price should be paid for it by the buying clerks."

"Well, why shouldn't each clerk who buys a store pay $300 or $400 a year for the name, and contract to use the name and make the payments for five or ten years?"

"Don't you see," interrupted the Judge, "that won't do. You want the name to be kept good, or its value will shrink and soon disappear. You must keep it good year by year. If you bind these men to pay for the name for five years, then at the end of any such period the name will be valueless. Good will and names have momentum, but they must be nourished and nursed and tended."

The sequel to this visit is worth mentioning. That vast chain corporation had its counsel prepare contracts for the sale of many thousands of stores to the managers or clerks. Lengthy detailed legal documents aiming at the breakup (not "down") of the chain were prepared and considered. That much I know. Just why the plan was never carried out, I do not know. My guess is that these mighty merchants thought the Supreme Court, then on its rampage of throwing out the NRA, AAA, Guffey Coal Plan, Minimum Wage legislation, and so on, was going to turn back the tides, restore status quo, revive the economy of Hoover and Coolidge. All the fears of what might happen to retail chain store businesses might safely be forgotten.

The plan did not go through. But putting it into the discard spelled out no basic defect in the thinking of that meeting. I have seen the merchant at odd intervals since that time some five years ago. It is not inconceivable that the plan of converting clerks into owners may still be his method of endowing the United States of America. He will get his money out, as he should. He may lose some future money gains. But his profit will be a short bit of immortality by adding to the democratic pattern of our nation.

I don't particularly favor chain store taxes, for they are levies on numbers of roofs. Rather would I progressively tax mere size. Integrated industries—such as oil—where a single company owns wells, refineries, pipelines and gasoline stations, boast of great economies. Let them give back part of these savings made possible by our grant to them of the privilege of freezing out little oil drillers and small gasoline pumping stations. Until we have enough wisdom to break them up—as we did railroad-coal owning companies—taxes are one of the available implements which can conceivably preserve individual capitalism. And then above all I'd exempt in any event from business income taxes the first $5,000 or $10,000 profit even though there is much merit in the idea of eliminating all corporate taxes provided a shift is made in our concept of capital gains taxes. Without a wide market place open to many ambitious people and usable by all, a few giants will dominate prices and supplies, and ultimately we will find prices go up by agreement, and then there will follow a push by the irritated public in favor of government ownership and operations.

More than fifty years of sporadic attempts to enforce our antitrust laws have been futile and deceptive. Except for the past decade, we never even stemmed the tide of monopoly. In addition, our course has been frustrating and unreasoning because no corporation was ever sure that its activities were lawful at any particular moment. I'd rather go back to our first century of practice—putting limits on size of corporations at the time when charters are granted. Size, of course, varies in relation to type of business undertaking. But there is an optimum point of economic value in each type of industry. Charles E. Hughes found it for insurance, but we didn't listen to him.

Our leading industrialists preach empty words in favor of competition but resent most of the effective efforts of the government which would give new or small units a chance to be born, compete and survive. If private capitalism fails, we can charge its demise to the leading capitalists. They are the economic schizophrenics of our day.

A WILL FOR A TYCOON

One of my favorite tough and very rich friends came to see me this morning. He's very old but has aged in the way that Clemenceau and boatman Captain Whelden aged. He never let on to himself that years were a thing of calcium and muscle. It's about time the psychologists found out the secret of proper aging. To die thumbing your nose, as Judge Holmes supposedly did, or to grow tiny and be blown away as happens to old people on Nantucket is a secret that should be exposed.

This tycoon, as *Time* magazine would call him, owns millions and an industry. He wanted a new will. As always with people sitting opposite me in the office, I'm interested in what makes them click. How did he make that fortune? Did it bring happiness? Was it a trouble? Did it make friends, or create envy and jealousy? Was he always tough and hard to the outside world? Where is his spot of humility?

My friend was simple in his tastes, at least as simple as one can be (save only a Brandeis) if one has more than a million or so. Of course there were several servants, several homes, several cars, extravagant wardrobes for wife and son, jewels for wife and sister, clubs galore, and travel de luxe at whim. But his own clothes and meals and hobbies required no great wealth. He was still a little surprised at being so rich and successful.

He wanted a trust fund for his only child, a lad of about seventeen. His other children had died. After taking care of the wife, giving a fortune to gather a speck of immortality by donations to hospitals and orphan asylums, he still had a fund left—after taxes—sufficient to garner an income of $40,000 a year.

This fund was to be set up for the son, income until thirty-five, and then outright. If the boy hadn't learned to guard wealth by the time he was thirty-five he probably never would.

It looked as if the boy would enter no profession but might enjoy business, even his father's business. It was at that moment of our chat that I asked the old man just when he had most fun in life.

"Of course it was making that first $10,000. The next $50,000 was not too difficult, and after I had my first hundred thousand the rest was a game without much kick in it. After the first million it got to be a worry, the mere holding on to it despite the avalanche that descends on all rich people to separate them from their wealth."

I got my friend to tell in some detail the story of the first $10,000. The usual pattern—energy, taking a chance, and luck. He knew his era of buccaneers was at an end. He knew that fortunes will no longer be accumulated in our land. He even knew that this revolution would not really reduce the joys of those with the potential of money-making. He had been to England since the war began and had seen the stately large homes on Belgrade, Portman and other fashionable squares empty, idle and for rent. It was obvious that the emotional revolution had taken place in England. The rich families (only six are left with $30,000 annual income, which requires $500,000 income before taxes) had found out that a seven-room flat with a part-time servant was less trouble than the old twenty-room house with ten retainers. They had discovered that possessions can be a nuisance as well as a joy, and that instead of possessions as a means of showing off they could find a substitute in devotion to the community.

But here was his son, to be the owner of this fabulous income.

I suggested that my friend was really a cruel, mean old father. Why should he deprive his only boy of the one single joy which marked the father's lifetime of effort, the joy of fighting against odds to make that first $10,000 rung in the ladder of economic success?

The old man smiled a sad smile, for he knew he had no

[27]

choice. By the very standard of living in which he had placed his son he had committed himself not to change the pattern for the lad. That would have been a breach of faith, a cutting of an implied promise. By gifts of a horse and a car and all the paraphernalia of wealth, the boy had been conditioned without his consent or request to a life free of economic battle and struggle.

That the son would be weaker than the old man goes without saying. Fiber is toughened by use, and the son might become a great industrial force but his quality would be far different from that possessed by his father.

My point in all this is that in a society of personal struggle, a society which, through profit motive properly controlled, produces, I believe, more wealth, plus freedom, than any other productive system known to man, this boy will be easy prey for other boys who are out to make their first little pile. He will not be able to keep his business. It will shrink in earnings, size and power.

There are very few instances of large businesses which survive in the United States. Robert Lovett, Assistant Secretary of War for Air, proved this to a fine point years ago with his story of a mythical investor looking for safety in our biggest enterprises. It wasn't there.

If the proponents of capitalism were wise they would glorify the one hundred or so still vital and profitable concerns which have endured for more than a century. Very few grew very big, very few cast an eye on Wall Street to issue stock to unconcerned investors.

I'll watch the old man's son with interest. I have quite a few like him in tow. Their lives must be steered a little so that they make contact with a few first-rungers. They badly need outside interests in which original capital is no emotional handicap. Many become publishers of books or magazines.

CHROME PLATE FOR ICEBOXES

I saw another old friend the other day. He was looking much better. A different man from that day in 1930 when,

[28]

down to his last three million dollars, he had developed melancholia. An amazing but not unusual bit of American folklore—contestants in a land of plenty, men with the separate knack of making money, successful, with no loss of their talents but with an immediate sense of defeat and emptiness of life because their barometer of success—dollars—had taken a tailspin down to hurricane levels.

I often wondered, during a tussle tangentially touching George F. Baker of the First National Bank, why he cared about wealth. He was old, and at most a bookkeeper showed or told him once a year: "You are worth eighty or ninety millions." Wealth must have had no relation to tangible reality. It was at best an optical or auditory illusion.

In contrast, there was Broun with $70,000 a year income and seldom any money in the bank. He never kept a checkbook, nor reckoned, and no one knows what he did with his money. Many a time I advanced him his first income tax installment and then he sometimes didn't pay the balance until the federal marshal came around to collect. What did penalty or interest mean? Money was to be used. What did he do with it? Almost nothing for those baggy clothes, a little tax on his Stamford home, no paid-for prize fight, theater or sports tickets, no organized charity contributions. But $100 a day at restaurants was sure, and then about $10,000 a year at roulette and poker and horses. But I remember going to the breadline with him during the Hoover Apple Era and, if a man's eye had some hope in it, Heywood's hand would go into his pocket and just as likely bring out $20 as a dime.

In our economy, what with the phony standards created by advertising and, particularly in the future, no more millions being accumulatable, we may well find that Veblen's Conspicuous Expenditure theory comes into its own.

Why must we have all that chrome plate on iceboxes? Or inconvenient oversized autos? (Page E. B. White and the New Yorker for their courageous editorials spoofing gargantuan cars.) Our homes, gadgets, clothes, all our tangible possessions are loaded with the evidence of lack of inner security. We are so unsure that we must show off. We must keep up

[29]

with the Joneses and if there are no Joneses we create some in our magazines, even going to foreign countries to find them.

There is nothing to the theory that all this waste expenditure creates national wealth by creating greater demand. This argument assumes that the money not spent on foolish show-off stuff would be put under mattresses instead of being deposited in savings banks, for investment, or spent on valid items.

Maybe someone will amplify Veblen. It is not enough to decry ostentatious waste. A substitute must be portrayed for the public mind. Maybe the appealing substitute would be leisure and fun. What if a decent small car, such as those used in Italy or England before the war, were offered for sale? It would have no fancy metal, no oversized fenders; it would seat five, it would not go over 45 miles an hour. It would require half the original outlay, and for gas and oil its expenses would be cut more than in half. The garage could cost less and on a rental basis would save many dollars a year. The difference between the show-off model and the adult model would spell a saving in dollars sufficient to buy a couple of extra weeks' fishing or sailing or golf; or even enough to send a kid to college for a half year.

I've talked with car manufacturers and they tell me that it can't be done; that below a certain consumer sale price it doesn't pay to make a car. Only a couple of million people ever buy new cars in any year. They like being suckers, for they know that a $1,500 car drops to about $350 in value after the first two years though it's good for ten more. These new car buyers, I'm told, are like private patients in an expensive hospital. The prices they pay carry the wards. And they want expensive cars and enjoy taking a big loss every year or so when they sell. This sounds like profit-and-loss rationalization. I should imagine that the American archparasites—the advertising agency boys—are slick enough to put over anything and, if they had a mind to, they could truly direct the American buying public into greater mass consumption of more items providing finer satisfactions for a better well-being of the people of our land.

Forty years ago we were told that the eight-hour day was impossible in the steel industry. Judge Gary, the dictator of steel, preached that nonsense.

Thirty years ago we were told workers could never be put on an annual contract basis. Please note what Hormel is doing competitively to the rest of the packing industry, and Hormel has annual contracts.

Twenty years ago we were told that a minimum wage would become a maximum. It just ain't so!

Ten years ago leaders of industry shouted that Social Security would destroy incentive. Silly!

The leaders of industry have been so invariably wrong on most matters of novel social impact that either the government or radicals in the real sense of the word, like Hormel or Ford with his original $5 per day wage, must shock industry into adventures profitable for business and healthy for the nation.

CHAPTER VI

WATERSIDE NOTES

WHILE EATING DINNER alone at "21" I was reading Yachting magazine. A fair-skinned Scandinavian waiter saw me looking at the picture of a schooner. I asked if he was interested in sailing.

"Yes, but I don't get much time."

"What do you sail?"

"Oh, I built a little boat myself up at Pelham."

"When do you sail?"

"Only on Sundays when a friend and I go up with our sandwiches for the day."

"Where do you sail?"

"Near City Island."

I told him that I didn't race and asked, "Do you like racing?"

"Oh, yes, I race whenever I can get into my boat."

After more talk I discovered that this waiter had won great prizes in the Star boat races in the Sound.

It was a warming American story. Star boats are sailed by men who get expensive Ratsey sails, who take their boats out of water every few weeks for polish and paint, who spend large sums of money for new gadgets, who devote their lives to the sport. And here was Servus—a "Sunday sailor" with a sandwich wrapped in paper—running off with prizes. It's a good land. And now the sailing waiter is off in our ski patrol skimming over snow instead of water to help us here at home.

I had never put foot into a sailboat until I came to Nantucket twenty years ago, but now it's difficult to imagine what would have filled that portion of my life if I hadn't been taken sailing by Elsie Cullman. Being lazy and less than a perfectionist, I brushed aside all the bewildering language used by skippers, and even today am less than articulate in the vernacular of the sea. As a defense I developed the idea that in seamanship, as in law and medicine and religion, those who are trained in the art use language as a fender, a means to scare off threatening competition. I know that whenever the medicos are bankrupt as to source or cure of a disease they give it a long Latin name, just as we lawyers bandy around words like "certiorari" and "hereditament" whenever clients catch on to the credited mysteries of the law.

It's easy to teach people to sail. Joan can take any child or adult and within four hours have them sailing her twelve-foot catboat, the *Comet II*, all alone. Of course getting up to a mooring or pier must be practiced just as backing a car into a parking space has little to do with driving along a straight road. In teaching, it seems to me, there are only a few principles of significance and these can be made intriguing rather than confusing by use of words such as "sheet" (instead of "rope" to pull in a sail) or "halyard" (instead of "rope" to pull up a sail). We usually start our friends off with the history of the Phoenicians and the use of a keel or centerboard, without which great invention of man people could traverse the seas only in the direction of the wind. Then we go into a very elementary (because that's all we know) discussion of the power of the air to pull or push. The suction over the wing of an airplane, the birds at rest always facing into the wind—leading up to the luffing of the sail. And finally we explain the jibe of the sail.

Fear is taken out of the sport in part by finally breaking through the meaning of the words. The starboard (steering board side), port side (free for loading at a port) or larboard (lading board side), schooner (in Norwegian to skim), sheet (the sail—later identified with the rope that pulled it in), bilge (which was the bulge), skyscrapers (used originally for high sails on clippers), binnacle (literally a little house for the compass to live in)—these and other explanatory waterside notes reduce the fear so early implanted in people of our earthy society.

To be an addict and not to be ashamed is a strange but satisfactory experience, for addiction implies a weird, weak and inexplicable compulsion. It is a kind of tortured or exaggerated habit, not always pleasant but quite unbreakable.

I am the proud owner of at least two violent addictions, both of a serious nature, both most punishing in a physical sense and both capable of causing momentary emotional distress of a high pitch: carpentering and cruising. Bodily weariness, discomfort, damaged hands are part of the game of sailing; tired muscles, lacerated fingers and sharp frustrations come from the saw, the lathe and the hammer. And still I would hate to give up either. Or rather, like all other habits, good or bad, none of us ever breaks away from one without being able to shift to another at the same time. Of the two slaveries the woodwork shop is the easier to understand. It fills a desire to create, it compensates for the daily verbal existence of a law office, and it brings at times prompt and visible completions. A desk which I made this summer, no matter how imperfect to the eye of a master craftsman, is to me an object worth endless minutes of adoring glances. Ditto from my wife, or I'll know the reason why!

Cruising is a subtler disease. Each cruise has an ending, but landfall is a different kind of completion, for the object of a cruise is never the home-coming. It's not like taking raw lumber and turning out a finished lamp or table. With wood there is finality; a boat and an endless sea are more than finite. Moreover, cruising engenders co-operation, while the shop at best arouses a relationship of master and helper.

Years ago that great mathematician Bertrand Russell, in his stimulating book on education and the good life, wrote that the fullest development of peace-loving man depended on sailing, the only sport the author could recall wherein man did not fight man, but nature. To do battle with tide and wind and current is fitting combat for homo sapiens. It brings strength and humility. In the final analysis, every skipper knows that the sea can do him in if it ever wants to. This combination of fortitude and humility is the germ of the disease. Unlike that low and mean abuse of sailing known as racing, cruising is the antithesis of competition between man and man. Those shabby characteristics which often arise when man tries to outdo his fellow man are all submerged when a cruising man puts out to sea. There are no tapes to be crossed ahead of other men. No gun announces the victory, for victory on a cruise is only that inner feeling, beating its smooth rhythm like that of a heart. There are no artificial rewards such as vain and ever boastful silver cups, symbols of the racer's insecurity which demands that evidence be in tangible form for constant display.

Even cruising has a semblance of a fault. It has a slight bend toward snobbery. I'll let you in on a secret—there really are few cruising folk. Of the 100,000 prewar privately owned boats in the nation, 93,000 cannot be slept in. Then from the balance of 7,000 we must deduct all the motorboats, those without sails. That's another 4,500 out of the class. Now, those 4,500 engine ships are all right—in a way; they give the male owner a chance to wash dishes and try out his new frying pan. Moreover, at times they provide a great social function. At times the owner graduates to sails but more often his weekend jaunt is adventure enough. On his ship he finds the joy of language nautical, and the cap marine. But the difference between the two types of skippers is clear though pathetic. The motor addict is usually a sure though minor bully. He wants an arena of power where his command is law. He therefore spends all week in trying to corral an audience for his next weekend trip to that harbor just around the corner. Statisticians have at last proved that there are 19.9 times as many people per over-all footage on power- as on sailboats. These pitiful dependents on Messrs. Ohm, Ampere and Watt need an audience not only later around the kitchen stove but during every minute of every trip.

Maybe I have been a trifle cruel, for I do remember seeing in a gunk hole—but never east of Casco—one of these regimented, impersonal, stamped-out hulls, occupied by a soft and tender family of five, without a guest or beer can aboard. This family, I will confess, was not rushing through life, but papa had only one arm and mamma weighed over two hundred pounds, and so these humble people traveled in gentle fashion, always resting in out-of-the-way nooks so as to reduce the pangs of suffering occasioned by the sight of a set of sails or two sticks shooting from a deck.

But to get back to canvas full of wind. Out of 2,500 sailing-sleeping ships, only 1,800 were truly made for cruising as distinguished from going places. The bigger ships, about 700 in number, were captained by the Big Boys and you can have them cheap, for the minute a paid hand comes aboard joy slips over the rail. Few men are able without money-helpers to cope with more than fifty foot of hull, and these paid hands, originally hired for just a little odd heavy work, all too soon are seen sneaking around having all the fun charting, hoisting, swabbing and pottering. And in time the owner develops suppressed envies, fires the crew, and has a helluva time engaging a new one.

In a way the gorgeous men on top of these exaggerated hulls were not unlike the big motor boys. Past the prime of life, inheritors of troublesome gold, unhappily married, commanders of cashless men instead of rulerless waves. Such are the charms of the men who own, not sail the vast hulls with or without canvas. Many of them were cruising people once upon a time, carefree and self-sufficient. But they never read Brandeis on Sailing or the Curse of Water Bigness. They never learned that size compensates for little in life, and that to have a bigger boat than your cousin or your neighbor is a sport belonging to the brontosauri, who died from it millions of years ago. Euclid long ago gave us the theorem of optimum point of joy in relation to length of keel.

Some years ago, while loafing in and out of the Maine coast with Maggie, Joan and Roger, I did a thorough research job on the giants' fleet. An accurate tally showed that 67.1 per cent of the owners were for Wendell Willkie for president and 32.8 per cent were against Roosevelt for president, or in fact any other job this side of hell. This makes a total of 99 per cent against Roosevelt. On these same ships the crews tallied 78 per cent for Roosevelt, 19 per cent never heard of Willkie—that was before his trip to England—and the remaining 3 per cent didn't care at all about government save for the lighthouse and buoy services. But among the real small-boat cruising fleet, economic new dealing seemed to fit in with the adventures and restlessness of the sea, and F.D.R. was overwhelmingly elected. As a postscript I must add that I think W.W. himself belonged in the cruising class but just couldn't get out of his old racing togs although he was trying hard during his last years.

And so, even though there are very few cruising men in the world, it is not an easy matter to diagnose the ailment. Cruising is a sport of three major variables: skipper, weather and ship, but the ship is the heroine of each story, more significant than the hand at the wheel or the set of the tide. Yet a truly great cruiser such as the former owner of my ketch, the *Episode*, who with his wife never lived off the ship for five years, would have a different set of impressions to tell about the same vessel.

It seems to me that there are five main spheres of impact of boat on sailor, and vice versa.

The first I mention not out of importance but out of courtesy to womankind. Men have in our society been led to believe that pastimes enjoyed by women should be disdained by men, even though the reverse is not so true any more. This results in many young boys wanting to play house and being afraid to do so because they would be called sissy. Along comes the boat, and I, for one, who resent a dishcloth or pot or pan at home, find myself more fussy and more intense about the galley than are any of my old aunts of whom I have made fun for years. I suffer now as the result of a suppressed desire to play with a doll at the age of twenty-six months. In a daze I find myself in Altman's housekeeping department on a bright spring afternoon. Except for my boat, I would no more have been found in that den of femininity than in the lingerie department. I leave with a pressure cooker under my arm. I sneak home, find some string beans in the icebox. In a minute and a half my beans are finished. They are my beans. I have a sense of pride in them such as when my old Buick climbs a steep hill in high. Just as if I had made the car or the cooking pot. As to recipes, it is not enough to explain that the great cooks of the world are male chefs. On a cruise I invent, I explore. If the labels come off the tins I am not disturbed. It's too bad that my wife never mixed apricots with lamb stew. Laugh, you phony females; have you never heard of grapes with duck, and oranges with capon? Of course, with the galley in its only proper place aft, it's easy to hand up the luncheon concoction. Not only handy but gratifying. Then also there is the joy of improvement. Tin canned food used to fill two shelves. Now it is hidden away, a necessary evil and the precaution of an overcautious, conservative sailor. Pancake flour takes the place of canned foods. Vacuum cream is a find worth reveling in one whole

[37]

summer. Toast for breakfast still isn't licked, as it should be, although rolls or biscuits are hot if put between the double Sterno cans or in the coal stove oven. My pewter plates are heirlooms, but what better contribution can my wife's ancestors make for my well-being? As yet no one has made the right dishes and bowls for cruising. This is something to talk about for endless hours—wider bases, deeper holding spaces, nonconductive material, and square. That Wilson pressed turkey was a find, but give me a new pot roast or fresh lobster and corn. The stove people are learning at last, but my old hunk of metal was designed only to get quick heat—if I don't buy slow-burning charcoal instead of my pet briquettes. But when it comes to cleaning this torture machine, the name of the maker and the number of the instrument are placed in raised letters just at the spots which make cleaning of ashes most difficult even with my new rubber dustpan. Of all the gadgets in the galley, I love best my garden trowel, to which Andy White tipped me off as the perfect coal shovel. I'm not ashamed of fire kindlers, and I bought two of the salt and pepper shakers in one, finally persuading the girls at home to put one on the home table. On motorboats there is usually a running inventory of foods on hand, with neat statistics showing the greatest peaks of demand. None of that for us. When we hit a harbor with a store, off we trudge to replenish, often forgetting to take the icebag along and always praying for the day when the kids will stop drinking bulky milk. Incidentally, washing and drying the dishes is not romantic but if done in twos has a rhythm of its own; a rhythm so definite and satisfying that if a guest sneaks on board and wants to help after the meal has been put away, invariably he disturbs the pattern of cleaning the dishes. Even if the guest's technique is more efficient than mine, I just don't like it at all, at all.

The minutiae of housekeeping bring endless thrills. Women must be dumb not to have thought of such and such a new idea. But on one score every skipper feels perpetually whipped. Nurr has the upper hand. Nurr is the sole universal

[38]

evidence of perpetual motion and growth. No doubt even out in the middle of the Pacific, forty days from shore, small piles of unanalyzable nurr start rolling up into corners. I promise you I have gathered enough nurr from the cabin floor of my boat to fill twenty mattresses and untold pillows. Where it all comes from is and ever will be a mystery. But the collection of it could be made less irritating, if not pleasant, if shipyards would learn that mills have long been turning out concave quarter-rounds. On my dream boat there won't be a right-angle corner. But every skipper is wiser than any manufacturer. That is the rule of the sea. For example, I'm still sore at the president of the Sterno Company. He turned out a neat job on his double-burner marine stove, but the flame damper is chained so that it will rattle even in the calmest sea. Some foreman must have studied long and diligently to devise that noisy devil. Also, the rails should be a trifle higher and should have pot holders. Out of affection for my warm morning Sterno I wrote to the president of the company to offer these suggestions. To my chagrin he called me on the phone and offered to make, specially for me, a set of pot holders. I spurned the offer, for I was interested only in the art and the welfare of seafarers. I bought me a set built for a Willis stove. They are not right but I wanted to teach Sterno a lesson—they couldn't bribe me. Reform was what I was after for all mankind.

Chapters could be written on the controversial use of sheets, the size and distinguishing colors of towels, brushing teeth during the morning swim. Within the small compass of a ship's galley, where all is diminutive, I have seen the huskiest of males play at keeping house. Some of the cruelest of men on shore have been known to give affectionate names to their favorite coffeepots or can openers and I wouldn't be surprised if they even petted with affection some of the gadgets of the galley. I imagine this must be so, for at times I'd rather see any one of my children fall overboard than lose Lucy, my Presto pressure cooker.

If there is woman in man, there is also a hunk of would-be

[39]

prophet in each of us. To predict the future gives a joy akin to control of the yet inexperienced. Prophesying and advocating are not so dissimilar at times. And so we start out on a cruise.

Leaving Nantucket we know the waters by taste, smell and temperature. The buoys nod to us as we go by and the bells play special tunes for the *Truant*, our cutter. But there comes a point when the charts, books and rulers are brought out. The charts, which have been put into boxes, special visible folders, and many other inept, expensive contraptions now are all creased, damp and disfigured. I'd rather buy new ones oftener than use any of the chart savers I have ever seen. I would like to whisper an idea to some smart merchant— cut charts into foldable sectors and mount them on light canvas. It's only on the creases that life makes for trouble. Out they come, all the modern counterparts of the astrolabe, and then thanks are offered to the government of the United States of America. Tides remain a mystery only as to cause, currents are just simple two-way rivers running through water rather than land. It all gets to be fairly easy. And there is no comparable thrill that I know of to charting a course, running through thick fog and hitting that buoy on the nose. That's when the skipper acquires a bit of godhood. It doesn't always happen. I remember violating all the maritime lawbooks by tying onto the Bell off Saddleback until some soup lifted. Then also I once hit No. 2 off Hyannis with such precision and unexpectedness that I wandered up and down the coast in search of another No. 2. Of course I envy the Einsteins of the sea but, from my perch, to be able to travel a thousand miles in a summer, getting places with fair accuracy, always seems like a special gift from heaven. It must be more than I deserve. Thirty miles in a fog, get what you're after, elation, suppressed surprise, fairly specious adoption of a take-it-for-granted attitude—that's fun, hurts no one, satisfies all the instincts of a crossword puzzler, and above all carries the gentle tickling emotion which develops whenever an intricate process turns into an unthinking, natural habit.

Some people sit and think, others just sit. And don't for a

moment think that it's easy to have a vacant mind. A useless
mind is a cinch, but an empty one is an art. To a degree
cruising helps toward that high goal. Sloshing along in an
even sea produces a slight dose of hypnosis. It's not unlike
the hum of a motor, or the thought-killing rhythms of the
worst of Bach. That special kind of monotony is not a distant
relative of sleep. And off on the boat, ties are severed. The
war in the rest of the world moves to another planet or,
rather, goes out of existence. The radio picks up only weather
report waves. Newspapers are mere mundane daily events in
the timeless aeons of man's history. Then when you strike the
breeze built for you, and all winds are custom-made for different types of temperaments, you stop thinking for a split
second and then you know for sure what the whole mad
world is about. Have you ever gone to sleep pondering an
intricate and difficult mathematical problem? It has stumped
you. But in the morning as you awake the answer is in your
mind. You are apt to think that it just came to you in your
first moment of awareness. That's not the fact. When the
old subconscious gets going it has sufficient power to frighten
mankind. And so at the wheel, flashes are shot from the subconscious which clarify all of life. Man's path is clear, you
even divine what Winston said to Franklin. Living a self-
contained economic life brings the feeling and power of self-
sufficiency. The modern ten dollar word for it is "escape."
But escape can be either a retreat or a forward march to the
rainbow of existence.

There is a further series of human experiences which on
the surface seems none too complimentary. The twin acro-
bats known as sadism and masochism are often two sides of
the same medallion, and cruising does a job on both, but
basically in a relationship between man and nature, not man
and man.

Sleeping in wet blankets, wave after wave trickling down
your frontal anatomy, days of never getting the salt out of
anything, fingers numb, eyes groggy with needed sleep, cursing at an unfriendly motor, becalmed in an objectionable

[41]

current, the toilet getting out of order, the fire refusing to get going—these are only a few of the perversities of life on the inanimate being called a ship. You get sore inside and out. You take punishment in the best tradition of the amateur spirit. You curse and complain and you detest the member of the crew who repetitiously announces that he loves discomfort. "For what?" you ask. All this brutality could be avoided. Certainly the easy answer is that the rewards of a fair wind and a landfall of the Camden hills are in the back of the memory and memory is for the purpose of spotting buoys in December. But that is only part of the story. Man likes a certain amount of beating—not by man but by the great phenomena of this world of ours. This is a true and efficient masochism, not the kind that is enjoyed for the sake of later make-believe brave recounting to timid friends. Probably the blood stream of man yearns for the toughening processes just as man loves the irritation of scratching until it hurts the healing scab of a wound. For in these days man must grow sensitive and hard, kindly and tough, imaginative and wooden, all at the same time. To balk the dictator boys we must be able to be cruel while at the same time realizing that such cruelty is not the object of life—merely a temporary compromise in order to subdue wild beasts. And in the process of taking a beating any crew shows a variety of capacities for endurance, with the strong one enjoying the additional sadistic pleasure of watching the more bedraggled ones suffer.

And then the trip is over. The entire crew looks forlorn and desperate. But appearances are deceptive, for, disheveled and abject, each and every one is dreaming of another cruise.

There are no objective tests of the beauty of cruising or of any harbor. Man's memory is tickled or not depending on the conditions of the approach. A friend of mine lost a rudder going into Christmas Cove—nothing could persuade him ever to return. Your anchor drags in Edgartown, you can't find scope in Sakonnet, it rains two days while you're in the Basin—don't tell me about trees, and shoreline, and beaches.

[42]

The softest sand, the tallest timbers, the ruggedest rocks are part of a setting of wave and tide and wind and rain and sun —and the picture can't be divided up. Each cruise develops its pets, often as a result of fortuitous events; the crew gathers experiences worthy of recall and re-experience. It's not like Conrad in quest of his youth. Rather is it the innate desire of man for intimacy. Maybe this explains why city folk go in for cruising more than do those wise people who live in small communities still capable of working out democracy. In fact, the most eager cruisers are the men who, born in small towns, moved to large cities. There is a compulsion which drives such men to go back and back to little harbors where the trees and rocks are as familiar as the faces of intimate friends. In such harbors the experience of being a part of an environ does not end at the water's edge. At Tenants you keep walking until you see the cow on the right-hand side of the road— then you know you can get your milk. At Acadia Mountain you look at the mooring—still without pennant. If a pennant should show up there some year we would all be lost, or, rather, have to learn to like a new friend. How are the rich tuberous-rooted begonias at Burnt Coat? Friendship with nature is merely a composite of myriad infinitesimal remembrances set in lucky scenes. But this desire to return to the favorites somehow does not seem to cut down the appetite for more and more experiences. At the Back Door a lady rings a bell as we get through the gut. Not for breakfast does the bell toll, but rather to express surprise and satisfaction that we ever made it safely. Where is there another bell ringer?

CHAPTER VII

ꞏ

A FEW REFORMS

EVERY TIME I SAIL over to the North Wharf in Joan's catboat *Comet II*, to see Joe and Miriam Price, I am reminded of the old City Club days. That club, to which
Joe Price devoted so much of his life, was a good teacher.
As a member of the Legislative Committee, chairman of
committees, and even a trustee over a span of fifteen years, I
got into the habit of reading all legislation of significance
introduced at Albany affecting New York City.

But the club lost its influence by not keeping awake. Organisms created by man are not unlike man. Excitement in
youth, holding on to what one has in middle age, resistance
to youth and the novel in late middle age, and then resignation in old age. I guess that's all that "shirt sleeves to shirt
sleeves" means in terms of generations. I rather guess General
Motors will have tough going after the originators pass on.
And so with the City Club—it made its contribution but
was unwilling to see the modern problems arising in their
new dress and outlines.

In 1913 I got excited about the waste of connecting men
and jobs, and the horrible expense and burden of thinking
that newspaper help and want ads were a satisfactory or efficient technique for handling employment facilities. England
and countries on the Continent had already created Free
Labor Exchanges, run by the governments. I went to Charles
H. Strong, then president of the club, and urged the club to
look into the matter. Strong appointed me chairman of a
special committee. I think he really wanted to get rid of this
overoptimistic youngster in that way. I asked Dr. Frank

[44]

Crane, the columnist, John B. Andrews, the wise and careful head of the American Association of Labor Legislation, and Mark Eisner, a then progressive young Democrat, to join me in the study. Eisner and Crane loafed along, but John and I prepared a report and a bill. A governor of New York State, now scarcely remembered, Martin Glynn, took up the measure and in less than a year New York established its first Free Public Employment Offices. When the war came, Governor Whitman asked me to consolidate through a clearinghouse all the public and private employment agencies. We were just learning that, short of a war, men could not be shifted like wheat, that a bricklayer in the Bronx was usually nontransferable even to Poughkeepsie. The mere time lag, the desire of the boss to interview, the exchange of references, all added dire complications to the transfer of jobs. But a start was made in dealing with the distress of connecting men and jobs—a preventable distress, a waste no decent society can afford.

Through this work I met Charles B. Barnes, with whom I lived for a year. In fact it was he who persuaded me to move to downtown New York. It was no slight shift as against an uptown background. Barnes was much older and wiser. He had come from the mining districts of West Virginia, worked for the Russell Sage people, and, getting $15 a week as an investigator, never understood the nerve of the Sage people in allowing him to use his judgment as to which families should get benefactions of $30 a week. This paradox gave him humor rather than irritation.

Barnsie knew that time changed many situations. He knew how to press for reforms of historic proportions without creating resistance on the part of the opposition. This quality is rare among liberals. Walter White, of the National Association for the Advancement of Colored People, has it to a high degree. To modify race bigotry against Negroes cannot be accomplished overnight. The ultimate objective must be kept in mind and still the daily battles must be fought as if all life depended on each little struggle.

Years ago when James Weldon Johnson and I used to go to lunch we found only two hotels which would admit us in all of New York City. And now I still represent some Negro every year or so in procuring admission to one restaurant or another. As a born Southerner, I've always been provoked at the supercilious attitude of many Yankees toward the Negro problem. They behave as if all Southerners were bigots and all Northerners were tolerant. It seems to me that the progress in the South is greater than in the North particularly when viewed against the rather valid fear of white people in much of the South where Negroes, if allowed to vote, might well capture the local governments, and retaliate for historic injustices practiced on them.

And the poll tax fight while in the hands of Congressman Marcantonio and other Communist front boys didn't help the cause of tolerance. They first dressed it up with the sale of stamps reading "Save America First," the only implication of which was to ask people to look at Russia. Whereas Russia has made a world contribution in the field of obliterating racial discriminations, such emphasis in the campaign didn't help with the legislation. Then for a time the anti-poll tax strategy was run from the North against the South, over-looking local Southern pride.

I'm not against a poll tax if it has a valid relationship to capacity to vote. In 1787 each and every colony had high property qualifications for voting. Property tests of $1,000 or 100 acres made sense in 1787. By and large the property owners were the literate, and were the only ones who could read one or more of the 93 newspapers then circulating through the 75 post offices. Out of four million people, 600,000 were illiterate Negroes and one-half the balance were illiterate women, for women's minds were thought unfit to educate, until more than a half century later. Of the balance, less than 25 per cent of the men could do more than read or write their own names even in sophisticated Williamsburg, Virginia. So naturally, the Founding Fathers, the wisest youngsters ever gathered in a meeting (average age forty-one, with six under thirty years of age), knew that a nation with such vast illiteracy could not possibly be formed if there were universal suffrage for all adults.

But now, with the miracle of free public education, with literacy well above 90 per cent, and the wide development of means of communication, a one dollar tax as entry fee for voting has no conceivable relationship to qualification for voting. No more relationship than if a state provided that only blue-eyed men and brown-eyed women could exercise the franchise.

I'm not sure what the immediate effect of abolishing the poll tax will be on our government. I suspect it will make little difference, just as when women were enfranchised. But as a matter of basic justice, as a proof that we believe in the democratic process, and as a symbol of hope for colored people, it is one of the "must" reforms for this nation. I have no doubt that the Supreme Court will invalidate state poll taxes if the case is developed with a Brandeis brief—full of factual information rather than mere quotations from outworn legalisms, nonrelevant opinions of other days.

"GET OFF THE SIDEWALK"

One of my most treasured possessions is my card of honorary membership in the Pullman Porters Union, otherwise called the Brotherhood of Sleeping Car Porters, dated 1927.

Jestingly, I tell my friends that with such a card I could throw any one of them out of a lower berth on any train. I've never tried it; but I've never failed to engage Pullman porters in conversation about our union.

The Negro problem is one of folkway dimensions. The South has no monopoly on prejudice. Employers are not alone at fault. Many trade unions up north refuse to admit Negro members. Nearly twenty years ago I represented the great scenic artists Lee Simonson, Joe Mielziner, Robert Edmond Jones and others, in working out the basis of their admission to Scenic Artists Local 829—amusingly enough,

[47]

a division of the Painters, Paperhangers & Decorators International Union. Here was an odd but effective union, this Local 829. It claimed as members the men with the brush, the creative designers, the employers and the contractors. This union was essential to protect its members from a few shabby producers. Too many shows had opened and closed without paying a cent for scenery. But with the admission of our greatest stage designers one would have thought that the color of a designer's skin would scarcely be the factor to determine employment by a New York theatrical producer.

Although I represented the union in many struggles against chiseling fly-by-night producers, I also took up the cudgels for Perry Watkins, the first Negro offered a contract to design scenery for a first-class Broadway production. Guthrie McClintic, one of our distinguished directors, wanted Perry Watkins to do a job. He held no union card—hence McClintic couldn't hire him. Watkins got his card, but not without a battle.

Gains for minority groups such as Negroes present problems of neat strategy. Walter White, of the National Association for the Advancement of Colored People, following the path of his great predecessor, James Weldon Johnson, and Thurgood Marshall, the eminent aggressive attorney for the association, do an outstanding job because in each separate fight they are tough and bitter, even though they think as leaders of their people in historic terms of basic changes of societal attitudes. Only recently, I went to Thurgood's office to celebrate with his staff his victory in the White Primary case. It was a good party. But we knew he had just begun that battle. He had taken only the first poll boxes. We had celebrated on other occasions, such as the victory of equal pay for Negro teachers and of admission to graduate schools without race discrimination.

There is one case I still want to bring, but I can't get any support for it. The Supreme Court has held that a railroad need not allow Negroes in diners or Pullmans with white folk, but at least must supply similar service in some other car. Until recently, many Negroes were unable to buy sleepers on our railroads. Now an old technique of railroading has been extended. A Negro wants a lower berth from Texas to New York City. The ticket agent tells him there are no more lowers. "Here is a stateroom. I'll give it to you at the price of a lower." Thus does the railroad avoid the democratic sight of a Negro in an open Pullman.

The case I'd like to try is this: A Negro goes to the ticket office, gets the stateroom, paying $11 for a $34 accommodation (in addition to the regular fare). The next man in line would be the plaintiff in my test case—a Carl Sandburg type of citizen. He asks for a stateroom. He gets one. He pays $34 —instead of $11. Then we go to court and say: "Judge, how come that railroads are permitted to discriminate against white folk in favor of Negroes on the price of accommodations?"

Truly, I believe that many railroads would welcome such a suit, and pray for our victory. They would prefer to cut through present discriminations, but are afraid to do so save under court edict.

In New York we have done badly with the problem. Harlem is the biggest Negro city in the world. In 1935 there was a riot, heads broken, stores looted. The Mayor appointed a commission to investigate. As a member of the Mayor's Commission on Harlem, headed by Dr. Charles R. Roberts, a leading Negro doctor, I held the hearings on housing conditions. Others looked into playgrounds, schools, police, hospitals, etc.

We found many houses—small brownstones, twenty-foot fronts—renting beds to fifty to sixty men each day. In each house there were about eighteen beds, but many Negroes live in shifts—three shifts to a bed. Sick or tired—get off that mattress! The next occupant claims it as his exclusive home. That cot is his castle. No wonder there are riots. It's to the credit of the people of Harlem that they have enough guts to break out once in a while. The report of our commission was suppressed. It still lies in the Mayor's office. It was critical of our city in its duty to Harlem. It suggested economic and civic reforms.

Many years ago, Will White of Emporia went to Haiti with Cameron Forbes and others to look into United States-Haitian relations. Will told me about one of the educated Haitians who acted as spokesman for the people of the island. It seems that Frenchmen in the old days, borning illegitimate children by Haitian women, did not sell the offspring at auction as was our practice before 1861, but instead sent the kids to Europe to be educated. From such ancestry much of Haitian culture and leadership stems. White was ashamed when the last spokesman said in effect: "I thank you for the roads and hospitals, and brick and mortar brought here by the great United States. But you have brought something else, in addition. Until you came I never was told 'get off the sidewalk, you damn nigger.' If you could take back the inferiority feeling you have put on our shoulders, I'd be willing to have you take back also all the buildings and improvements you have given us. Thank you."

This is the essence of the problem. In the past decade we have made great strides. We have great distances still to go.

CHAPTER VIII

A DEMOCRATIC LAWYERS' GUILD

ABOUT A QUARTER OF A CENTURY AGO Nelson Spencer, a stoutly liberal lawyer, suggested that I should not join the American Bar Association because it refused to take in Negro members. At about this same time I received a perfunctory circular from that great organization asking me to join. I wrote back: "Do you take in Negro members?" The reply I received read: "Sorry, we did not know you were a

Negro." Quixotic, maybe, but I've never become a member, even though in 1944 the color bars for admission were slightly bent although not quite broken down.

This association has for decades represented status quo. Change is usually anathema to legal luminaries. Why should they scrap all their tried knowledge for experimental ideas? Surely they have a vested interest in old lady Stare Decisis. Aside from its great Committee on Civil Rights, the Association has stood fairly consistently for reaction.

With this in mind I drew up a plan in 1937 for a liberal lawyers' guild. Frank Walsh, a giant liberal, Governor Charles Poletti, Judge Ferdinand Pecora, Judge Jerome Frank, George Bowden, of Chicago, Judge Samuel Null and a small group of us got it started. Membership grew by leaps and bounds but mainly in New York City and along the eastern seaboard. I rode the rails to Philadelphia, Baltimore, Chicago, Boston and elsewhere addressing small groups of lawyers who were interested in personal liberty as well as in property rights. I found fertile fields. The American Bar Association had stood as an advocate for Big Business and Big Law Shops.

Our group was concerned with the new liberal social legislation. We thought we might be the answer to the Liberty League, which was guided by lawyers who dared incorrectly advise their clients that the National Labor Relations Act was clearly unconstitutional and hence should be resisted. We had a golden opportunity.

But we were asleep. I was chiefly at fault. The Communists sneaked in, never saying "Here we are—the Commies." Their tactics of wreck or rule became evident after the first convention. Outside of New York City the Lawyers Guild units were still naïve about Communist tactics, but the New York membership controlled the Guild. All too late we saw what was happening. A lawyers' guild—dealing, we thought, with problems of our craft—was being converted into a mouthpiece for American Communists. With undemocratic caucuses in advance of meetings, with controls held and orders being issued by Joseph Brodsky, chief counsel for the American Communists, with naïve liberals allowing themselves to be used as window dressing, the independent undisciplined liberals—no doubt a majority of the total—were outvoted time and again, by organized secret Commie caucuses.

A resolution introduced in February, 1939, stating our faith in democracy and our opposition to totalitarian forms of government, Fascist or Communist, was defeated. We had no choice but to withdraw. Frank Walsh led the way. Judge Pecora, the retiring president, refused to be a stooge for the Commies, and the heart and core of the organization resigned.

The remnant of the Lawyers Guild is probably still in existence somewhere. I doubt if the Lawyers Guild has ever repudiated its former stand on antidemocratic forces.

But every year lawyers write in to suggest a new national association of liberal lawyers. Some think that the American Bar Association can be converted from its stodgy path. Others desire a society of limited membership to examine as craftsmen of the law the legal social problems of our day.

We still must find the technique for handling secret, underground, undemocratic minority controls of democratic organizations. Teachers Union, American Labor party, Lawyers Guild, are a few of the projects frustrated by Communists and fellow travelers (innocent or otherwise). The American Civil Liberties Union woke up just in time. We can thank Roger Baldwin and the Reverend John Haynes Holmes, its chairman, for preventing that institution from falling into totalitarian hands.

THE AMERICAN CIVIL LIBERTIES UNION

For twenty years the weekly meetings of the American Civil Liberties Union have been a joy and an education. I've not been too regular at the luncheons lately, what with much time in Washington plus trips abroad. At the law office we usually have a full half dozen civil liberties matters in work at all times, and each year a new flock of exciting young lawyers come in to see me about a job in our office because of their desire to get into some kind of law other than chattel mortgages, leases and corporate reorganizations. Law is a kind of Robin Hood game, with nonpaying clients, mostly people unjustly pushed around, taking the place of patients at the clinics and wards of the medical profession. Much of which joy the big shots of the Bar are missing entirely.

The Union is Roger Baldwin's life, and to a great extent vice versa. On its toes to protect the rights of a Scopes to teach Darwinism; to fight against our shocking acceptance of racism in the compulsory concentration of Japanese citizens; to resist the improper expulsion of a trade-union member because he opposed with ideas the leadership of the union; to contest the breaking up of Communist or Christian Front meetings. Minorities, often composed of the neurotic fringe and the fanatics, need special support and legal representation. Otherwise the state, the big industrialists, the vigilantes ride over them, and in time threaten the liberty of us all.

On a meager budget the A.C.L.U. has made a significant contribution to the cause of freedom of the human mind. It has done a vast amount of worthy work. It is still quite inexplicable to me why so few people join the organization. Is it that they have no taste for defending those with whom they disagree? If so, they fail to grasp our American religion— the Bill of Rights. Is it because we have done a poor job in explaining our cases and our philosophy? Is it that our periphery of attack or defense is too vague or wide? Whatever the reason, I should imagine no other group with so exiguous a budget has done so much work.

Of course, the associations of lawyers should have carried the burden. But it was only recently that the American Bar Association became actively interested in freedom of thought. As a striking exception, in the case against Mayor Hague of Jersey City, Grenville Clark's Committee on Civil Rights of the American Bar Association gave great aid, and once in a while that organization files a brief amicus in a civil liberties case. But in the main it is excited exclusively about property rather than liberty of the mind.

THE RIGHT TO READ, TO HEAR, TO SEE

One of the miracles of this war is the preservation of civil freedoms. We succumbed to no such hysteria as during World War I. No outrages of any significance by local police. With Francis Biddle as attorney general, lovers of civil liberties could not have a better friend in power. Even restraints on news for military security have been deftly and generously administered by Byron Price. Some of the Leftists are truly disappointed—it's been difficult for them to conjure up bugaboos against the Roosevelt administration.

But there is an increasing need for constant vigilance over the individual right to read, to hear, and to see. Of late years I have become persuaded that an aspect other than defense of freedom of thought has been overlooked by most of us. I've spent a good portion of my life defending books and movies and radio and unpopular left-wing movements from governmental restraints. But I'm convinced that the impact of state controls—postal, movie censorship, sedition laws, obscenity statutes, police ordinances—all together exclude from the market place of thought only a negligible number of ideas. Much more material is banned through consolidation into a very few hands of the controls over communication —movies, radio, and the press.

Our faith in freedom of speech is predicated on only one theorem. We hold that, in the clash of ideas, truth will rise to the top in the market place. But there must be a market, wide as possible and free, in which case we believe in the people's judgment. They can go wrong for a time, but who is sure enough of himself to know what in the realm of ideas is incontestably "wrong"? We trust no one person or group to make the decisions, no matter how wise they may seem to be.

Hence, if in any town one man owns all the halls for speakers, the only local radio station and the only newspaper, there is no longer a market. Clash, conflict, matching of ideas are dead and finished.

Originally freedom to speak was deemed a gift from heaven, and the Founding Fathers talked about it as a "natural" right of man. This was in the era of town meetings. A century later Judge Holmes and Judge Brandeis gave the concept a new connotation. No longer was it the right to speak—rather, it was the right to hear. For only by the free flow of ideas does society become enriched. Only by the back and forth of controversy do we gain that capacity for critical analysis which tends to correct errors.

In the meanwhile the Industrial Revolution put its dirty monopolistic hands on the merchandising of thought. Chain newspapers, syndicate columns, boiler plate pages, radio chains, agreements between the Movie Quintet of Giants, monopolies of movie theaters—these and other developments spelled the closing down of hundreds of newspapers, the devitalization of local radio stations, the subjugation of independent motion-picture production and exhibition. The result of this pattern must be either the domination of the community by the group which owns presses, and often also the microphones, or the spiritual uprising of the people with a profound distrust of the few people who control these vital instruments for creating public opinion. Either course is disastrous to our Bill of Rights.

Much can be done to reverse this curve of ownership in fewer and fewer hands. If incentive taxation is the order of the day, why not also incentive subsidies? Telephone rates should be reshaped to help small radio stations withstand envelopment by the four big chains. Taxation should be framed as an incentive for more media of expression. Paper rationing, now aiding unduly the giants with the greatest amounts of advertising paper wastage, should be put into reverse gear.

Even if there were diversity in this market place, a further trend threatens our concept of freedom of the mind. For my part I would not ban a line from the mailbags but I would allow no quantity publications in the mails unless the name of the responsible author or publisher was printed clearly on the material. I would go further. In order to protect dollar investors, we call for complete disclosure through the SEC of all facts behind the sale of bonds and shares of stock. This, to stop a Jack of Diamonds—"Robbing my pocket of silver and gold." But there is something worth more than silver or gold. The wealth of a people depends solely on the development of thought. We should apply the same theory of full disclosure to prevent fraud in ideas and to reappraise the value of caveat emptor in the field of ideas.

Our theory of the First Amendment rests on the ability of the public to appraise and weigh ideas presented to it. In this busy world none of us is able to examine all the facts underlying each important public issue. Of necessity we make up our minds by reading the opinions and research of others. This the anti-American forces are aware of. This is the basic Hitler weapon. Hence, we find evil movements—that is, the cowardly ones—pumping millions of pamphlets and circulars into the market under phony names or anonymously. This is a prime deceit on our way of life. Our Bill of Rights gives each of us the right to speak our mind, and hence negates the need for anonymity. Who put up the money for America First? Had we known, it would have died young. Who supported the Franco movement in America? Was it the Chase Bank gang? Who is back of the anti-Catholic K.K.K.? Is it true that Henry Ford financed Father Coughlin? Who are the leading oil company officials contributing large sums of money to Gerald L. K. Smith? Who gave Tom Dewey, while he was prosecutor in New York County, thousands of secret dollars with which he could soften up pimps and prostitutes to be used as witnesses?

I have supreme faith in mankind and the democratic process. I'm not afraid of any movement so long as we are informed as to its source of income and are aware of who gets the money. By the way, what did happen to all the money collected to defend Bridges and to free Browder? Was it spent exclusively for those purposes?

Two out of many pertinent trivial events come to my mind.

I was at Town Meeting of the Air one evening. I wanted to see and hear Verne Marshall, the man who in 1941 as head of the "No Foreign Wars" Committee, was urging immediate treaties with Hitler. Just before going off the air George Denny, the moderator, happened to see me in the audience and suggested that I ask a question. I merely asked Mr. Marshall where he got the money for his campaign. Mr. Marshall said he would make the contributors' names public. Later he refused to do so except for a few unimportant ones. But the question over the nationwide hookup started something. We followed Marshall up at other speeches—Boston and elsewhere. The query "Who's backing Marshall?" tagged after him. In no time at all he was done and finished. He couldn't risk disclosure. But he asked his followers to support Gerald L. K. Smith, and we still don't know the names of the half dozen backers who put up no less than a couple of hundred thousand dollars for Marshall.

Years ago, when the defense of the Scottsboro boys seemed to me to be most important, the Communists had stolen the show. Earl Browder asked me to get together a group to help raise more funds. I did so, and to my office there came one day representatives of the churches, the Negro movement, the Civil Liberties group, and others. I prepared a United Front agreement, but insisted on inserting a clause for audit of books and full disclosure. The Communists could not refuse; they could raise no more money over the bodies of the Scottsboro boys, if they pursued their old tactics of concealment.

After the meeting, I said jestingly to Browder, "Whenever I do a chore like this I want a personal favor in return." He assented. I suggested that I wanted to be sure that the *Daily Worker* would not stop calling me a Public Enemy and Fascist every other Tuesday. Browder turned me down. He

[57]

said that they couldn't keep on calling me names because of the new collaboration program. They would even have to be friendly with the Catholic Church. This was in 1935.

But we never did find out what happened to all the Scottsboro money previously donated by the public. The great job done by Judge Samuel Leibowitz, who served as attorney for the boys, was without a single penny of fee; and so I suspect that the *Daily Worker*, other Communist publications, and many activities carried on to destroy or capture unions were financed by the siphoning off of "Scottsboro" nickels and dimes.

Disclosure of sources of income and public filing of tax returns should be required of all purveyors of propaganda. The best of our labor unions make full reports. There is no corporate report so complete, so simple, so clear as the annual financial statement of many of our unions. Corporations should also make separate disclosure of contributions to propaganda movements. It took a Senatorial committee to dig out the fact that, from 1934 to 1936, General Motors had spent close to one million dollars on labor spies and private labor detectives.

I would apply the rule to one and all who sell ideas, including churches which leave the spiritual pulpit to campaign for or against child labor laws, the public teaching of evolution, or for a political Jewish state in Palestine. I know no satisfactory definition of propaganda. I confess that I always feel that my own writings are purely educational and that the opposition is nothing but propaganda.

CHAPTER IX

,

THE BATTLES OF RACE AND RELIGION

TODAY WE ARE IN POLAND and close to Vienna, that is, we the Allies. I've been to Poland only once, going up from Vienna in 1921. I went over as adviser to James N. Rosenberg, the artist-lawyer, who was heading up the work of the Jewish Joint Distribution Committee in Europe. Some of us youngsters had persuaded generous Felix Warburg, socially minded banker, to turn toward financing the stricken by aid of a constructive nature rather than solely by charitable gifts. We knew that under either course currency fluctuations would take a heavy toll of any funds in transit in all those inflated nations.

Before going to Poland to help set up a rediscount bank for the innumerable little loan societies which peppered that country, I spent a few exciting days in Vienna. The first night there I had dinner with Sir William Goode, who was then representative of the League of Nations, or at least the Allied Nations, in the running of Austria. Walter Lippmann was there and also a beautiful slender blonde reporter girl, Dorothy Thompson. This was the first time I met Dorothy Thompson whom I love despite or maybe because of her violence of feelings.

It was Thompson who, the next morning, was out in the mob in front of the Hotel Bristol which was then being attacked because, as the residence of Sir William, it had become the symbol of the unreachable price of bread. In these days no mob would attack a hotel. Revolutionaries look at waterworks and radio stations instead of symbols. Thus does the world progress!

[59]

I moved up into Poland, cold, bleak and dreary. All through my life I have regretted my language ignorance but never enough to buckle down and work on learning the means of communication with other-speaking people. Hence I have increasing admiration for Henry Wallace who, walking to and from his office with a teacher, has learned Spanish and Russian, so that on his trips he is one of the few Americans who is able to talk with and to address the masses, for whom he is one of the international hopes of the future. In Poland I was peculiarly handicapped with only English and inadequate German and French.

We set up a kind of two-named paper rediscount bank. This bank would take the notes of local loan societies which in turn had received notes from borrowers, much in the fashion of our industrial loan type of bank. Thus the funds from American benefactors flowed to the cobbler and the farmer with dignity; the shoulders of a borrower are always a little straighter than those of a beggar.

From Poland I went through Germany to England to work with the now Lord Nathan of Churt on the charter of a Palestinian Bank. Here I lost out on the one issue of deep interest to me in connection with the setting up of the bank. I wanted the bank to be limited to the handling of accounts of co-operative societies, with no loans flowing to individuals direct.

That J.D.C. experience was valuable. It made me read up widely on co-operatives throughout the world, and above all, gave me my first insight into the regrettable but understandable nationalist, rather than merely religious, feeling of Jews. Even in Poland, where persecution had of course developed solidarity and strong racial feelings for the sake of protection if nothing else, I noted innumerable Jewish leaders who, though more religious than myself, which takes very little, were far more interested in national political Jewishdom than in its religious or spiritual content.

Here I became convinced of the evil of Zionism as it was being sold to the world. Chaim Weizmann, strong, silent and realistic, has done an extensive job. He has dramatized the need of a haven. He has led the movement which proved the Jews' capacity, despite centuries of condemnation as Luft-mensch, to become creative farmers and producers. But a better and bigger Weizmann must soon come along to let the world know that Jews are people; they need no isolation. They need decency and praise and condemnation in quality and kind not different from those meted out to all other peoples. A new Weizmann will shout that Jewish people now should go back to Europe to live. One of the tests of the fruits of victory in this war is the capacity of those who were pushed around by Hitler to go back and replant their feet on their old soil and proudly say: "Here we are, pitching in to make a joint new world of sorry Europe."

There is no need for a separate state in order to bestow on civilization the contributions of Jewish culture. Those are or aren't bestowed by now, just as the Greek culture is part of us in our daily lives even though the old Greece has been dead and finished for centuries.

It's about time that the Protestant world stepped into this Jerusalem squabble, as an arbiter at least. It might have a sobering influence on both Jews and Arabs to the end that power politics might be submerged. The United Nations, going beyond UNRRA, no doubt will announce that one of the first duties of the peace is to aid all refugees—Poles, Greeks, Jews, Catholics, Freemasons, etc.—to go back to their homes and farms in Europe. Surely the war is primarily rooted in the indignation of the world at Hitler's pushing people around because of race, creed, color and political beliefs. If any refugees, on returning to their old farms, homes and shops, find them occupied by decent nonbigots, there will be no need to dispossess these civilized new tenants, for reparations in Germany can easily supply homes and stores and farms for all those pushed around by Hitler, and at the expense of the Hitler followers.

The Jews have a chance to cross a Jordan, but a Jordan of the mind and the spirit rather than one pointing to different soil and borders.

This same basic problem, race-religion, is the main sore of our world.

When I was in Montreal in March of last year on my way to England I wandered around the town. The variance in language in different sections of the community seemed on the surface to create no problem. But the social need for separate schools, English-Protestant and French-Catholic, makes for less than homogeneity. Until recently, the French schools taught little English, and vice versa. Canada, with its one-third French-Catholic population, is decades away from the kind of unified folkway that is necessary for the full functioning of the democratic process.

On an earlier trip, I was held over a few hours in Ireland, on the River Shannon, not far from Limerick, having flown in from Lisbon on the way to England. I looked up the hill and saw an attractive schoolhouse. With Douglas Poteat, lawyer-economist, I climbed the boggy path to the school. It was a three-classroom building. Up to eight, eight to twelve, and twelve on. There were two teachers. We went into the room for the eight-to-twelves, where a tall, twinkle-eyed, middle-aged man, with rod in hand, was giving instruction. After the usual introduction, we're from New York, et cetera, I asked why he taught Erse in these days of a dream of Basic English. Obviously to this man, dedicated to teaching, and a good job he did, I'm sure, the purpose of Erse was to educate the people of Southern Ireland to isolationism. A separate language did more for nationalism than a flag or national anthem or salute.

When we were about to leave, the teacher's fifteen-year-old daughter appeared on the scene with her father's lunch, not much, but well wrapped. We walked down to the little village with this bright, sharp Irish girl and her friend. "Why do you hate the English?" was my opener. "No such thing," came the answer. "I have a brother in the RAF and next month I'm going to London to work as a secretary. I can do better there than here. I can get two pounds a week to start with."

[62]

I made inquiries and found that a high proportion of South Ireland men were in the British military services and many more working in the war factories of England and Scotland. But still it's the same problem. No matter what the historic causes, religious or racial nationalism has made and still makes irrational, cruel and costly enemies of mankind. South Ireland wants to own Protestant North Ireland. I tried to find a rationale for this desire. According to the census of 1937, about one-third of the population of Northern Ireland is Catholic. Do they get shabby treatment? Are they not serviced by police and garbage collectors and roads just the same as the rest of the population? The mass of people, as distinguished from the leaders, had no answers to these queries. As for the leaders, I suspect they are concerned primarily with a yen for power and political campaign issues. And so Ireland is torn with dissension which throttles all progress.

India—what a mess. Deep-dyed old religious fanaticism going so far as to create a religion of inherited ostracism. The existence of untouchables is an extension, without cause or trial, of a Devil's Island on the mainland.

Puerto Rico, with its dark-skinned population, raises obstacles to an economic federation of the Caribbean. If we can't integrate trade, shipping and industry in those few scattered interdependent islands, what hope for a confederation of the Balkans? England, France, Holland, United States truly desire to institute economic planning in the Caribbean. Resistance is racial. The Puerto Ricans in measurable numbers demur at going into new close relationships with those "niggers" in Trinidad.

In our own land, the 14 million Negroes, even with the strides made since 1900, live in inequalities which should make us humble in trying to teach other people how to live in amity.

Even with a world of free trade in goods and ideas we would still have the basic problem of the planet—bigotry, unreasonable loyalty, religious fanaticism, and belief in color superiorities. Probably all these petty traits result from basic inferiorities and insecurities. But we know they can be eradicated. This has been proved by the Soviet government. Within a quarter of a century, racial and color discriminations have been substantially rooted up in a land of dozens of creeds and races, although the problem was simpler than elsewhere on our globe since no such fanaticisms had existed in Russia as in India or the United States, for example. The all-pervading century-old hatred of the czars had gradually diminished the temperature of internecine hates. Maybe someone will whip up a new world hate which will reduce the virulence of all local hates. No doubt Hitler, without aiming to, has done much in that direction. I doubt if love can take the place of hate. It seems to me more likely that man will develop a new hate—the bitter hate of bigotry, of injustice, which might have the power to destroy all racial and religious hates. Maybe love as a mass instrument is too soft and tender and individual in its connotation to beat down present mass hatreds.

PANDORA'S BOX

There is no question but that Hitler has performed a Pandora. From all the insecure, unhappy and unsuccessful he has invited forth venom and hate for minority groups, particularly for the Jewish people. In our land, in different decades and sections, we have had violent anti-Catholic, anti-Irish, anti-Negro and anti-Oriental movements. Only a century ago Boston, the home of our Bill of Rights, burned down a convent.

The anti-Semitic forces have been aided by the lack of Jewish leadership. Between Stephen Wise, with his flamboyant bravery, and Joseph Proskauer, with his brilliant timidity, there is little forthright statesmanship. On the one hand, there is extreme frightened racial consciousness and, on the other, a policy of closing eyes and whispering hush-hush.

Wealthy businessmen and poor neurotic little people have financed the Gerald L. K. Smiths, the Father Coughlins, the

[64]

Pelleys and Edmondsons. These and others have poured into the stream of our reading matter millions of vile documents, bitter and false, fanning race hatred. It was only natural that well-wishing people should try to suppress this material. They didn't quite dare make it a crime to utter racial hatreds —a vague concept at best—so they proposed legislation which would deny mailing privileges to any "defamatory and false statements which tend to expose persons characterized by race or religion to hatred, contempt, ridicule . . ."

At the recent hearing before the Post Office Committee of the House of Representatives I appeared in behalf of the American Civil Liberties Union in opposition to the measure. I put forward the usual stock arguments. It wouldn't be effective. Falsity is a vague concept. What does "tend" mean? As a prior restraint on freedom of the press it was unconstitutional. It would set a dangerous precedent. I agreed with Postmaster Walker that there was no clear line that the Posmaster General could draw between hate, ridicule or contempt and mere criticism. But the Union had no affirmative remedy to suggest other than the long pull of public education, and faith in the ultimate wisdom of the American people.

During the hearing I went on to set forth my own opinion that the evil of organized hate was more than negligible. Much of the anti-American racial hate literature is distributed under the protection of anonymity. It travels as first-class mail. I opposed all suppressions but took the occasion once more to propose a program of full disclosure. All printed material except books must, under present laws periodically set forth details of ownership in order to qualify for cheap second-class postage rates. It is irrational to continue to allow secrecy and stealth for publications just because the distributing organization can afford to send its printed words widespread through high-cost first-class postage. Contributions to election campaigns are subject to public reporting. This hasn't worked without subterfuge but it has accomplished much good. Surely issues discussed between elections are often as important as the elections themselves.

The Treasury, rather reluctantly, had at long last in 1942 compelled the filing of tax returns of information from all nonprofit-making organizations except only trade unions and religious groups, for which new legislation would have been needed. These returns show names of officers, income and disbursements, and the names of persons giving to or receiving from any such organization over $4,000 in any one year. I favor making such returns a matter of public record.

All legislation has a plus and a minus. No statute is an unmixed, unanimous blessing. If it limits no one, then legislation is not needed. I'm willing to see some of the taste and comfort removed from the decent desire of donors for anonymity, in return for the exposure of the fortunes now pumped into the mailbags contra to our way of life. I've seen no statistics, and I doubt if there be any, but I should imagine that the total spent on propaganda of all kinds, in printed form for general public distribution, would exceed a half billion dollars per annum. Of the more than 50,000 nonprofit-making groups operating in our land, 49,000 find no problem in reporting and would not oppose disclosure. Furthermore, great additional income taxes would flow into the national treasury as a result of publicity of such returns. Many gifts to nondeductible organizations have no doubt been allowed on individual returns because of our governmental ignorance as to the changing activities of such organizations.

I would not allow a single piece of mail of one hundred or more copies to go into our postal pouches without disclosure as to source. We applied such a rule to literature of foreign agents even before the war. We still have internal agents who should be smoked out. If they can stand up in the open, then we can argue them down.

But to ban all material capable of creating ridicule or contempt or hatred of a religious or racial group is absurd. I explained at the hearing that I wanted for myself the right to hold up to contempt the Baptists when they outlaw teaching of evolution, the Catholics of Boston when they fight freedom for birth control, the Jehovah's Witnesses group, in their un-American attacks on Catholicism, or the Zionists when they urge a political Jewish state. To create disdain for the anti-Negro group is a public duty. The line between criticism and inducements to hate is not always clear and neat, and Frank Walker, the Postmaster General, was sound when he advised the House he wanted no such responsibility as the legislation would give him.

No bill passed our Congress, but in various communities local restrictions on racial and religious hate literature have been established. I wonder how many of the wealthy supporters of bigotry would continue their support if their names and contributions were made public? It is the organization of hates on racial and religious grounds that is objectionable. Private individual preference for Italians rather than for Serbs, or for Frenchmen rather than for Mexicans—all such attitudes are merely evidence of the ease with which unfounded and usually unreasoned generalizations are made by man.

At Exeter Academy recently I discussed with the students the sources of bigotry. I asked the boys to dig into their early lives to discover when they first heard about "dirty nigger" or "nasty sheenies or wops or polacks." When did someone first engender hate for "papists." The boys started such researches as games of individual solitaire and later swapped such experiences with roommates. For some, I am told, it was the first appreciation of the fact that bigotry was the lazy man's tool; generalizations of that sort were foul and stupid. I asked, "Did you have any evidence to support the charge? Why did you fall for it? Have you checked up since then? Why be a lazy push-over for ideas which condemn groups of people?"

I think this is a persuasive approach to the problem— certainly better than sentimental pleas for so-called tolerance. Catholics, Negroes, Jews—minorities need no tolerance. Oppressors of minorities are in need of reappraisal of their evidence—and public disdain for groundless hates.

CHAPTER X

LEFT-HANDED ROBINS

A STRAY SPARROW, not one of our regular visitors, was on a branch of the ailanthus tree in the yard at 11th Street. I recalled having watched for hours our robin family in Nantucket. It did seem to me that, whereas one of the robins was left-handed, the direction in which the sparrow turned its head showed no preference for either side. I can find no study of left-handedness in animals. I know that, except in rare cases, we can test man for left-handedness by examining the eyes in order to find out if there is a dominance in one eye or the other, and a concomitant dominance in the opposite side of the brain. Is the characteristic of dominance, which we think makes for great convenience—people don't become confused as to which hand to use—something peculiar to man? I suggest that only sophisticated forms of life develop the kind of confusion which makes necessary the dominance of one side or the other of the brain, the eye and the hand.

The Jewish people centuries ago must have been left-handed. Hebrew is written from the right-hand side of the page to the left, an easier way for left-handed people to write and read. Statistics seem to show that there is more left-handedness among Jewish people than among some others. It is perhaps an odd kind of acquired characteristic which in time became an inherited characteristic. Maybe gradual acquisition over centuries spells inheritance. There really isn't much difference between a 999-year lease and a deed to a piece of property. We know little about one-side-brain dominance or the ambidexterity of other races vis-à-vis the writing of such races, as for example the up-and-down script of certain Oriental groups. Latin seems mature in this respect, since it was written one line from right to left and then the next line from left to right, alternating every other line. Is that evidence of an unconfused people? Maybe the old Romans were all mirror writers in addition.

Our 11th Street birds, whether right- or left-beaked, don't seem to migrate. Migration has always seemed to me to be one of the most intriguing problems facing the mind of man: the salmon going up the river to spawn and die, the hummingbirds flying ten thousand miles, the eels leaving Nantucket to go to the Sargasso Sea—but most of them conducting a two-way voyage. It is amusing how people at each end of the trip look on the migration differently, except in those cases where animals go home to die. It's not easy to find out which is the home port of a migratory animal and to which port it travels.

I am disinclined to follow those authorities who think that birds migrate for food or warmth or because of mere climate. That theory seems to me to be denied by the millions of birds which fly over and past rich lands of comfortable temperatures to migrate to places where there is little food and a hard life. And in some areas where many birds of different species go, there is deadly competition for food and survival, while an extra day's travel would bring ease and luxury. Nor do the theories which are predicated on the glacier concept appeal to me. It's too easy for man to blame everything on an unknown glacier. I wouldn't be at all surprised if someone someday disproved the entire glacial theory. It does not make much sense to say that when the glacier plodded along it pressed the animal life to the south and when the glacier receded, the animals started to come back, at least for temporary trips, out of preglacial habit.

It is not impossible that this great homing instinct bears similarity to an airplane traveling on a beam. I can't believe that animals have memories sufficient to go back and forth over thousands of miles year after year to the identical places

[69]

at two ends of the run. That birds wait over on their trips at our fogbound lighthouse at Great Point proves little. I can't imagine that any of our known five senses—touch, taste, smell, hearing and sight—exist in any form of life with sufficient potency to act as the sole directive power for these migrations. If little man can invent a machine which can send a ray on which an airplane can travel across the world, surely animals may also be working on a beam of nature. This idea intrigues me because so much of the migration has a direct relation to procreation. Can it not be argued that the great urge of sex and procreation is more potent than a tiny radio box made of metal and wood by mere man? Or have the birds a religious image—a Mecca, a Zion for undisclosed emotions?

The inner temperature of birds and other animals may not be unrelated to migratory urges. The uniformity of man's temperature at 98.6 is less than a fully answered riddle, it seems to me. Aside from cases where the human organism goes out of kilter, there appears to be little evidence of major deviations in temperature among men. Man's temperature might well have deviated comparably to his capacity to see or hear or taste. Moreover, just as young children can hear sounds that older folks can't hear, we might expect comparable variations in temperature as one grows older. I've not been able to find a full table of the temperature of animals, with a breakdown by different types of birds and fish. I don't know exactly how they take the temperature of a bird, but the last figure I saw indicated that certain birds have a steady temperature of about 110 degrees. This, of course, makes them much lighter and therefore makes flying much easier, in so far as heat rises. On the way back from Scotland in December the temperature in part of the plane was about 35 degrees below zero. In a very light plane possibly some new kind of synthetic concentrated heat chambers might be of flying value.

This constant migration of birds to the south is not unlike the migration of people. Not only the well-to-do birds, but also the low-temperature birds probably go south every year, just as people who can afford it and who feel the cold most acutely, go south first. I don't mind cold and I dislike Florida.

REPLACEMENT OF OLD PARTS DEPARTMENT

When, on Sunday mornings, Margaret and I go walking in sections of New York which we scarcely know, Margaret usually gets something in her eye. This may be the result of a weak muscle in the lid or it may have something to do with eyelashes or even eyebrows, although I don't know any reason why the eyebrow should protect the eye. If it does, certainly John L. Lewis never gets anything in his eyes, and our beauty parlor plucking will lead to feminine blindness. It is funny that Margaret doesn't get anything in her eye in Nantucket, where there is more wind and sand than in New York. Our upper lids are much more mobile than the lower. Many animals work their lids from the bottom up, or even sidewise. No doubt this motion is related directly to the dangers of living, and if airplanes become a way of life then the upper lid may be little more than a nuisance. Up to now, man has looked down, while some animals more often look upwards. If I ever get to the desert areas of Africa, I will take a good look at the eyebrows and eyelashes of the natives and ask them if they have any trouble with particles of sand getting into their eyes.

I seldom notice the eyelash factor in animals although sheepdogs have hair long enough fully to cover their eyes and their whole faces. Maybe they are just trying to withdraw from life altogether rather than merely gain protection from morsels of dirt. While dictating to one of the girls in the office, she reminded me of the fact that at a luncheon the other day one of the women present lit a cigarette, found that her eyes watered but kept on smoking. No doubt this girl enjoyed the irritation of the tear gland and the sensation of compelled crying. Not all irksome events are unwelcomed.

In looking at paintings and pictures of centuries ago, I can

[71]

find no signs of a greater growth of eyelashes, brows or lids than exists in these days. This whole question of growth is most confusing and, like most scientific matters, is written up in such stilted form that I can't understand it, and in any event seldom does the authority touch on my basic excitement about the relation of growth to the concept of life itself. I remember years ago, when a youngster, I wrote that stones don't grow but shortly thereafter at high school I actually saw a crystal growing. When the crystal was put in a certain solution, it became bigger and if it had lost what we would call a section or a limb, the part that had been previously lost would be the first to grow—a kind of passion for totality. This might spell some great power of attraction not unlike magnetism and not unlike the power of the magnetic pole to pull the needle on my compass in its constantly moving direction. I can't find out whether the magnetic field is growing or shrinking. With that great power of attraction of parasitic metals in tune with the pole, gradually over millions of years there may move in the direction of the pole all kin metals, even my lost keys and razor blades.

Man, unlike crystals, runs his own artificial Recrystallization Studios: camouflaged as beauty parlors and manicure shops. They are our concession to the power of the human body to re-create. A neat category of animal species listing their powers to replace might show that this capacity is in indirect ratio to the ability of the animal to think and feel. In the main, all we have left that regrows is hair, nails and skin, with a partial capacity to replace teeth. In American Indian folklore we might discover much wisdom on problems hirsute. Does sunlight accelerate or retard such growth? And then again we run into the glacial school—with the absurd theory that hair was a concomitant of cold climates. Page the Eskimos!

Much of animal life has us licked on this score. A crab of course can regenerate a large claw, and many an animal can regrow an eye or the capacity to hear. In a way the ability to re-create and replace is an abundant power and I can't find

[72]

any theory, unless it be complexity plus specialization, which explains why the higher forms of life have so much less of it than the lower. I once read that the very lowest forms of life can re-create sensory organs even if all of the animal is destroyed except one little remnant. Incidentally, what's the explanation of growing new tonsils after an operation? I wonder if other organs in the body could not rebuild if cut in the same fashion as used to cut a tonsil, which regrows later. Maybe the regeneration of a tonsil does not depend on the vitality of the tonsil seed alone but also depends in part on the impact of the incision.

Now that the doctors have ridden to affluence on the tonsil fetish and the appendix threat, they are going strong in the direction of sinus. I don't know what people called that ailment before the doctors scared the wits out of modern society by talking sinus. Of course, sinusitis is merely a disease of the sophisticated. I wouldn't think that anyone who used snuff could ever have sinusitis.

But certainly the modern idea of a handkerchief has a direct bearing on the ailment. When I worked on labor problems at Hog Island Shipyards during the last war, I fully noted for the first time the technique of stevedores blowing their noses. Man cannot get anything up into the sinus, if the technique of blowing the nostrils is one at a time and with a stout finger lodged against the other. There is probably no better way of pumping unfriendly particles back up the nose and into the head than by the modern use of a handkerchief.

THE DOCTOR'S DICTIONARY

The last time I was ill was when I was ten years old, being a victim of the early appendix vogue. Although afraid of hospitals and not peculiarly of use to ailing friends or relatives, I have nevertheless been interested in a painless, informal way in the mathematical incidence of diseases. For example, as I read the figures, for every 1,000 males who have leprosy there are 500 females. The proportion runs nearly mathematically two to one, and no animal has leprosy, and to date we have been unable to inject it into any animal. I'd like to see a list of all the diseases which do not exist in the animal world, those which cannot even be given to animals by injection. Only recently I saw a table correlating male and female susceptibility to each disease. No wonder women have longer lives. As against their environment they are the stronger sex in terms of living.

The medical field is most forbidding for a layman. Of all vocabularies the medical is the most impossible. I understand that a student of medicine must learn at least five thousand new words during his first year of instruction.

During each winter new bewildering words find their way out of professional closets into the daily press to smack an innocent public between the eyes. It isn't, I am sure, just the effect of cold weather that brings on this deluge. Rather does it arise because in winter the scientific brain boys of the nation have their annual junkets known as conventions. There they read their papers, get misquoted by the press, and amaze the public.

But often it takes less than a decade for new gibberish created by scientists or lawyers or doctors to become accepted by the *Saturday Evening Post* or *Collier's*. "Complex," "neurosis," "schizophrenic" are etymological newcomers. "Pragmatism" is no longer discussed—it is accepted. "Defense mechanism" has no relation to war and "overcompensation" does not stem from the Beveridge plan. Such words come in a fumbling way from the laboratories where searchers after new truths slip gently upon a vague new idea not yet fully born but desperately needing a name to create a semblance of legitimacy and existence. Man can't operate without names. At times a profession uses unpronounceable combinations of letters to fend off public assaults or to confound the lay audience. The use of Latin by the parish priest of old placed him above the hordes, in part because Latin could not be understood. In the law game whenever a client catches on to too much of the legalistic rigmarole, a satisfactory effect can be created merely by letting drop in a casual way a reference or two to "stare decisis," "certiorari," or simple old "demurrer." If these don't terrify and put the client in his place, what about trying out a little "incorporeal hereditament"?

Every once in a while styles change in words. Only recently I have noted that that old phrase "dementia praecox" has become too clear to the mass mind of man, and we now have to call it "schizophrenia." Please try to get some psychiatrist friend to explain the difference. And just because the public had difficulty pronouncing "schizophrenia," the victim of that impossible word has been given an affectionate nickname such as "schizie."

Incidentally, all I know about my schizie friends is that they are usually young; they can't forget their dreams while awake; they carry on and live their dreams while most of us remember our dreams only once in a while and then try unsuccessfully to find relatives or friends who will listen to us repeat them in incoherent and boring sentences. But what interests me most about my schizie pals is that their pulses, temperature and blood pressure are lower than mine, which is just the opposite from the fast body gushes of all my epileptic acquaintances. I am told by sources usually reliable that neither group can be much or uniformly helped as yet by psychiatric or psychoanalytic therapeutic measures. How's that for using three bewildering terms in one sentence! But if freezing the "eps"—my affectionate abbreviation for them— in order to reduce their temperature gives relief, as it does at times, why shouldn't boiling the "schizies" be in order?

We certainly are a conceited people if we think we can leave to God or nature, or coffee or aspirin or Scotch, the equalization of our internal heat and cold. Someday we ought to cut down about four thousand square miles of luscious trees in order to make paper to be used for ads which would read: "Buy our Anti-Schizie Tonic. It will shove up your blood pressure, raise your temperature and increase your pulse. You don't have to be a Schiz."

[75]

Some time ago I wanted to get a hundred of my friends of both sexes of the age of eighteen or thereabouts to give me their average temperatures, blood pressures and pulses. I'd look over the list, checkmark those of subnormal or schizie tendencies, and then just sit back and wait to watch these daytime dreamers start praecoxing and dementing all over my favorite saloons.

I read recently again about the royal Spanish family and their tendency toward hemophilia—a peculiarly male failing. I recalled that Leviticus, our first great public health historian, might have been of help to Alfonso and his relatives. The old Jews certainly had a wide knowledge of public health in its best terms. They discovered the dangers of eating pigs and oysters. They learned much about bleeding through their art of circumcision. I have read that a circumcision can be performed successfully on the first day but not at any time between the second and eighth days for fear the boy will bleed to death. I wonder how many little Jewish boys died until some wise man discovered that fact.

This isn't so far removed from the wisdom that must have prompted the spanking of a child so as to get air into the lungs. The first spank was probably fortuitous. Some prehistoric woman probably dropped a baby in a cave and the mere shock let air into the lungs. Surely, no one at that time could have imagined that the baby embryo has gill slits and lives in a liquid until birth, and hence that the possibility of air in the lungs is quite inconceivable until after birth. I am quite convinced that no mother ever said to herself, "I'll spank this kid to get air into the lungs which never had air in them." Incidentally, isn't it possible that the method of getting air into the lungs by making the child gasp, or what not, may have some relationship to pneumonia and pleurisy in later life? First impacts such as a spanking and air in the lungs are probably more important psychologically than all the other spankings a child could ever receive from a parent. Maybe there is even a proper choice spot to spank.

Our embryos tell of our historic physical past. If we had wisdom, by the same token, we could foresee the future of man. I ate a banana the other day, the first one in a long time, and I really wished I could have sent it to friends in England where a whole generation of children has grown up never seeing a banana, a lemon or an orange. As I ate the banana I cut it with a knife and there saw the cross-wise figure. I don't know whether it's really what I think it is, except that I was told as a child that if you cut a banana in half, you will see a figure of Jesus on the cross. I'd like someday to have someone publish a picture book, showing the cross sections of acorns and other seeds which, if cut in half, show a picture of what the ultimate plant or tree will look like when full grown. I'd like to see those pictures magnified. Someday we will take an X-ray photograph of a cross section of a seed, blow up the picture, plant the seed and then in later years take a picture of the tree full grown, and check it back against this cross-section picture of what was to develop from the seed. One of the bases of distinction, if we feel we have to make distinctions between plants and animals, is that plant cross sections foretell the future, whereas animals are lacking the geometry of a cross section. Someday Stumpp and Walter, our seed house, will sell seeds with future photos, guaranteed or money refunded.

CHAPTER XI

HEYWOOD BROUN

THIS EVENING I HEARD Quentin Reynolds do his great GI Joe broadcast after the landing in France. Margaret said Quent learned much from Heywood Broun. And Quent would be the first to admit it. Quent didn't know him many years but he knew what Heywood Broun was about. Heywood had few friends and Quent was one of them.

At high school, more than forty years ago, Heywood and

I first met. We were bound together then through Heywood's aunt, Belle Baker, my English instructor and one of my few inspired teachers. He went to Harvard and I to Williams, but he came to Williamstown several times a year for a course in poker with Alan Rogers and other boys we had both known at Horace Mann High School. I didn't play. I was unsophisticated. I envied these men of the world.

Heywood never graduated from college and maybe his initial disdain for Walter Lippmann—climaxed at the time of Broun's discharge from the old *World* because of his Sacco-Vanzetti column, which was engineered, he thought, by Walter—arose from his envy of Walter's success at Harvard, an institution of learning. But Heywood learned at Harvard and everywhere else he lived. In love with a slender dancer, he got his blow early in life. He married the opposite —violent, strong, mathematical Lucy Stoner, Ruth Hale. And the dancing lady married the opposite of Heywood Broun—one of the world's notable economists.

No one, least of all I, can tell the tale of Heywood, even though I spent two or three evenings a week with him for fifteen years. I held his hand in all his scrapes and escapades. I represented him as lawyer and I befriended him as friend. He was courageous in the original sense of the word. He was soft and tender and understanding. He was a gentleman because he couldn't help it. The strength of his pen and person scared his editors—Roy Howard, Lee Wood, Walter Lippmann. He never could organize his own life. He was gay but seldom happy. He was brave but full of fears. He wanted friendship more than anything else on earth. If he was ever petty it was toward himself and not toward his fellow man. For twenty years he was our greatest newspaper figure.

One night at Jack and Charlie's "21" he passed to me under the table a slip of paper concealed from the two or three women present. I have the paper somewhere. It reads: "I need you—for no less than two hours and no more than twenty." We met and stayed together much more than

[78]

twenty hours. He wanted my advice as to whether he should join the Catholic Church of which his wife, Connie, was a member. His first question was: "Will people think that Connie made me do it?"; to which he himself replied out of his insecurity as to what people thought of *him* (not his shape or his clothes): "Of course I'll have to make her go to confession and mass."

We talked that night of Heywood's life. His pathetic sexual insecurity stemming from bits of still prevalent gutter folklore which circulated, at least in New York, at the turn of the century. We reviewed Heywood's desire for certainty. His search for authority in the Socialist party, which he found less than overwhelming. His playing with the Communists until he felt contempt for their dishonesty and chicanery. His long life with his former wife, vital Ruth Hale.

We went over his neuroses, his years of panic when going into crowds or theaters. His taxi rides to Stamford, afraid of trains. His $70,000 doled out to psychiatrists and psychoanalysts. His one-man art show of cardiograms. His ever-present fear of death because he loved life, particularly after dusk.

He was upset and serious. I kidded and suggested that he might become a Jew. Why not join our boys? We were being beaten all over the world, and Heywood was a star masochist.

I'm glad I told him to join the Catholic Church. He got much out of it. Connie, with her native humor, and her foot clamped on all little checks (Broun grabbed the big ones and spent them gathering up tabs at saloons for twenty years) gave him a background of comfort and ease. The Church gave him the kind of discipline he wanted, even though during his instruction and later he jested about how he had comprehended the concept of the Virgin Birth along the scientific lines of high-church Romanes but could not quite understand the Immaculate Conception.

I thought of Heywood only a few days ago when the Pope in liberated Rome spoke to fifty thousand people, and of what a voice Heywood would have used in these days of Westbrook Peglers and Fulton Lewises and that tribe of men who do not know that life is a changing adventure.

When Roy Howard, the big boss of the *Telegram*, fired Heywood from the paper, Heywood understood with that tolerance which often irritated his friends. "I've been a terrible pain to Roy in my work for the Newspaper Guild. He feared the Guild and all unions and I don't blame him for firing me." Heywood had understood why Roy Howard had censored his columns, put him in positions of lesser importance on the feature page and hired Westbrook Pegler, with his early column in favor of lynching, to do combat with Heywood.

Years before, when the New York *World* dropped Heywood for a time because of his Sacco-Vanzetti articles, I had suggested to Oswald Garrison Villard, editor and owner of the *Nation*, that he take Broun on for a weekly column, and so once more I turned to a client and friend to grab this great reporter and writer. Dolly Thackrey of the *Post* bought his column, at a temporary loss of about $50,000 a year to Heywood compared to his old syndicate pay. Heywood wrote one piece for the *Post*. The column was dated Friday, December 15, 1939, three days before his death. He discussed the Roosevelt Third Term, ending his last column with this final paragraph:

Depend upon it, there won't be very much of a show when Roosevelt makes up his mind yes or no on the third term issue. He'll go into a room and there will be three persons there: the President, his better nature, and his devotion to his country. That should be a committee quite satisfactory to anyone.

He wrote it in my office on a borrowed typewriter. Like many of his columns, he had tried it out the night before in his round of night clubs. As usual it took him only twenty minutes to put it down on paper.

But Heywood was particularly sore at Carl Randau and Milton Kaufman and other Communist-line Newspaper

Guild boys, for and with whom he had worked for years. He felt that they deserted him at the time when he attacked the Stalin-Hitler Pact. About a month before Heywood died he telephoned me in near tears. I must meet him for a drink around three o'clock in the afternoon. He had been to the *Telegram* to pick up his papers, a euphemism, for Heywood had neither papers, records nor checkbook. The pro-Communist Guild leaders down there had shunned him. Not one had come up and said, "Sorry you're leaving, Heywood." But a little copy boy had grabbed the Big Boy's hand and said, "Too bad, Mr. Broun, but thanks to you I'm getting two dollars a week more and a vacation with pay." Heywood was deeply touched, but very, very low. It hurt to see his beautiful face on the verge of weeping. I told him I'd get up a party for him. I actually hired the top floor of Sardi's restaurant for midnight of January 8th. We would have a new kind of party. No more than about three hundred people, though thousands would want to come. It would cost 50 cents to get in—the price of one drink. Beyond that each could spend what he desired. I wanted to get away from the racket of the $5 cover charge for the usual banquet in this overdinnered New York. I wrote letters to Jack Dempsey, Secretary Ickes, John L. Lewis, Helen Hayes, Walter White and many of Heywood's wide list of friends. I included his favorite taxi drivers, waiters and bartenders. I added the name of his priest at Stamford, and of Father Ryan of Washington, whom we both loved and who had helped so much to get the Guild started, and then sent the list to Heywood for cuts or additions. A postscript on my letter said, "How about Margaret Sanger?" Heywood answered, "Of course bring Sanger, but *I* didn't invite her!"

The party never took place, for Heywood died. Just before he died he asked the doctor, "How am I?" The doctor said, "Getting along." Heywood whispered, "Have you sent for the priest?" The doctor had to be truthful: "Yes, but you are some better now."

And then Broun drawled, "If I pull through, I'll remember

that Ring Lardner would have lived longer if he had only written what he really wanted to write. And I will write only about horse racing, night clubs, baseball, gambling and life."

And so the great monument of Heywood's life, the union of newspaper writers, seemed to him at the moment of his death as little more than an overlay, far from important. Since that time I have noted how often man's greatest contributions are fortuitous, and remote from the ordinary expected patterns of one's conscious life design.

I don't cry often. But I could scarcely complete a broadcast about Heywood after his death. My daughter Connie was at the station with me and I was ashamed, foolishly ashamed, to have her watch me sneak into a doorway after we left the WEVD broadcasting studio while I bawled.

I loved Heywood. We were friends. I still miss him often.

CHAPTER XII

THE NEWSPAPER GUILD AND THE FOUR HORSEMEN

ONE EVENING, before the Guild was organized, about a dozen newspapermen had gathered in Heywood Broun's penthouse flat on 58th Street. The door, never locked day or night, opened, and in came a couple. I wondered why Louise was coming to this secret meeting. Bill, her husband, was and still is one of the top newsmen of the nation. I knew Louise hadn't been invited. Later she told me that she had come to protect Bill—not from us, but from his boss, the New York *Times*.

This gathering—one of a dozen or more—was set up in order to discuss the formation of a society of journalists, a guild of newspaper writers. Louise had come along so that in case the bosses learned of these meetings, Bill might save his job by saying he and Louise had gone to Heywood's just for a social drinking evening. I'm confident that the *Times* would not have fired Bill, but the distressing part of this episode lies in the fact that dozens of other Bills lived in similar fear —fear of loss of employment if it were known that they desired to create an organization which might someday have sufficient bargaining power to trade with publishers. If men working for the *Times*—in most ways the best employer in the field—lived in such fear, imagine the state of mind of reporters working for less objective and socially minded papers. No wonder the Wagner Labor Act was needed in our nation.

The gap between publisher and writer exists even among top-priced journalists. Years ago I ran into Stanley Walker, encyclopedist of insignificant trivia, not at Bleeck's, his pet saloon, but at "21." He showed me a dollar bill on which was written, as nearly as I recall it, in ink: "With more like this William Randolph Hearst purchased the soul of one Stanley Walker." Signatures followed—of Stanley Walker, and either Hearst, Brisbane, or one of the high officials. I ordered a round of drinks, telling Walker, "As long as you can show that bill, your soul isn't completely lost." In a few months Hearst put Walker on ice. His fabulous salary was paid regularly, but he was given nothing to do. Finally Walker went back home to the *Tribune*.

It's a miracle the Guild ever got on its feet. Some years earlier, Lewis Gannett, McAlister Coleman and a few other newspaper writers had made a similar attempt. The time wasn't ripe, and there was no Broun to dramatize the movement. But the disappearance of the New York *World* did much to help the Guild concept. Moreover, the papers of the nation had been shrinking at a terrifying pace. Munsey had bought and destroyed great properties, dozens of papers were folding up. The remaining press of the nation was being boiler-plated. This meant thousands of workers were being fired. Salaries stayed below decent living levels. Publishers still traded on the romance of the reporter's job. They offered glamour instead of dollars. But grocers would not swap food for romance. As the papers lost in public esteem, with the abdication of editorial pages and the distortion and suppression of news, the reporters realized, probably before the owners, that the American public had lost faith in the integrity of the press. The integrity dwindled through omissions rather than through false reporting of news. There is little glamour in working for a boss whom the public treats with disdain. There is scarcely an election, local or national, in which the public does not rise up and vote in direct opposition to the advice of the owners of our press. And the publishers, banding together for still greater power, opposed the Wagner Labor Act, as well as child labor, minimum wage and most social reform legislation. Freedom to hire at $15 a week was confused with freedom of the press. Special profits for publishers were decreed to be guaranteed by our First Amendment. The American Newspaper Publishers' Association looked only at advertising revenue and daily increase of total circulation, became scared of the advertising shift to radio and was blind to the essential fact that the public was buying funnies and entertainment instead of editorial opinion or news on which it could rely. They still don't comprehend the wide difference between Freedom of the Press and A Free Press.

Many of my liberal friends are apt to scold the mass of newspaper readers, calling them stupid, sheeplike, unthinking. These critics are dead wrong. There is no greater evidence of the thoughtfulness, vigor and independence of the voting public than its ability to see through the selfish distorted portrayal of news by the leading newspapers of the land. Candidates now run for office on little more than a slogan: "No newspaper supports me." Here and there a great editor is disturbed by the public's rejection of the nonentertainment pages of our papers.

But in 1934 most newspaper ownership was arrogant and blind. In that year I wrote, as counsel for the newly formed Guild, to the association of newspaper owners of New York

City suggesting a conference. They never even acknowledged receipt of my letter. On this kind of shortsighted resistance the Guild throve, just as the continued opposition of leading newspapers today adds to its vitality.

Joseph Patterson, the bad boy who runs the News, was a tower of strength for the workers. He told us at our first talk, "I'll tell my reporters only this—'If I were working for Patterson or any other publisher, I'd join the Guild.'" He did that. A unit was formed. David Stern, owner of the New York Post, had a social record which the Guild found of great value. But for the rest in New York City, they were scared and stupid. They thought they could smash a society of journalists. They resisted, they sniffed, they jeered, they bribed by giving better wages and shorter hours. They would do anything but recognize a guild of their favorite and most important workers.

This type of employer behavior—still carried on by some of the owners in different fashions—drove the Guild to the left. No moderate leadership can survive on continued rejection by the bosses. For a time the Communist faction took over the national organization. It is the usual pattern of American trade-union development. Union leadership, responsible and honest, holds power only if the bosses deal with labor on decent bargaining levels. This we should have learned from England, where trade-union relations are decades in advance of those in our land. Rejection of labor organizations invites crooks or Communists or demagogues to take over the power. Moderates, like Broun, can't hold power if the bosses will not even confer with them.

The Communists had an eye on the Guild from the beginning. From the outset Broun was worried because he thought that one of the paid union officials was getting a supplementary secret salary from one of the C.P. subsidiary organizations. Bob Minor and Earl Browder, top Communist party dictators, had a suite at the Hotel Astor at the time of one of the early conventions. Toward the end of his life Broun was kept in office as a symbol—but the power had been shifted. From a society of journalists, the Guild was converted into a left-wing trade union by the constant opposition of the publishers. Roy Howard and Helen Reid, among others, did that job without intending to.

At the time of the shift I withdrew as counsel. I couldn't stomach the Communist controls. Before the C.P. took over we had our great Watson case, testing out the constitutionality of the Wagner Labor Act. This case arose against the Associated Press—that great co-operative national, international and world-wide news gatherer—which came to court urging that it never was engaged in interstate business. Watson, an energetic, highly neurotic, though capable newspaperman (now but not then on the Communist line), had been fired because of Guild activity. The referee—now Judge Charles Clark—sustained our complaint in behalf of Watson, and the United States Supreme Court handed down a bill of rights for newsmen when it declared that Associated Press's plea of freedom of the press was without reality as an excuse for resisting the unionization of newspaper writers under the Wagner Act. It was a good fight, and as it went on many publishers became ashamed of the AP position. But some never learn.

Only this year I was greatly flattered when the National Guild, having thrown the Commies out of power, asked me to pitch for it once more.

Life Magazine, the New York Times, Scripps-Howard and the Cowles papers were resisting union maintenance contracts for the Guild. These four great publishers and a score of other papers took the position that, whereas all other American workers were entitled to protection against destructive antiunion tactics by employers, newspaper writers must be left without this protection because of "freedom of the press." One of the most important news services, King Features, went so far as to urge that trial by jury and the right to bear arms, and in fact all of the first ten amendments to our Constitution were violated by the Guild's plea for union maintenance. Thus does the concept of Freedom of the

Press become confused, diluted and tainted in the public mind.

The writers had given up the right to strike during the war. This single greatest weapon of workers was abandoned as a contribution of newsmen toward victory. In return they asked that any worker—a member of the Guild—must leave his employment if he withdrew from the Guild during the period of the contract. Without such union maintenance clauses employers could decimate the union. Such protection was necessary only because of employer anti-Guild attitudes. Many papers, large and small, had agreed with the union on this issue, but these four leading publishing firms, with an array of eminent attorneys, argued that freedom of the press was in peril. We made clear that no worker would be compelled to join the Guild, and every member could within fifteen days from the signing of the contract withdraw. But the Four Horsemen of so-called "Freedom" resisted. The War Labor Board hearing, held in the great auditorium of the Labor Department Building, showed how little the publishers had learned about trust and faith and confidence in the men who write their sheets. The Board decided for the union, but I'm inclined to believe that the Big Four are heading for more serious trouble. The issue of the closed shop for writers—a problem of deep and subtle implications—will be fought out on the picket lines unless publishers like the Big Four wake up to what is happening in the world today.

At the opening of the hearing Elisha Hanson, attorney for a Harrisburg publisher, brashly announced that he would defy the War Labor Board and would not abide by its decision. When my turn came to address the Board I merely said that I wasn't happy arguing in an American forum against an adversary who shouted defiance of our democratic government. It reminded me, I said, of a certain bushy-browed labor leader.

If the Guild or any union representative, even John L. Lewis, had uttered such a taunt, the press of the nation would have headlined the event. But the following day's stories in the papers were in the main silent about this lawlessness of Mr. Hanson, and amusingly enough *PM* went all out in the other direction with a headline indicating that all the papers defied the War Labor Board.

In the election of 1940, over 80 per cent of the writers on the *Times, Herald Tribune* and many other papers voted directly opposite to the urgings of their papers. The employees of *Life-Time-Fortune*—the men who make up the words that fill those magazines—are pathetically apologetic for the confusion and illiberalism of Luce and Larsen. Only recently I was asked to aid one of Harry Luce's top writers who was scared into a dither because a Washington columnist was about to call him a New Dealer—which he thinks he is. Mr. Luce wouldn't like it!

This situation is less than healthy. It can't endure for long. I doubt if reforms will come from within the publisher groups. The Thackreys and Marshall Field are crusading for a shift, but I doubt if they can persuade the men who run the Publishers' Association. No signs of leadership from within the dominant groups are on the horizon. Elisha Hanson is still the leading legal brain for the owners of the press and he really believes that all legislation benefiting newspaper writers on wages, hours and working conditions is somehow in violation of freedom of the press.

During the remarkable expansion of the Guild in membership and in contract relations with publishers, most of the moves taken by the Guild—deplored by the publishers—were in fact forced on the workers by the publishers. Here was a middle-class group of writers, cartoonists, reporters, anxious to improve their working standards. "Go away," say the publishers. "You can't get a following, and even if you do, your power will be too scant to bother us. We can always hire scabs and if necessary we can increase the salaries of your leaders and wean them from this Guild." But the Guild grew—unrecognized. It needed additional strength and power to overcome the employers' offishness. So William Green and John L. Lewis bid with dollars and aids to gain the Guild as a unit of the A.F.of L. or C.I.O. Still the publishers sat back on their nineteenth-century haunches. More heat was needed to get a nod of recognition from the bosses. So these writing men took into their Guild the employees of the business departments of the papers. That made a big mass—not always homogeneous in interests—but a mass that had weight and power. Maybe the writers should have had a separate local and the business department employees another local, both operating through a joint board. Maybe some other setup would have been conceivable. I'm not sure. But I'm certain that the publishers gave the writers no alternative. And who are the publishers to talk of homogeneity of interests when they stick together in anti-Guild

distrust and disdain for each other in

s the annual Guild
ificant union in our
ignity. Milton Mur-
great union leaders,
ublishers will realize
e much in common.
inevitable clash, that
ckholders and labor.
ther can work to add
g.
contracts alone. There
tificate, ceremony and
g toward agreed-upon
iticizing each other—
enduring industrial peace is estab-
the distortions of our press would de-
took Guild representation into their
highest council. Neither side is ineluctably right. The single great hope for a useful press as educator rather than as mere entertainer lies in the influence of the writers on the men who own the presses.

Under our theory of freedom, the man who owns the presses (it takes millions of dollars in a metropolitan city) has the right to spread his own prejudices. He can be wrong-headed and even malicious. He can distort by omission. But as the press shrinks, the men who write the papers will be less than happy to find the ultimate product which reaches the readers so far out of tune not only with what the readers believe but with what the writers desire.

The pipelines of thought to the minds of the nation are being contracted and squeezed. About thirty men realistically dominate the conduits of thought through the ether, the printing presses and the silver screen. Without wide diversity of thought, freedom of speech and press become idle bits of a worn-out shibboleth. The cartelization of the mind of America is well on the way. No wonder we have a cynicism toward the press that shows up in every important election. F. D. R. running in 1944—an overwhelming re-election—had only 17.7 per cent of the nation's newspapers supporting him. Surely cynicism to that extent is less than wholesome for a free press of a free people. Hundreds of cities which formerly had several papers now claim only one, and that one, in more than 120 cities, owns the only local radio station. What price free market place in thought? As for movies, the five giants—Metro, Paramount, Warner's, RKO, 20th-Century-Fox—own theaters and rake in 70 per cent of the box-office money of the nation. No independent can get full distribution except through the giants or their satellites. Sarnoff, Paley, McCosker and Noble are the overlords of the ether.

Once a year the Stock Exchange turns over its management and the entire running of the Exchange for a single day to the messenger boys and other minor employees on its staff. I'd like to see some newspaper owner give the completely unrestrained editing of one day's issue to the Guild—to the men and women who get up the paper. If I had my choice, I'd pick the day before election each year for an Employee-Edited Edition. That would be more than a stunt. It would be an education to publisher, Guild and, most important of all, to the public. Heywood Broun would smile from his grave.

CHAPTER XIII

,

REFLECTIONS ON THE HOUSEWIFE'S LOT

I DON'T REMEMBER THE LAST TIME I was alone for more than a day. Certainly not during thirty years—the period when I started picking up Heywood Broun for late afternoon and evening rounds. Not that I was ever in need of company or crowds as was Heywood. Many a time at four in the morning I'd say I was going home, couldn't take it, had to get up at eight because Maggie had to go to work. Even then Heywood would go to the telephone at Texas Guinan's or wherever we were and call up any one of fifty people: "Hello, Bob, what are you doing, come and meet me for a night cap."

But this spring after sailing my new shoal-draft cutter from Mamaroneck up through Long Island and Vineyard sounds to Nantucket, I had three days at the house before Maggie and Jo arrived. I enjoyed it, every minute, though I don't know whether I could have stood it for three weeks. I haven't the kind of inner security that Maggie has. But I learned a lot. Entire new crafts had to be explored and licked. That hot-water stove, with its updraft for starting the fire, and the mystery of the downdraft when the stove was banked for the night. The oven in the Pyrofax with its slow motion compared to the burners on top. It was fun figuring out with practically a slide rule what Kitty knows but never learned and can't teach to anyone else. Maybe intuitive knowledge is so deeply embedded that it can't be articulated and passed on. Timing, that's the fun of cooking potatoes and chops in the oven; eggs, soup, coffee, all on top. The art of simmering, so that everything comes out on the table finished and hot.

Bedmaking, with the hospital corners, is also fun after watching the army movies; and the magic of the carpet sweeper, wielded with that perseverance which spells perfection as the last bit of thread disappears from the rug.

But the entire process of keeping house is one of the problems of the future scarcely touched upon by any theorists to date. I suppose in our folkways men will continue to go to work and women will be considered the better equipped to bring up children and run the table and the home. And still this way of life condemns many women who could be of great service to the community as schoolteachers, bank vice-presidents, supervisors of precision instruments (to mention just three jobs trained women do better than men) to give up that fuller life and live as housewives. This, assuming that domestic service is as unattractive as it is today and that few, if any, would choose it out of preference. The eight-hour day for cooks and houseworkers, infinite new gadgets of simplification, living out for domestic workers, all will reduce the objections to domestic service. But even more pay than for working in a factory will not give us the answer. Nursery schools will help, but when one adds up all the kitchen dreams of tomorrow there is still a problem.

I've always had great faith and hope for young girls who studied professions, particularly law. If they stay feminine and use their own sex appeal and don't try to ape the masculine, success is theirs. But what a tough time of it they have if they marry and have one or two kids—even with the best of houseworkers and nurses. In many cases a job for a lady lawyer nets no income at all after paying income taxes. At a starting salary of $2,500, with a nurse to take her place at home, there is at most a gross gain of about $1,000, but then come business expenses and on top of that the federal and state income taxes. Maybe the government should give an extra special allowance to working mothers (with dependents at home) who have to hire help at home while they are off working. I wish the equal-rights women would plug away at such important trivia all in the direction of overcoming existing disparities operating against a full economic life for women.

CHAPTER XIV

DEMOCRACY AND LADIES' SLACKS

EVERY TIME I WORK with Dave Dubinsky I'm increasingly aware of the meager spread of information about our great labor leaders compared to our leading bankers and industrialists. I'll match for competence, selflessness, ability and public contributions Clint Golden, of the Steel Workers Union, Walter Reuther, of the Auto Workers Union, Emil Rieve, of Textiles, John Green, of the Shipyard Workers, Matthew Woll, general A.F.of L. factotum, and quiet Phil Murray, head of the C.I.O.—to name a few—with all the presidents and ex-presidents of the National Association of Manufacturers and Chamber of Commerce combined. But labor leaders usually are publicized through adverse criticism. Phil Murray, in any of his proposals or plans for future America, just doesn't get the favorable and extensive publicity of an Eric Johnston. Is it possible that newspaper publishers have more of a liking for Chambers of Commerce than for trade unions?

We are several decades behind England in our union relationship. Although our leadership has improved greatly since 1933, it is still true that until industry and the press raise their labor sights, incompetents, racketeers or Communists will find opportunities for advancement in labor ranks. Only by dealing, day by day, in the joint solution of industrial problems will labor leaders develop and procure the education needed for responsible intelligence. Wherever there is peace in an industry instead of war, unions perfect their own democratic life—with secret ballots, regular meetings and honest published financial reports.

Of all the antilabor drives made in recent years I know of none more absurd than the suggestions for compulsory incorporation of unions. Every businessman knows that the corporate concept is primarily a device to avoid and limit liability and responsibility. The vast networks of utility and banking subsidiary and holding companies often rely on the use of corporate subterfuges in order to milk creditors and public. Labor surely would be smart enough to follow management's suit. Labor knows that, although branch banking is unlawful in New York State, the Marine Midland Trust Co. circumvents our legislative intentions by the interlocking of twenty separate banks through a parent holding corporation. Unions can give birth to hundreds of corporations just as easily as does a motion-picture company, such as Paramount with more than six hundred member corporations.

Union responsibility must flow from sounder sources than legal corporate devices. We have seen it rush freely from good will, disclosure and understanding. The International Ladies' Garment Workers Union, which Dubinsky heads, avoids strikes and stoppages; it finances honest hard-up employers; it helps finance and plan the future of the ladies' garment industry. It is responsible. It has built up the lives of its members—with summer camps, health clinics, educational classes, and the production of public entertainments of high success, such as *Pins and Needles*. That union's financial statements are more explicit, honest and complete than any corporate statement I have ever seen distributed for general public reading.

The problems of a union are in quality identical with those of our democratic government. A few years ago I sat with some of Dubinsky's labor engineers and tried to find out just how the great Ladies' Garment Workers Union handled the revolutionary problem created by the introduction of women's slacks. This garment—whether glamorous or not— was being adopted throughout the land by women young and

[94]

old. Factories which made waists or dresses or skirts were anxious to convert to making pants for women. But not only were the manufacturers concerned; the workers of each local union of the International were pressing their leaders because future full-time work might depend in many shops on orders for work on slacks. Some leaders grumbled because the new garment was uncomely. Other equally irrelevant arguments were injected, but in the final analysis "claimants," to use a governmental term, arose in many quarters for the work as well as for the orders. This appeared to me to be a typical ever-recurrent example of the development of interunion management. Here was a jurisdictional problem. Which local of the I.L.G.W.U. should take on slacks—skirtmakers, waist-makers, or negligee workers? Out of this controversy and conflict, a solution had to be reached. There was waste of time, energy and money, all of which could have been avoided by a dictatorship of the union. No single official, no boss made the decision. Conferences, arguments went on for days. Out of the debates there developed a meeting of minds. Such a democratic method of reaching solutions does not always leave all participants completely satisfied with the results. But the process of using ideas instead of sheer power to resolve issues permeates a democratic organism such as this great union.

Here we have the essential difference between Communist- and democratic-led unions. Out of the constant educational process of "claiming" we find the development of a strong intelligent union membership. Under the Communist tactic, decisions are flicked off Browder's cuff—no explanation, no reason, no use of the mass mind. The Communist technique is valuable only for those who desire short cuts. It develops a race of unthinking sheep whom any new "ism" can eventually capture.

Our government is daily going through the same process in order to reach solutions. In the midst of this war the various military agencies have created a formula for governmental military decisions: "Joint Chiefs of Staff." A plan is proposed. The Navy might say: "We cannot afford to lose the 27 ships required by the proposed strategy." But the Army and Air Services say in effect: "You'll damn well lose them." And so a decision is reached after listening to "claims." Likewise with Lend-Lease, Joint Purchase, et cetera.

In a nation as big as ours some such Joint Chiefs of Staff concept must be carried over into the operations of our civilian government. This is much easier to urge than to set up in our vast democratic framework.

There is scarcely a problem of even negligible importance that does not call for decisions by at least three bureaus or departments. This being the case, who is to decide as between the different claimants? Which one of the bureaus should be given the responsibility for selecting the wisest solution? Surely our Cabinet setup is no answer. Thousands of such problems arise every month. Cabinet officers, if concerned only with policy matters and relieved of all administrative duties, could not cope with these situations. A policy man out of touch with daily operations would be incapable of appraising and solving interdepartmental conflicts. It's no answer to juggle our Cabinet concept by splitting every Cabinet officer into two persons—one administrator, the other a policy maker. Policy is often made through the day-by-day operations of the bureau staffs.

A year or more ago I prepared a study on Anglo-American relations, concerning myself only with trivia, minor items by which folkways are disturbed or welded. A joint visa office, a new consular convention, exchange of patents, the freer flow of books and teachers and students between the two nations, etc. Visas concern State, FBI, Labor, Treasury, etc. Copyright touches on the province of State, Commerce, Library of Congress, Customs, etc. In England, as in our own land, not one of these problems is the exclusive concern of a single governmental department. Wise public officials like Sir David Scott, Sir Hugh Walton, Ernest Bevin, Richard Law, among others, are pondering this same structural problem for little England.

I am quite aware of the irritations to the body politic because of delays and confusions embedded in the nondictatorial machinery of the government we now operate. But our choice in broad general terms is between expedition plus dictatorship or delays plus democratic arguments and pressure in pursuit of the best solution of any specific problem. Seldom have I lost my perspective on this problem even when urging decisions for clients. I know that many of my friends and clients complain most freely when decisions are not in accord with their own then special interests. Portions of the press, of course, have inflamed the public on this subject as much as possible. Seldom have I seen an editorial comment in favor of the process of "claiming" and the necessity of all angles being heard. Who should control the civilian gas supply—the bureau which has the responsibility for production of all fuels, or the department which is charged with handling transportation of workers to factories, or that branch of government which is impressed by Congress with the over-all duty of all other rationing problems? Much can be said for each position. A decision has to be made. And at this point the very newspapers which attack F. D. R. as dictator are the first to castigate him for not jumping in at once with a decision. It is the rare patience of F. D. R., his desire to have his appointees work the thing out between themselves rather than take orders from above, that makes him the leader of our people. Informed as to the minute details of our government, the President believes in the process of interbureau argument, pressure and claiming. Only out of such conflict is there a chance for truth and wisdom to win out. It should not surprise us that the President, when he does depart from this policy, pounces with what seems like unexpected and disproportionate vigor.

This basic problem of making decisions between forces of society urging various solutions is a concomitant of bigness. It helps not at all merely to shout for prompt issuance of directives. Judged by over-all results, our government during this war has been comparatively free of undue delays. I should imagine that the confusion in government is not so great as will be found in the insignificant operations of our largest bank, the Chase Bank with billions of deposits and innumerable branches. Any one of the big casualty insurance companies suffers from the same essential weakness. Only a few of the giants in our economy have established techniques for besting this problem: for example, the American Telephone and Telegraph Company; and at that no one really knows at what terrible costs to consumers the efficiency of the telephone company is achieved.

I sat in at an interdepartmental conference in Washington once on a matter of trifling significance, but a matter which affected seven different bureaus. The decision to be made would change records and procedures of each bureau. No one bureau was in a position to order the other bureaus around. I left the room for a few minutes and when I came back suggested, "Why isn't this the way out of the dilemma?" To my surprise my proposal was accepted without demurrer. I couldn't understand why all parties had agreed with such alacrity. Later I was told that all the people at the long conference table had thought that I had got instruction from the White House. Of course, nothing of the sort had happened. But the formula worked. Everyone was happy.

It was this incident that has encouraged me to suggest the need of a special secretariat close to the President to function exclusively on interdepartmental problems. Those of a minor nature could be handled without reference to the President or Cabinet officers. Real snags would have to be referred to the President. Of course, such a secretariat would be in a tough spot, dealing as it would, in the final analysis, with Cabinet officials. The job would require a man of high caliber. The Director of the Budget does much of this task today and does it with great success. But the process must be expanded outside of budgetary items.

Our danger lies in the direction of dictatorship rather than the boring delays of democratic pressures. But after democratic forces have played on a particular problem, then somewhere someone, other than a busy president, must make the final decisions. I'm not referring to decisions of extreme significance such as apportioning pulp paper between military and civilian needs. But after paper has been allotted for military needs, the pulp for civilian use affects hundreds of producers and thousands of workers. Decisions must be made hurting or benefiting different claimants—and never without effect on the public weal. Paper is used for aprons, bird-cage bottoms, fireworks, laundry shirt boards, poker chips, napkins, notebooks, and pie collars. Books, magazines, newspapers, advertising circulars and hundreds of different items must be appraised in terms of essential needs, amounts of paper needed, labor used, location of labor, convertibility of plants, and innumerable other factors. The knowledge and judgment of many bureaus is needed for the best possible decision in each case. Who would trust such decisions to one man or a single bureau?

Few if any problems fail to touch either Treasury or State, and so in a way these two old departments dominate many scenes, and all too often are the least adventurous and open to new ideas. A refugee is to be got out of Rumania. That needs money (Treasury), negotiations with foreign governments (State), shipping space (Shipping Board), and above all, co-operation with the military authorities operating particular theaters of war (Army, Navy). Policy questions such as the right to political asylum and quota immigration laws arise immediately. And so, as in innumerable other cases, a special committee of Treasury, State and Army is set up. John Pehle, head of the War Refugee Board, tough and able, carries through with the operation. Maybe we will solve part of this problem of government by expanding the number of such operating committees of department heads. It's not perfect. It creates no functional setup which can be spread out on a blueprint of government. But with a nation this size we will have to go through years of painful experimentation and change before we hit the answer which avoids both dictatorial decisions and undue delay and confusion. We can learn much from women's slacks and the International Ladies' Garment Workers Union.

CHAPTER XV

OUR EXCITING PROFESSION

Maggie's exhilarating interest in words—their history and shadings—has made me increasingly suspicious of what we call $10 words. "Truth," "morals," "ethics," create less than lucid, succinct images in the minds of all men. In my profession there is a great lather of talk and writing about "ethics"—which often has little if anything to do with right or wrong or even morals in the most generous use of that word. What we lawyers are really talking about is trade conventions, a comfort of practice.

Charles Burlingham, a kind of G.B.S. of the Bar, asked me years ago to go on the Ethics Committee of the Bar Association. Working with Irogen Seymour and Walbridge Taft as chairman over nearly a decade I learned more of the selfless decency of leaders of the Bar, sitting one night a week answering inquiries from hundreds of lawyers, than I have learned in all the rest of my practice and in the rough-and-tumble of the courtrooms.

In a real way this group, concerned with unprofessional conduct, was the radical sector of the Association. It tried to get down to the roots of the discomfort of clients in relation to their legal advisers. It was aware of the growing need for joint co-operative activity by laymen in those many situations where no one alone can afford to test out a law, or press a grievance against a giant corporation. It considered with conscientious dignity the many situations which involved conflicts of interest between clients in a lawyer's office and the need of a solitary accent in the vigilant advocacy by a lawyer of his client's interests.

[100]

Wally Taft, a hefty sailing man by the way, was ideal as chairman, possessing all the qualities of a good arbiter in a needle trades union. He let all of us talk ourselves dry and never let us fully know how much of each decision he sponsored with warm humility. William Roulston, an encyclopedist of professional conduct, was a true historian in the field. We had clashes, close decisions, but real intellectual matching of wits and prejudices.

But our committee was hamstrung by the top Executive Committee of the Association. We wanted to be more than a surface committee. We did some deep digging, but the little group that runs the Association was satisfied with its respectable surface mining.

Only slight changes have happened to the able great successful top lawyers over the past quarter century. It's only yesterday that women lawyers were kept out of the Association—on the last-ditch plea that the spacious building which houses the Association did not have female toilet facilities. To which some of us answered that we would contribute a special fund to erect a special Mae West Toilet for Women Lawyers.

But the Bar of New York has a grace and charm that springs in part from the joy of being engaged in a livelihood game that is truly noncompetitive. Clients come or don't come. There is nothing a lawyer can do to attract a clientele other than make speeches in churches, as a former president of the American Bar Association advised the neophytes. The absence of the curse of advertising—common to many professional groups in our nation—gives a better ride for the small and impecunious. It means that ingenuity has a chance against masses of money used to invite a flow of consumers into a few rich offices. Still, not many lawyers will claim that the Bar has attained its proper stature of communal leadership. Indeed, the Bar is far behind the judiciary in independence, vitality, courage and vision.

Some years ago I was invited to be the guest speaker at an Atlantic City weekend gathering of all the Federal Judges of the Third Circuit. This is the nearest I have come to getting an honorary degree.

It was after President Roosevelt had cleaned out the horrible old gang that sat on the Circuit Bench of that district. It was flattering to be so invited by Judge Biggs, to give an address in the presence of his conferees, with Judge Owen Roberts sitting in as the United States Supreme Court Justice attached to that area. I wished that Allen Wardwell, Charles Evans Hughes, Jr., Kenneth Spence, and the other leaders of the New York Bar could have witnessed the conference. They would have been shocked and bewildered. They might have gained some courage and some idea that the law they learned in college forty years ago has changed, and that the secret of the law lies in its ability to mold an influence to fit the changing needs of our society.

Someday there will be a renaissance of the Bar. Our great profession—trained to think, grounded in the stream of jurisprudence—should lead societal adjustments and reforms rather than befuddle and resist as is our present mood. Holding society's hand in its relationship to government, it could attain a preferred position in aid of the community as well as the individual.

It's less than wise to fetch for an analogy between our Bar and that of England but for odd historical reasons we fail to achieve leaders such as Lord Greene, Master of the Rolls, in England. In England the Bar more than lives up to its title "Officers of the Court." There, it is a sober guide in the tenuous paths traveled in the making of an adjustable world.

CHAPTER XVI

'

"SANITIZED FOR YOUR PROTECTION"

ON THE WAY TO THE 1944 August Convention of the
American Newspaper Guild in Milwaukee I stopped
overnight at the Statler Hotel in Boston. I was
shocked and amused at the drinking glasses in the bathroom
tightly wrapped in elaborate tissue paper. A band of paper
was wound around the toilet seat, marked "Sanitized For
Your Protection," with a Red Cross emblem.

I am not opposed to sanitary practices but it does seem to
me quite silly to waste all this paper during a war in which
paper is an essential for making and shipping material to our
boys at the front. Shortage, so called, of paper is so acute that
thousands of tons of paper are being used to try to sell to the
public the idea of collecting waste paper. It looks as if we
preferred toilet seat wrappers to books.

I know of no more phony and inexcusable campaign than
the American Waste Paper Drive. In England paper had to
be conserved and collected because that island at all times
must import all its pulp. With the invasion of Norway, England's main source of supply was cut off; a small amount of
esparto fiber was still coming in from Africa. While Africa
was owned by the Axis, that source also was cut off. But in
England the great newspaper owners bought with their own
funds three vessels (two were sunk in short order and the
third was shortly requisitioned by the government) in order
to get paper from Canada and the United States to keep the
presses going. At the same time the British publishers pooled
all their stocks of paper, put limits on circulation, eliminated
all return copies, and placed limitations on the amount of

this rare commodity that could be used for advertising: 45 per cent in newspapers, 55 per cent in magazines. The sole purpose of their entire program was to preserve the press during the war, not to keep corporations as such alive, nor to consume more of this precious material in advertising than was necessary to keep the publishers financially solvent. No preferences were given to large papers; in fact, small units—even *Punch*—procured extra rations. Publishers with many magazines or newspapers were not preferred over singleton houses. Books, containing no advertisements, were never cut so much as were newspapers and magazines. Advertising circulars used by merchants were severely curtailed. Freedom of the press was never put into question.

Under this program the newspapers, raising their rates on advertising space, prospered as never before, even though paper used for other than news and editorials was violently cut as compared to prewar patterns. The papers shrank to pitiful dimensions, but the people knew that a war was being fought.

Our problem presented a very different situation. Here the main objective was to see that the advertising content of the press not only held up in acreage of space used, but increased proportionately to the total size of each newspaper. Large publishers were preferred in innumerable indirect ways. Small or large units which did not carry advertising were put at a comparative disadvantage. Tons of circulars and advertisements kept pouring into the homes of the nation, substantially unaffected by the military needs of paper. Full-page institutional, quasi-political advertisements with pictures of General MacArthur—not intended to bring in any business —were placed in leading papers. The balance of the advertising took on an inflationary mood: "Buy War Bonds—That's Your Duty—But if you ever expect to buy another sweater—this is your last chance. Buy from our store."

It is all thoroughly disgusting because at the same time a constant bitter stream of attack on waste of paper by the government agencies is the main crusade of much of the press. Naturally, in our miraculous expansion of govern-mental production and military personnel there was waste of paper, but of minor dimensions compared to the waste by the press itself. Of course, the government's answer to such attacks was not given preferred space in the press.

We have learned much from paper rationing. The use of needlessly heavy paper was discovered and corrected. Size of magazines, size of margins in books, for example, compen-sated for much of the cut ordered from Washington. And as a nation we are slowly becoming conscious of the economic burden of excessive advertising. Our total national advertising bill runs close to $3 billion a year; and many a company which never advertised much before the war found that Uncle Sam was paying for the advertising, and hence there was little incentive to cut down on this kind of waste. Corporations with 80 per cent tax rates were buying space with 20 cents of their own money and 80 cents of Uncle Sam's. I estimate that the position of our Treasury, with which I heartily dis-agree, costs the taxpayers about 65 per cent of the $3 billion advertising burden of the nation. Slowly we are seeing adver-tising replace news and commentators' columns and edi-torials. Some publications have climbed up to 80 per cent advertising content, news being squeezed out of existence. And the big nation-wide advertisements—for so-called good will—such as Pere Marquette Railroad (I don't know where it runs and its ads didn't tell me) go mainly to the large papers of the large cities.

Some time ago I started to compute how many square miles of trees were cut down during this war in order to run institutional or inflationary ads in newspapers and magazines. I estimated that enough manpower was spent on cutting trees, logging, transporting and making paper for advertising pages to make unnecessary the entire draft of all married men with children in the United States. But the paradox of the entire shocking newspaper and magazine war saga is that there is no doubt that all publications would have made much more profit if there had been space limits on advertising. Rates would have been raised for the advertisements carried, and the saved space might have been employed for what I imagine is still the prime purpose of the press—news and entertainment. But once more the publishers of the giant publications dominated the situation and failed to see the enduring social impacts of the policies they urged. The sole benefit from this entire paper rationing is the trend to higher prices for circulation. This, if continued, might mean the liberation of the press from advertising pressure. It is better for consumers to pay directly for their reading, rather than through Pere Marquette tickets or Timken Roller Bearings.

Having made an investigation for the War Production Board in England for Donald Nelson and Leon Henderson, maybe I'm a little piqued because my suggestions were politely disregarded by the newspaper and magazine divisions. I still wish that various clients of ours such as *Omnibook*, the *New Yorker*, and innumerable other nongiant publications, could have banded together to make their voices heard.

But it's difficult in our economy of gargantuan controls to have the mass of democratic forces band together against the giants. The usual tactic is for the giants to buy off the opposition of the pygmies. In paper rationing this was done by allowing small papers using a score or so of tons per year to go without any cut. Thus maybe a thousand potential objectors were got out of the way. But beyond a little relief to the smallest papers there was only scant and all too late recognition of the fact that a 50 per cent cut of all paper used on Sunday editions above fifty pages would have brought less misery to publishers and public than a 20 per cent cut to big and small papers alike.

It still nauseates me to read in a Sunday paper which is 55.5 per cent advertising a lot of balderdash about the patriotic press and its campaign to save paper to win the war. Why not put up electric signs on Broadway and on the main streets of each city—burning away power and coal all night long: reading "Turn off your lights. Save Coal. Save Power. Win the War. The suppliers of these signs and power are contributing at the expense of Uncle Sam the power used to run these signs."

And then I can't forget the thousands of men whose war effort is to get more paper for advertising. What price total war for the press!

CHAPTER XVII

WE WENT TO SEE JOAN GRADUATE

WE LEFT NANTUCKET AT SIX in the morning after a brief coolish swim, and journeyed without barometer or Kenyon weathercaster to Northampton, Massachusetts. We traveled via three trains, a boat, a car and three taxis. It took me a little longer than it took to go by plane from Fisherman's Lake, Liberia, Africa, to Natal, Brazil, South America. All of which merely points to the ease with which we get spoiled by saving minutes, never quite knowing what we will do with the time thus hoarded. Often I've noticed that my most rushed clients are the people who stand on the street for long minutes to watch a safe being hoisted or a ditch being dug. To many of these "rushy" people I've told the story of the farmer who was approached by a salesman offering pills to be fed to pigs in order to accelerate the period of littering. "The pigs will have a litter in three weeks instead of four months." To which my favorite busy farmer replied, "But what's a hog's time worth?"

Like most parents, I am not at ease at my kids' schools, under any circumstances. I'm a little afraid of the teachers, much embarrassed with my children's friends, and certainly feel alien to my offspring in these surroundings. I know of no occasions of greater artificiality between parent and child than at a visit to school.

Whatever might be said about ordinary visits, graduations

are still worse. The unholy emphasis laid on these so-called definitive ends of chapters in children's lives creates tears, mercurial emotions, and fears of the next chapters to be lived.

But this graduation had a different quality. Joan was getting a diploma from the Clarke School for the Deaf at Northampton. The miracle of lip reading never can be reduced to meager proportions. I never quite forget that Joan blew out a candle a hundred hours to learn to say P instead of B. A good stout P blows out the candle; a decent B leaves it unquivered. For years I've tried to distinguish, by lip reading my friends, the letters "P," "B" and "M," or the words "eight," "nine" and "ten." To me they all look the same. All speech learned other than through audio-memory still seems quite improbable, but Joan can say any word in any language perfectly if she wants to. However, if she needs the word again the only way she can repeat it is by acute remembrance of where she held her tongue and teeth and lips the last time she said it—maybe a year or more before.

And so at the exercises the audience of parents and friends heard the prayer, listened to the award of prizes by gracious Mrs. Calvin Coolidge, and even the graduation speech. The kids only saw these events. In fact, the speech had been written out and distributed in advance so that the graduates could read it beforehand. To lip-read a speech from a platform, with the speaker turning his head from one side of the audience to another, was too much for these youngsters. It's nearly as difficult as lip reading a three-cornered conversation.

For a few early years of Joan's life I was worried for her, and for us, but soon she licked deafness. Everyone has a hump—in the terms of Katharine Butler Hathaway's discerning *The Little Locksmith*. Some humps are concealed and some invisible even to the owner. In a lawyer's office, which can partake of the confessional of a parish priest, all kinds of humps sit before his desk. My profession has the privilege and joy of smoothing out humps.

Joan has licked hers. Once a year maybe there is a little exasperation when she says, "I wish you were all deaf." Never does she say: "I wish I could hear." Not hearing has compensations. None of us knows fright except from grownups, and Joan, uncorrupted in her youth by fearsome adults, dove off ten-foot diving boards before she could swim, and sailed a boat alone at the age of seven, upsetting, sitting on the sailing dinghy's bottom, waiting for rescue, and laughing. She had not yet acquired the concept of "drowning." For years she was confused about the meaning of two words—"frightened" and "surprised." Tripping over a cord or wire she would say, "I was frightened." She no doubt felt surprised. She will never put into the word "frightened" the significance attributed to it by most people in our kind of society. Her frame of reference will always be different.

Only recently I was kidding Joan about the many beaux who take her to parties and dances. Joan's only reaction was to say, "Of course I'm lucky because most of my boy friends are deaf, and girls with hearing find that most of their beaux are in the Army."

This capacity to take life as it is goes so far as to give her a real amount of joy from the fact that I have a certain amount of hearing difficulty at times. She does not hesitate to tell me that it makes her feel better.

With Joan we came to the edge of a miracle. I flopped. I didn't have the guts to go on alone. A dozen doctors offered me cynicism, but no hope, and all the teachers for the deaf, except one, Dot Wood, failed to understand what I was talking about. As for engineers, the big ones were too busy. Most of my friends thought I was plain nuts.

When Joan was about ten, after years of the usual unimaginative jabber of despair in doctors' offices, and they seem to me to have a greater vested interest in ignorance and old textbooks than have even my brother lawyers, I made up my mind that there is no such thing as total ear deafness unless the organ has been physically mutilated. My starting point was nothing but the wishful thinking of any parent. My theory, rejected by medicos, was to find some wave length that could get into Joan's nerves, through either the bone or

[109]

the ear. Maybe the wave was such that human beings could not ordinarily hear it. Maybe it was way beyond the 10,000 cycles ordinarily audible to man, or the higher ones heard by some children. Why not convert sound into light, then back into sound at any vibration we want, amplify it (not enough to destroy distinction of sounds) and then see if Joan would enjoy it?

In no time at all our top floor looked like an RCA-NBC radio station. I had no scientific training and was too old or something to take on the learning of modern electronics and acoustics. I should have. Lazy, no doubt.

The first box was a radio keyed to 1,300 cycles as the peak. Joan listened for fun an hour or so a day. We don't know if or what she heard but after six months she said, "That's beautiful." Here was the opening wedge. Joy of experience is so often the introduction to knowledge and even wisdom. After a few months more she could tell the difference between speech and music. She noted the difference but of course did not know, in hearing terms, what speech or music meant to hearing people. She could no more describe what she sensed than I could define the color "blue."

We made other contraptions. A phonograph, peaked at a certain cycle. This was a failure. Joan couldn't do a Berlitz job. She wasn't ready to co-ordinate reading—"Mother, Roger, Delia" and other words—with the concepts of the sounds which hit her eardrums. We put a silver microphone on the phonograph and talked through it. By this time Joan had read stories about a dog barking, a telephone ringing, the water running. She had learned to lip-read, talk and read by a single process. This is a glass—the object before her to see, the printed word on a card to read, the teacher's lips to follow and her own lips to use either by following the teacher's, looking in a mirror, or by joining phonics which she had learned. But she had never heard such phenomena until one day Margaret took the microphone to the telephone and asked central to ring our number; the water running in the tub and a dog barking in the yard sent their stories into the mike over the wires, through the tubes and out over wires to Joan's earpieces.

Joan was delighted. A totally deaf friend, a first-class sculptor, was there. He tried the apparatus. He could distinguish two- from three-syllable words by the number of blows on the ear, but he could not decode the actual word spoken. Joan looked at him and said to us, "Poor man, he's deaf."

And so we went on, cursing the doctors and teachers who had delayed us for a half dozen years. Finally Joan got to the point where the concepts of a hundred words were distinguishable by sound alone. After hours of practice with Dot Wood, Joan could repeat or write down words talked into a microphone out of her sight, even in the next room.

For my part I was at home plate. If with certainty she could distinguish even two words by sound alone, she could do two thousand, which is as much as most people need or use. The rest was practice. But practice is tough. We hearing people are deaf in Arabic or Latin—at least most of us are. It's a great chore for hearing people to learn Russian without an environmental capacity for mimicry and correction.

And so, with doctors and teachers uninterested, we had to wait until Joan came home from boarding school. This year she is at Parsons School of Design in New York, living at home, and will have time to learn to hear. The first six months will be tiresome, hard work but with hope of learning to hear those hours will go by. New instruments will come out of the war, not out of medical laboratories. The attitude of the human race toward deafness is where it was toward eye trouble thirty years ago. I remember when glasses were considered de trop for women. In New England, spectacles in time were accepted as a symbol of erudition; in the South, there are maidens who would rather squint; and not until the horn-rimmed job was sold as a stylish accouterment did women of the United States accept glasses and start to see.

And so hearing aids are just getting out of the cellar of taboo. As counsel to a New York State Legislative Commission inspired by Judge Jacob Livingston to investigate deafness, we found that probably ten million people need hearing aids in the United States today. Thousands of children flunk their grades and are treated as feeble-minded because they are not put in the front row, or taught to lip-read, or given hearing aids.

It's a great saga—the story of lip reading—a recent saga, a saga of people who reject the isolation of finger talking.

We have learned more from Joan than she has from us. And that's the way it should be.

Joan has just read these notes. She was amused. Her only comment was: "What were you worried about when I was young?"

CHAPTER XVIII

THE CENSOR MARCHES ON

IN 1870 A PITIFUL DIRTY-MINDED MAN—Anthony Comstock —backed by J. P. Morgan shifted the course of our national pattern on censorship. A decade previously, England had for the first time started to define obscenity. Comstock engineered through Congress with less than ten minutes of debate our first censorship on the grounds of sex. All states except New Mexico followed suit. And then until 1915 publishers were enslaved, often sending manuscripts before publication to Comstock's Society for the Suppression of Vice for approval or editing.

In 1915 the tide turned when Mitchell Kennerly contested the ban on *Hagar Revelly*. It has been one of the profoundly satisfactory portions of my life as a lawyer to be called upon to represent dozens of authors and publishers against the censors, private or public. I happened to hit a tide, a stream which made it easy to win all the cases save only two: one an early volume, Donald Henderson Clark's *Female*, temporarily banned only in Queens County, New York; the other, John Herrmann's *What Happens*, published in France. Both would be approved by the courts if retested now.

It has been a useful crusade—much of it without financial compensation. It has involved classics such as the *Decameron*, brave new themes like *The Well of Loneliness*, historic writing such as Joyce's *Ulysses*, sex educational writings such as Mary Ware Dennett's pamphlet "The Sex Side of Life," and "The Birth of a Baby" article in *Life* magazine. Magazines, novels, fiction, history, etchings, radio programs, theatrical productions, art exhibits—a gamut of human expression.

Each case raised a different aspect of the censors' fears—Anglo-Saxon words, glorification of adultery, pioneer treatment of the theme of homosexuality. Obscenity is still a vague concept. Censors shout that all impure ideas of sex which are capable of corrupting the readers should be banned. We asked: Corrupt whom? Children? If so, is adult reading to be reduced to the level of youth or of the feeble-minded? What kind of ideas are impure sexually? To the pure all things are pure. And what does corrupt mankind? For years I made inquiries in the professions to find evidence that reading had any objective traceable effect—corrupting or otherwise. I followed tests showing the reading of prisoners arrested for crimes of passion. If we used their testimony as a guide, then the daily papers and all movies would be the first to be blue-penciled. Even the Vice Society has no worthy testimony bearing on the relation of books and antisocial deeds.

We know little about our sexual folkways. Soon it will be proved that homosexuality, masturbation, and petting are more prevalent among the sophisticated, or what is called the upper stratum of society, than among other people, who show a higher percentage of premarital sexual relationship. The figures on sexual relations with girls under eighteen years of age—which acts, no doubt, run into millions of incidents a year—may cause a reappraisal of headlines concerned with juvenile delinquency. But the law in the main and particularly in the police courts is administered by judges stemming from one stratum of life, unconsciously applying their codes vis-à-vis the other stratum. All of which not yet reduced to scientific terms is nevertheless the ever-changing basis of the law of changing obscenity.

We had fun educating juries and judges. We never argued a case without trying to bring home the fluidity of sexual standards and the constant shift in man's fears of ideas. Originally censorship was applied to protect the church—blasphemy was the charge. As the church's power dwindled, man feared any attack on the king, the state, and the crime shifted from blasphemy to sedition. And now, in the main, the current insecurity in our society is in sexual matters.

After twenty or more years of such cases before courts or government agencies I am convinced that there is no book openly published, reviewed by reputable publications, which will be banned by our courts. I am disturbed, however, at the new rampages in Boston and at the Post Office Department. All these cases can be won only if the publishers and authors believe in their product, stand up and fight unafraid. It is also important that the publishers' advocates never apologize, never blush, never feel ashamed. They need not identify their own taste with the manuscript they defend. But stoutly they must believe in the right of the public to hear and see all.

Once more the censor marches on. In Boston, *Strange Fruit* was withdrawn by agreement of booksellers on a mere unofficial threat by a police official. What timidity on the part of these merchants of our most precious commodity; even though it's unfair to ask a retailer to stand the brunt and expense of a test case! His financial stake in the sale of any single title is negligible. The book doesn't carry his imprint. It is not of his making. Freedom of thought would be better served if retailers in peril, rather than submit to a cop's appraisal of literary crime, called on the publisher and author to stand up openly in support of what carries their names. Certainly, agreements between merchants to withdraw an

[114]

article from sale seem to be clearly in contravention of our state and federal antitrust laws. Recently I wrote Attorney General Francis Biddle and suggested that conspiracy to withdraw a book—in this case, *Strange Fruit*—seemed to me to be a more antisocial restraint of trade than an agreement not to sell wall or toilet paper. Words on paper should not deteriorate the value of pulp in the eyes of the law.

A test case was brought by vigilant Bernard De Voto. His attorney, acting for the Civil Liberties Union, has been in our office to look over all our briefs and records in other cases. The surest way to lose that case—involving, as it does, a single word—is to be apologetic for the use of any word or concept in a book of such dignity and distinction. Dozens of recent books have used the same Anglo-Saxon word which the Boston authorities object to in Lillian Smith's great volume.

The most amusing legal instance on this score that I know of occurred during the defense of James Joyce's *Ulysses*. In 1925, dealers had gone to jail for selling it in sophisticated New York. In 1933, Random House had courage enough to decide to publish an American edition. We advised that obscenity, a vague concept at best, is always subject to reinterpretation against the changing mores at the day of trial, and that we thought we could clear Joyce's much-discussed opus.

As in all these cases, hundreds of people turned out and went to the courtroom. This figurative burning of books under modern juridical blessing can well be compared to the burning of heretics at the stake four hundred or so years ago. One of the government prosecuting attorneys, intelligent, generous and capable, came up to me before the hearing. "The government can't win the case," he said. I asked why this defeatism. He said, "The only way to win the case is to refer to the great number of vulgar four-letter words used by Joyce. This will shock the judge and he will suppress the book. But I can't do it." "Why?" I queried. Prudishly he replied, "Because there is a lady in the courtroom." Sure enough, when I looked around, there was Maggie, taking a day off from school to hear the argument.

"But," I said, "that's my wife. She's a former newspapergal and a present schoolteacher. She's seen all these words on toilet walls or scribbled on sidewalks by kids who enjoy them because of their being taboo."

Well, the government didn't pick up the "word" argument. The second day of the trial gave me an opportunity. I told Judge Woolsey about all these words unused by the polite. I tried, after going over the etymology of each word with Margaret, to trace the convention in words. Tastes change, taboos vary, but man has always found a new combination of letters to convey a concept if the old word was deemed disgusting. No better series in our own generation can be found than in the travelogue of bathroom, toilet, water closet, W. C., gentleman's room, john, can, and now "I'm going to telephone." No one is ever really deceived.

When I got to the word "fuck," I explained how one of the possible derivations was "to plant," an Anglo-Saxon agricultural usage. The farmer used to fuck the seed into the soil. I told the Judge I liked the word. I didn't use it in parlors because it made me unpopular, but the word had strength and integrity.

"In fact, your Honor, it's got more honesty than phrases that modern authors use to connote the same experience."

"For example, Mr. Ernst?" asked the Court.

"Oh—'they slept together.' It means the same thing."

The Judge smiled. "That isn't even usually the truth."

At that moment I knew that the case was half won.

The other half of the battle gave rise to one of those rare experiences which make court work involving ideas such a joy.

Many times Judge Woolsey, a man of great culture and wisdom, asked whether I had really read through the entire volume. I feared he might tend to condemn on the theory that it would do society no harm to suppress a book so long, so dull and so dreary. I had to answer this potential state of mind.

I decided to wade in on a personal note.

"Yes, Judge—ten years ago I tried to get through *Ulysses* but couldn't. This year in preparation for the trial, I *had* to read it. And while reading it I was invited, in August, to speak at the Unitarian Church in Nantucket on the New Banking Act and the reopening of the banks after the Holiday."

"What's that got to do with my question?" said Judge Woolsey.

"Well, I addressed about four hundred people. I was intent on what I was saying. And still, when I finished, I realized that while I was talking about banking, I was also thinking at the same time about the long ceiling-high windows on the sides, the clock and eagle in the rear, the painted dome above, the gray old lady in the front row, the baby in the sixth row, and innumerable other tidbits.

"Judge," I said, "that's *Ulysses*. I went back to my reading with a new appreciation of Joyce's technique, the stream of consciousness put into words. And now, your Honor, while arguing to win this case I thought I was intent only on this book, but frankly, while pleading before you, I've also been thinking about that ring around your tie, how your gown does not fit too well on your shoulders, and the picture of George Washington back of your bench."

The Judge smiled. "I've been worried about the last part of the book but now I understand many parts about which I've been in doubt. I have listened as intently as I know how but I must confess that while listening to you I've also been thinking about that Heppelwhite chair behind you."

"Judge," I said, "that's the book."

The next summer Margaret and I were in Paris and picked up Joyce—nearly blind—for dinner at Fouquet's. Joyce was interested in the trial. I told him how Martin Conboy, the Federal District Attorney in New York, had opened the argument by describing this book as one day in the life of a Hungarian Jew. One would have imagined that the scene was not

Ireland and that the trial was for blasphemy instead of obscenity. Conboy had been counsel for the Vice Society for many years and it had done something to his attitude toward writing. He had looked too long and too often for dirt.

I paused to ask Joyce just when he had left the Catholic Church. He said, "That's for the Church to say." Which to me meant that inside himself he had never left the Church, try as he might have.

This tale I related to Judge Woolsey at a later date when we both spoke at the opening of an exhibit of Banned Books of the World, a great exhibit put on by the New York Junior League under the direction of Mrs. Tex Moore, oddly enough Harry Luce's sister. Judge Woolsey then made what seemed to me to be a profound observation, not picked up, so far as I knew, by any of the Joyce students. "Maybe Joyce's inner conflict as to Catholicism explains why the secondary streams of the non-Catholics in the book are penciled with more clarity than are the inner thinkings of the Catholics."

Judge Woolsey's decision legalizing *Ulysses* spelled out a new approach to the appraisal of works published in the open by established publishers. For years judges of all courts have in their written opinions on censorship cases referred to authorities for support of suppression or clearance. Although Sainte-Beuve and the Encyclopædia Britannica, among others, were cited in the *Mlle. de Maupin* case, the same court suggested that defendants might not call living authorities to the witness stand to testify to the literary, educational or psychological impact of an attacked volume. Judge Woolsey broke through this monopoly of jurists. The jury henceforth may gain wisdom also from experts. His decision, wise and epoch-making in this field of law, was enjoyed by many who never read *Ulysses*. It will no doubt be quoted for years, at least for two brilliant sentences:

The words which are criticized as dirty are old Saxon words known to almost all men and, I venture, to many women, and are such words as would be naturally and habitually used, I believe, by the types of folk whose life, physical and mental, Joyce is seeking to describe. In respect of the recurrent emergence of the theme of sex in the minds of his characters, it must always be remembered that his locale was Celtic and his season Spring.

SEX IN E-FLAT

Recently the New York censors were out sniffing once more. D. H. Lawrence's *The First Lady Chatterley*, the hitherto unpublished first version of *Lady Chatterley's Lover*, was attacked, though cleared. Will we never get over our fear of the Anglo-Saxon vocabulary? I've always thought that Vizetelly's memorial to Parliament, written from his jail cell after publishing Zola in England in 1888, was an important and telling document for censors to read. The great lexicographer, while serving the jail sentence from which he died, collated outstanding samples of the sexually provocative lines of the great British authors from Chaucer through Congreve and Shakespeare to Swinburne. He asked: "Why don't you suppress all these classics? Or are the dirty words or thoughts of dead authors unobjectionable? How long must an author be dead to be a legally obscene classic?"

In 1930 I appeared before a soft, considerate magistrate in behalf of Simon & Schuster's *Casanova's Homecoming* by Arthur Schnitzler, the deft Viennese author. In order to persuade the Court that the condemnatory opinion of Judge Robert Wagner in 1924 should be reappraised, we prepared a separate brief containing the opinions of prominent Americans on the book in question. Columbia University used it; Edna Ferber, Carl Van Doren, Sinclair Lewis—many leaders of our literature approved it. The argument implicit in these letters was: If these people who lead public literary opinion oppose suppression, then surely the Court should admit that the volume did not jar our present mores sufficiently to be condemned.

After submission and argument against sorry John S. Sumner, the director of the Society for the Suppression of Vice, we waited while the Judge delayed for weeks handing down an opinion. We were at a loss to understand the delay. One bright day the Judge called up the office: "I have read over the testimonials and I don't find any letter of approval from Heywood Broun. How does he feel about the book?" Within a few hours a brief blessing in writing, signed Heywood Broun, was in the Judge's possession.

The decision was announced promptly thereafter. It read:

... there had been submitted to this Court the written opinions of such writers as Henry L. Mencken, Theodore Dreiser, Herbert Asbury, Heywood Broun, Dr. Harry Elmer Barnes, Sinclair Lewis, John Cowper Powys and others, recognized as leaders in the field of literary art. . . .

This court has come to the conclusion that the book in question is not obscene; that there is nothing within its covers which tends to impair the morals of any one reading it, and that process will not be issued for the arrest of these defendants. . . .

I never understood this request for a Broun letter until weeks later, when I ran into the Judge on Madison Avenue. I suggested that we needed all the testimonials once more for use in another court, since Sumner was going to proceed against the book in an adjacent county. To which the Judge replied smilingly, "You can't get them. Why do you think I called up for that Broun letter? My son is an autograph collector."

Another Schnitzler episode which brought me into engaging correspondence with the great Viennese author arose out of the attack on his sharply defined play *Hands Around* (*Reigen*). This brief drama, a circuit of love affairs, had previously been staged under the auspices of Otto Kahn, an American Maecenas. I had not handled the case below when the book was first attacked and, in fact, appeared only as amicus curiae for the author in the hearing before the Court of Appeals. The book was suppressed, but two judges dissented. Many years later, when buying some secondhand books, I ran into the clerk who had been convicted, and was happy to be able later to plead for his pardon, which was granted by Governor Lehman. Judge Cardozo had voted for suppression, which led me to ponder the fears of judges. Judge Cardozo, afraid of obscenity, was never scared by allegedly seditious or revolutionary writings. Judge Woolsey, brave on *Ulysses*, had suppressed an amateurish paper, the *Militant* written by pseudo revolutionists.

Years later, when I reviewed a life of Judge Cardozo, I explored the paradox of general unanimity between Judges Holmes, Brandeis and Cardozo. Holmes, lusty and free-flowing—never reading economics; Brandeis, brought up on a slide rule and less than a "good fellow"; Cardozo, ascetic and lonely and shy with people. And still time and again, despite different backgrounds, glands and emotions, they united in declaring the law and their dreams for our nation. After the review appeared in the New York *Herald Tribune*, Judge Cardozo wrote to tell me that my review was the only compensation he had felt for this unauthorized biography.

In researching *Reigen*, I read the evidence adduced at the original trial in Vienna years before, when the performance created a riot, a debate in the Austrian Parliament, and a world-wide controversy among literati. The Austrian trial discussed at length the possible obscenity of the music accompanying the dramatic performance. This approach struck me as fantastic except as against man's ancient fear of exciting music. For ages certain churches would not allow music in houses of worship, and music is still recognized as an agent provocateur of amorous behaviorism. Quakers and others still ban it.

From the testimony taken before the tribunal in gay dancing Vienna, I found that the music was written in the key of E-flat. I went back to the days when I played the cello —and badly, I may say—and the more recent period of pounding the piano, chiefly with *Lohengrin* and Williams College songs, and then looked for pieces of homely virtue written in the same key. I had enough to make a point, or at least raise a query. Was there such a thing as a special gonadic key? Or did each person have a special key? Or were extroverts susceptible to one key and introverts to another? Although treating the subject lightly, I nevertheless felt that an interesting test, or at least an amusing and somewhat spicy parlor game, might stem from the idea.

As often with odd tidbits of this nature, I sent a note to E. B. White at the *New Yorker*, the keenest commentator we have in the United States on man's tender irrationalities. He did a swell piece in "Talk of the Town." He wrote in part:

The court . . . gave the music a clean bill of health on the ground that it was written in E-flat. Nobody, said the court, could be corrupted by anything in E-flat, "an especially gloomy and heavy key which has no power to define the rhythm of sexual intercourse, if music can ever do that."

White also pointed out that E-flat was the key of "Drink to Me Only with Thine Eyes," "My Man," and "Every Little Movement Has a Meaning of Its Own."

In 1935, Philadelphia rose up against Shostakovich's opera *Lady Macbeth of Mzensk*. The furies subsided after Alexander Smallens, who was conducting, deleted from the score four measures of trombone music which were supposed to depict the final stages of bedroom love. And when the Junior League of New York put on its exhibit of writings banned through the ages, from Tyndale's Bible up to date, there were also displays of banned music. How sophisticated we are. How remote from sheer, free-flowing primitive days. How complimentary it all is to music and musicians!

CHAPTER XIX

STEPCHILDREN OF THE PRESS

JUNE AND SEPTEMBER IN NANTUCKET are the times of year when I make up on my reading, particularly fat volumes such as the *Holmes-Pollock Letters* and Mott's *American Journalism*. Maggie, I'm glad to say, keeps her list of books, and of movies which someday we may want to take in. We now know there is no such thing as timeliness for most books save only for the purpose of idle chitchat at dinner parties, which we go in for less and less. But the books come in by mail from many quarters: authors whom I have met, publishers' galleys to read for libel, and an increasing number of requests for boosts or blurbs.

Every time I mail a book I'm reminded of the sixty years when books were treated like stepchildren of the printing press. For decades, magazines and newspapers have received subsidies of tens of millions of dollars a year, through postage rates pegged much below the cost of carrying. But formerly books cost 8 to 26 cents, by zones, for sending across the nation, as compared to about two or three cents for a magazine or newspaper.

Most exciting adventures of the law stem from fortuitous events, but none more chancy than my interest in outlawing discrimination against books. I had read that 20 per cent of the American public lived more than thirty miles from a bookstore. This, coupled with the fact that we in the United States have a lower book-reading public in relation to literacy than any other portion of this planet, got up my intellectual dander. We explored how this came to be. Obviously bookstores had been decimated by the fraudulent practice of loss-leader selling. Macy was the archdevil in the field of price wars, at times selling Modern Library books costing close to 50 cents for as little as 11 cents. This come-on game of selling goods below cost resulted in sucking customers into a store and then of necessity making up for the below-cost sales by extra charges on other items. But no such averaging game against customers could be carried on by little retail bookstores. So, when Macy sold Modern Library books below cost every bookstore in the district put those volumes under the counter. Thirty years ago, when I first represented some publishers, book salesmen traveled from East to West, New York to San Francisco, back and forth, stopping at many cities and towns. Now there are less than five hundred important bookstores left in the nation. Mail-order business had come into our pattern of distribution and postage rates became increasingly significant.

I assigned the law end of the research to a smart lawyer girl in our office, just fresh from the *Columbia Law Review*. I have always envied the Phi Beta Kappa and Law Review people, since I had no decent law education, what with sleeping at night school five nights a week after a day of shirt manufacturing on the Gowanus Canal in Brooklyn, or later selling golden oak furniture on the installment plan in one of the Baumann stores. This associate of mine found that the President had the power to modify book postage rates by proclamation.

We prepared a brief on the economics and the law. I saw the President. In a jiffy the agile mind of F.D.R. saw the point: "The more they burn books in Germany, the cheaper we should make them here." So books became mailable at 1½ cents per pound, the same as newspapers and magazines all over the land, irrespective of zones. Later the President said, "You had better not rely on the whim of a president. Go to Congress for statutory relief now that the trial periods have shown the results." Senator Jim Mead sponsored a bill and Postmaster General Walker and his assistant, Mr. North, supported the move. And now books get a subsidy of about

$9 million a year, still mere chicken feed compared to newspapers and magazines. Congress jacked up the rate to 3 cents a pound—a little higher than magazines and newspapers even though books carry no paid advertising.

The discrimination against books was easy to dramatize. I sent the President a package of books including the Bible and Shakespeare, and in another package of equal weight I sent some of our most tawdry magazines. The book package had cost 60 cents to mail from New York to Washington; the magazines cost less than 15 cents. At the time I sent these gifts, I wrote the President advising him that two packages would come to him so that he would be sure to get both, knowing which of the two might be purloined in his outer office!

I'm of the opinion that cheap books, a prime tool of an informed democratic people, cannot be available in a nation our size except by use of the mails, and subsidized postage.

But I'm still disturbed at the vast gifts made to *Reader's Digest, Time, Life, Chicago Tribune* and others out of the taxpayers' nickels and dimes. I favor increasing subsidies for units which merchandise ideas—radio, books, magazines, newspapers and movies. But surely the subsidy might be graded just as our income surtaxes are upped for the higher brackets, the lucky ones in life. Why should DeWitt Wallace or Harry Luce or Colonel McCormick get a subsidy by cheap postage after one million or more of their copies have been carried by the Post Office at far less than cost? I would rather encourage every little country weekly by practically free postage, just as we do books for the blind, and then charge maybe ½ cent a pound on the next 100,000 circulation. By the time a publication hits a million or so it should not need any further gifts from the taxpayers.

The giant publishers claim great economies due to mere size. Let them spend some of those savings out of their own treasuries rather than out of the national till. What do Luce *et al.* say about free enterprise without government intervention in this field of economics? Captain Patterson, of the

New York *Daily News,* is the only publisher I know of who has spoken out against government grants of the nature now extended to the big circulation newspapers.

But more important still, by increased subsidies to small units, to thousands of dailies and small weeklies in little communities, we might be able to save them from bankruptcy and thus stem the tide of evaporation of our press. A few years ago dailies numbered nearly 2,600 and now we are down to about 1,800. About 90 per cent of our cities have only one newspaper left. Reversing this trend will demand all our ingenuity.

CHAPTER XX

ENGLAND'S PECK'S BAD BOY

IN THE LATE SPRING OF 1944, down at Welwyn Gardens, his home near London, George Bernard Shaw, who prefers to be called Bernard Shaw or G.B.S., told me about his latest book, recently finished. Ever quixotic and provocative, Shaw had outlined the unfitness of the average man to nominate and vote for his government. Doctors took tests before practicing; lawyers had to pass their Bar examinations and ministers to be ordained. But, said G.B.S., for the most important task of man, electing his rulers, we think that all adults are qualified without examinations. Hence he was proposing a test so that those who passed would be members of a panel which in turn would nominate the candidates for Parliament and all other offices. The rest of society would still have the right to vote, but only from the list of candidates chosen by the qualified few. It all seemed quite out of line with his *Guide to Socialism,* which I pointed to on the near-by bookshelf, but in keeping with his admiring comments about Mussolini. I was embarrassed in the face of the inconsistency of his philosophy, but perhaps excitement is sufficient to expect from any one such person.

I asked, "What are you writing next?" Eighty-eight years old, sprightly, vital, with gay gillies on his feet, and knickers, he answered, "I don't know. I'm two years behind in my writing." What a man! Two years behind at eighty-eight.

Tea was served. I started to kid him about his abstentions —wine, tobacco and meat. The first two elicited an easy and ready explanation. His father once had said, "Don't be like me," and G.B.S. gave up liquor and smoking. On cross-examination he did confess to a jug of wine once in a while. It didn't pay, he thought. While not imbibing he could fight off and eliminate 90 per cent of his ideas before they got on paper. When drinking wine, 90 per cent got into his writings and then had to be cut out later.

"But how about this vegetarian stuff? Are you sentimental about killing animals?"

"Of course not."

"Do you lay off meat for health reasons?"

"Of course not. I might be healthier if I followed the practice of my contemporary, Sidney Webb, who was born with a pound of beef in his mouth and has not stopped eating meat ever since."

"What's it all about then?" I asked.

His blue eyes twinkled. He had the question he wanted.

"People who keep dogs get to be like dogs. People who own horses take on in time some of the qualities of horses. The entire human race is valet to the cow and gets to be more and more cowlike. I'd rather eat my grass direct than through a cow."

It wasn't true but it contained a trickle of sense. We all are affected beyond our comprehension by immediate environment. I thought back to one of my favorite books, *Wolf Child and Feral Man*, by the Reverend J.A.L. Singh, where at last we had the proof of the Romulus and Remus legend. I have always believed in the verity of folk sagas, such as that

[127]

of the seaman carrying a caul for luck, and the glories of
Atlantis, the lost continent.

Amala and Kamala, female babies, were picked up in a
field by a milk-full wolf mother, after they had been deserted,
as is often the practice in India, by a work-weary human
mother. These two human beings lived in a cave with the
wolves. In far fewer than ten years they had taken on the
habits of a wolf—running on all fours, seeing in the dark,
drinking by lapping, howling at night, fearing men, feeling
kinship to animals, eating live raw chickens. They were
unable to stand upright, had long tongues, calloused feet and
hands. It's too bad the heroine of this story, the wolf mother,
was killed. She is my favorite in this bit of history. But these
two human beings prove the adjustability of man, the overwhelming capacity of life to change within one span. Their
progress in the mission to which they were taken where they
mixed with other children, shows the flexibility of our race.
Within a decade, Kamala stands up, overcomes her fear of
light, becomes friendly to human children, and in time
accepts and adopts the human race's fear of other species.
Before she died she was able to think in adverbial terms.

Some people reading this diary of re-education—authentic
though inadequate—come to a tiny despair. How quickly the
human race could slide back a million years and once more
live in trees and caves. But to me it indicates rather the untold capacity of man to grow and change and conquer nature
and life.

The present wide advances of gadgetary science have led
many to believe that we as a race are nearing the end of our
historic development—which is only a bit of species conceit.
Feeling color while blindfolded, as is the power of Eileen
Garrett of extrasensory perception card fame, reading a distant mind, as has been done by the great Greek scholar,
Gilbert Murray, are merely gentle ticklings at the universe we
haven't caught hold of as yet.

I wish I could be around when the lost continent is rediscovered. I'm betting it was, and is. We have only started on our way.

MISHMASH

Once in a while, as I fall asleep, I make up my mind to try my ability to wake up at some precise moment without an alarm clock or a knock on the door. Recently I did it within about 32 seconds. This is a baffling trick of nature. That the human mind can keep in exact rhythm with man-made springs and gears and dials known as a clock is quite inexplicable, especially since the power exists peculiarly while man is asleep. It's a unique capacity. I know of no similar power possessed by man asleep or awake.

I tried in vain to find out if anybody has ever explored to see if this particular ability exists among primitive races which never heard of time or saw a clock. Can a native of a Pacific island wake up at the exact chosen moment when the sun reaches the second bough of the tree under which he sleeps? I'd like to see some such experiments with a clockless native. If he has a sun-time power, then let him sleep a mile away from his pet tree and once more decide to wake up when the sun reaches the second bough of the tree under which he previously slept. How many nights would he have to sleep under the new tree before the sun crossing a bough of that tree would become the equivalent of our man-made clock and become deeply enough embedded in his chronological sense to permit him, while asleep, to know the position of the sun?

This power is so naïve, intense and simple that it must have seemed like a miracle when first discovered by man. Most such miracles lie in unsophisticated organisms. Just so with the major inventions of our civilization.

Probably one of the true scientists of all time was the man who first realized that there was just one star out of the billions of stars that was fixed and immutable—at least for a short time. Man could not have traveled this globe without the discovery of such a star. It was not always our North Star.

Astronomers say that the North Star, Polaris, will be out of our heavens in a short time. Five thousand years ago, when the Great Pyramid was built in Egypt, an opening was left in its center for the frosty light of Thuban, then man's North Star. We know which star will take this place in the future of man's history—it will be Vega. Vega will be used to steer my *Truant* about ten thousand years from now.

Incidentally, the North Star wouldn't have done navigation much good unless another genius had discovered the steering board, the centerboard or the keel. With the major windflows of the world as they are today, and probably were long ago, the migration of man without the centerboard would no doubt have proceeded but the travelers could never have gone back home. Recently I played with the charts of world winds and figured where man could have roamed always with the winds, and how, if at all, he might ultimately have returned to his place of departure. I am quite sure that by the time he would have returned home through sailing only "full and bye," he would never have known in any kind of recorded history that his ancestors thousands of years before had left that very place.

There is one place on earth I know of where there is a symmetry of wind—Lake Como. I remember sailing in a clumsy dory with outboards, and how we had to go up the lake in the morning and down the lake in the afternoon, and how all the cargoes of the communities along the shores travel up with the wind and down with the wind. I wonder if anybody has correlated the time of the shift of the wind at Como with other phenomena? It may shift with the regularity of some distant tide at some spot antipodal to Como— say in the neighborhood of New Zealand. It must be correlated to something.

The great discoveries of man, such as North Stars and keels, were surely made by people who could not read or write and who didn't even have the concept of addition. These great explorers of nature were probably even more ignorant than 60 per cent of the world's population today, which is totally illiterate. They were poets without laboratories. Some very wise person—and I have always thought it was probably a child—first captured the idea that grain grew from a seed. I don't know how that concept could ever have pierced the mind of man, because to us it is such a simple one, so taken for granted. My theory is that outside of an old cave a Stone Age tribe stored its grain. Around the edges of the pile, outside of the rough stone wall, new grain started to grow, and then people expected grain to grow wherever there was a mound of grain. And then the wind carried a seed a little distance away, and eventually a child formulated the simple idea: new grain had something to do with old grain. Original planting must have been of whole stalks without any idea that life was contained in the seed. After millions of years, surely by 5000 B.C., seed was a "thing." In the days of the earliest religions, the concept of seed existed to some extent, although in the translations we, in our sophisticated knowledge of seed as distinguished from grain, may have injected our own knowledge into the original language carved on the stones which tell the stories of olden days. I would like to touch some of the seeds which recently were found in the old tombs, seeds which have lain dead, if that is the word, for thousands of years and which, when planted now in 1945, still contain life. Discovery of the relationship of seed to grain and seed to planting is a more profound flash of the human mind than the present ones that indicate that food will come from coal and trees and air, and that plants of the future will grow not in the soil but in separately prepared beds of chemicals, or possibly be compelled by radio and electric rays. We are getting close to something on that score except for the tomato, and somebody ought to find out why the tomato's growth cannot be artificially accelerated as readily as the growth of other foods we eat. The love apple is a vegetable individualist which refuses to add cubits to its stature for the highest-watted electric bulb invented.

Some years ago I made my own list of the important steps in the rise of the human race. I do not refer to insignificant inventions such as automobiles, radios or radar. I had in mind the Neanderthaler who, dragging a dead animal through the woods, happened by chance to find that a round log helped him to sledge along. And then his cousin invented the round wheel.

I put near the top of my list the woman who first discovered fire. Even in the warm climates where some people think life began, the nights are cold. Man might have developed a thermostat which would have created complete adjustment to great heat and severe cold, but instead he lived near volcanoes and live coals were cherished as tribal heirlooms. "Keeping the home fires burning" meant something very different in the days when fire was made only from fire and no one knew how to start a new one. I should think this discovery was just as fortuitous as the round wheel, and the keel. I see a couple of cave men fighting with stone weapons which clashed and showed a light, or a pair of kids playing with pebbles near some dry material full of gases which invite heat and fire. A woman sitting near by saw a chance to get relief from toting live embers wherever the tribe migrated with the seasons. No doubt many simple discoveries came originally from play instead of work. I hope that's true.

In this year 1945 there are surely many more simple phenomena of life waiting to be discerned and perceived by simple people who look and hear and sense. It's absurd to think that the advance of our race from now on depends on large laboratories. The significance of life, the meaning of the spirit of man—for example, the simple art of telepathy between people—will first be recaptured by uncomplicated poets, just as two out of three of all important inventions of our day come, not from corporate laboratories but from the passion of people who invent because they have to, uninfluenced by patent monopolies or profit motives.

Tiller or wheel, and sea—these provide a fit setting for a free-roving mind and a loose-footed spirit. Then if ever it's possible to get outside of one's own frame of reference.

Margaret, who is a good reporter, on two successive evenings said "the sun shot down." It seems to be the general impression of traveling people that in certain parts of the world the sun goes down like a shot. Up in Nantucket I watch the sun with some care as it travels over the course of a summer, from one church spire to another, setting far to the north as we are about to leave the island at the end of September. I try to catch the change in solar pace. I wonder if anybody has made a map of the world in relation to the speed of the setting of the sun as seen by man's eye? I know they say that the sun has set eight minutes before we think it is down, because it takes eight minutes for the light to get from the sun to this planet. If the stories about the relative speed of the actual setting are reliable, might they not depend upon the communicative powers of our atmosphere? For if the eye is not fooled, so to speak, by the speed of a setting sun, then there may be something to the theory that light travels at widely different speeds in different climates or atmospheres. If that is true, what's all this talk about the speed of light being computed with such accuracy as to determine the distance of Vega, and all those other bodies which are, so astronomers tell us, millions of light years off, some in fact gone out of our ken ages ago. Heaviside waves may change all our thinking on the courses and speeds of light.

Maybe only certain eyes can see the speed of a setting sun. Eyes certainly vary greatly. I have always felt that an artist is mostly a pair of eyes. I remember the story of how Titian's father trained the young boy to be an artist. According to the legend, the old man walked the kid down the streets of some Italian village, took him past dozens of horses, and then some days later made the boy describe in detail the nose and eyes and hoofs and mane of each and every separate animal. That's good training because to most of us, particularly in city streets, all horses look alike except for a rare Percheron or a white mare. Years ago I had a law case involving some Chinese and the question I was asked by my Chinese client was merely: "How many witnesses do you want?" This question made sense, if not ethics, because my client knew that to the average white man all Chinese look alike.

The Titian technique for art-eye training can't be laughed away entirely by pointing to some modern artists who paint what looks to most of us like objects which have never been seen before, and hence independent of eye memory. No matter what imagery the mishmash of modern art invokes, it's true that no one can imagine anything he hasn't seen or heard about. The combination of colors or objects or lines may be changed by the artist but in essence the mind, which subserves the eye of man, is no bigger than life as comprehended by man. All of which neither explains nor makes more delectable the madness of many an art exhibit to which mink rushes in hordes.

In a recent exhibit which I went to—the name of the artist is protected by libel laws—I saw some interesting distortions. From the gallery I went to an eye doctor, and this wasn't just cause and effect. At the doctor's office I saw in a magazine some colorful, strong Tom Bentons. Faces, legs, arms, trees, all seemed elongated to my eyes. There were no stout, plump human beings. Even the horses were rangy. Just the opposite of the fine lines of Adolf Dehn, whose men look to me like pouter pigeons and whose women are shaped like paunchy eggshells. I'll bet a Dehn against a Benton, or vice versa, that this particular variable in their respective arts will show up on an astigmatism test. Those lines which appear on the chart in the doctor's office running up and down and left and right, look very different to each one of us. Rubens with his three-breasted women, El Greco with his lank faces, all fit into the pattern of astigmatic art. It might be amusing to make an eye test of a hundred artists and then, concealing the name shown on each report, see if the degree of astigmatism is not directly related to the work of the artist. This might be a good game for the Museum of Modern Art.

The only generic deviation I can think of in this respect is in the drawings which appear in the comic strips. Maybe the size of the box into which the so-called funny has to be placed further distorts the artist's distortions.

The present theories of speed of light and sight irritate me—for no rational reason. I don't know why but I resent computations of distance based on speed of light in atmospheres remote from our own. I don't like to believe that the stars and sun and moon are as far away as the astronomers tell me. I am less than comfortable when told that a star is 62 million light years away, when I am supposed to know that a light year is light traveling at 186,000 miles per second. I don't want to believe that so many of the big stars have gone out thousands of years ago. It all seems to me quite silly to judge space by our standards of speeds. There might be atmospheres in which a light ray cannot travel at all. Or it might get tired and just go around in circles. It might even just sit down on one of its twinkles. Maybe it dawdles along at a mile an hour or shoots forth at a million miles a second. We know that light is capable of being deflected, and so drawn off by all kinds of powers innate in stars or forces that we cannot see, so that the light from Vega is not only bent a little, as some people now seem to think, but possibly comes down to us in a spiral or at a clean right angle. And when Miss Harwood at the Maria Mitchell Observatory lets me look in the instruments to prove that astronomers know the contents of the stars, I merely ask, "How do we know that the color shown as hydrogen on the plate is not the same color as shown by an element unknown to man on a distant star?"

Sight and hearing are not alien to each other. Someday they may be directly interchangeable without any mechanical interweaving contraption made by man. Some animals feel and see with the same organ. Can we hear or see with either eye or ear at certain speeds? What if the speed of light and sound are propelled at the same pace? Do they become identical and interchangeable?

The capacity of dogs to hear sound up to sixty thousand vibrations per second gives man something to aim at. The

[135]

American Indians certainly had a better receiving set than the balance of the people now living in the United States. Maybe they remained eye-strong, like children. Many a child in our civilization can hear up to forty thousand vibrations per second. Why children lose this power is difficult to find out. I should imagine that Andy White of the *New Yorker* can hear much more than most people. I doubt if he can hear more of the sounds emitted by human beings than most of us but certainly he is sensitized to the communication system of all animals.

This loss of hearing capacity from childhood to adulthood runs counter to many other developments of man because one would imagine that constant use of hearing by a child would develop the nerves so as to increase rather than lessen the capacity to hear in the higher ranges. Are the sounds which hit the embryonic ear all in the upper ranges? Or is the hearing range of youth an historic hangover? Possibly in this world of ours, we don't much need the use of hearing and consequently the little we have at birth shortly becomes atrophied. But some of the leading medical men in the hearing field in New York have assured me that there is no such thing as atrophy of hearing, when I argued that there might, in fact, be an analogy between the nonuse of Joan's hearing nerves and a broken arm being carried in a sling. I should imagine we could develop greater hearing powers by playing on the idea that there is a kinship between 256 and 512 vibrations. This identity of octave affinity makes me feel that within the vibration of 256 cycles there must be a core, call it "X," which same core is developed at the 512 range; and likewise up the line to 1,024 and 2,048, etc. If we could find the constant X, it might help in the development of all hearing aids because the confusing merger of 256 with its neighbors 255 and 257 may not derive only from the failure of our perception and the proximity of the vibrations. There may be an analogy to be drawn from the field of color where blue and yellow make green. Incidentally, I think that green should be a basic color since in many ways it is the base of life and in an odd way is identified with chlorophyll. The leaves are green only because the balance of the colors are bounced back into the air and the whole rainbow that the sun emits, shunts off the leaf and the only thing that is left is green, the great resister of all color.

On a clear day we cross-examine light and sound. I am told that whenever the air is clean, light and sound will travel better. I am quite convinced that sound travels worse on a clear day. Give me a good, moist fog in Nantucket and I should think that a voice would carry farther than on the clearest autumn morning. Water certainly is a good conductor of sound up to a certain point and maybe other liquids are even better than water. This must mean that the elements of sound bounce better when moist. I wonder what a violin would sound like if played and heard underwater?

My rejection of all theories of light or sound which do not provide a basis for the denial of blindness and deafness irritates beyond measure all my scientific friends. They are often smug and self-satisfied. But I keep up my dreaming and postulating, unwittingly encouraged at rare moments by Dr. Foster Kennedy or Dr. Abraham Stone, who don't even know they are setting me off on romances which fill hours of idle thinking in the garden at Nantucket.

In an antique shop recently I saw an Oriental pipe with a bowl. I smoked it and realized again that smoking through water or a base of water has a cooling effect, and I know from experiment with Joan that hearing through salt water has a different quality from hearing through our kind of air. When Joan is swimming underwater, if somebody clinks two stones together many yards away, the impact sounds to her like a cannon shot and much louder than the noise made by two stones banged together on earth in our air. Someday I will get a new hearing box made for Joan, allowing the waves of sound to travel through water. Or possibly the earpiece should have a water cell. Maybe it ought not to be water. Some other liquids might have a greater kinship to sound. Scotch should work delightfully. Alcohol loosens the brain. Kinship usually means little more than clean and precise relationship without jagged edges. Some summer I'll try experiments on sound through water because, after all, the ability to hear is more than vibration and really depends on the ability to receive a concept and concepts depend more upon clean precision than upon inflection, volume or pitch. I wish to believe and hence I do believe that there is no such thing as a deaf human being unless the physical ear has actually been destroyed. And even that is less than true, for much of our hearing is not through the ear at all. All we mean when we say "deaf" is that the sounds that man can utter or create cannot be received by the deaf person's receiving apparatus. It is about time we did more experimenting with the dog whistle and the sounds that animals can hear and which we can never hear. Some deaf people no doubt have a receiving set which can't receive the ordinary waves created by man but could hear a bud breaking open or an oyster gasping for air. All we have to do is to convert our sounds into light and back into sound on the wave length of such a person. Someday I'll have to write up our experiments with Joan and the way the doctors looked on me as a madman. As long as Joan doesn't agree with them, I'm content.

CHAPTER XXI

THE BIRTH OF A BABY

IT'S NOT EASY for a lawyer to write about his private practice. The poignant is privileged. Camouflage never fully conceals. In all these ramblings I have dared touch on only one or two private professional episodes and then only because death or decades or permission of the client has intervened, or the secret is mine and mine alone.

[138]

But once in a while an incident of significance develops within a frame which permits divulging. I was reminded of such an instance when only recently Roy Larsen, publisher of *Life*, kept hitting at me below the belt. His cowardly disregard for correcting falsity in his magazine seemed inexplicable against what I knew of him in my professional relationship.

He's a gay, affable, direct person. When defensive he is a "tell you" type, but when secure he's an "ask you" type. I first sensed this ambivalence during the delightful overnight trips I took on his speedy yacht *Karen* from and to Nantucket. He's more articulate than his associate, Harry Luce, and far more factual in a simple way.

When called in to represent *Life* at the time of the wholesale prosecutions of that magazine for running the "Birth of a Baby" pictures, I knew that various Catholic organizations, particularly the Knights of Columbus, were the prime instigators of the stir.

I explained to Roy the difficulties in the case. A majority of the court of three judges would probably be Catholics, and without any insinuation of orders from the Cathedral, they might nevertheless subconsciously find themselves in tune with the Catholic position. I had talked to many priests who were my friends. What was the objection to pictures prepared by leading doctors to help reduce the mortality of mothers and children stemming from inadequate knowledge at the time of birth? The initial answer was that all such public education should come from doctors, teachers, clergy and parents. Agreed. But, I asked, "What if all those groups were ignorant or uncourageous? Must thousands of mothers still be condemned to misery or death?" Finally one of the clerics said that such information in family magazines would take the romance out of life. I couldn't resist asking, "Since when are you interested in romance?" Of course, I made clear that the story of birth was, to civilized minds, the most beautiful romance of all of living.

After telling Roy that the odds were against him, rather in jest I suggested that I was damned weary of seeing impecunious booksellers and insignificant newsstand dealers taking the rap for mighty publishers. All too often the authorities pounced on the near-bankrupt retailer, realizing that he couldn't afford to defend, had no motive for putting up a fight, and hence could easily be persuaded to plead guilty with a light fine. Thus a mass of bad law was being written to be used as precedent in future battles against freedom of thought.

Newsdealers find hundreds of magazines dumped on their stands by delivery trucks. They don't read them. They could not appraise for obscenity even if they read. They are only conduits; they should be viewed no differently from the delivery truck which also helps to bring the material from the publisher to the reader. I said I'd like to find a publisher who would dig his heels in the ground and stand back of his material.

Without hesitation Roy said, "Come on, I'll give myself up and make clear that I alone am responsible."

He scared me. I begged him to call up his wife and talk it over with her. I'm no martyr type myself and never ask clients to be martyrs. I'd hate to have Roy all through life, when asked "Have you ever been convicted of crime?" be compelled to answer, "Yes, for obscenity."

Roy wouldn't dream of calling up his wife to ask her judgment on surrendering himself. I insisted that Harry Luce be consulted as a matter of publishing policy. Luce came down into Roy's office, and promptly approved Roy's attitude.

And Roy went to the court and won his own case. The entire atmosphere changed when I was permitted to plead for the person who took the credit or blame for the material. Roy was proud of his editorial selection of this article and the pictures. It would not sexually corrupt the readers. It dealt with an important subject in dignified terms. It was not obscene, or filthy or indecent or lascivious. He had not printed a single extra copy of the issue in order to capitalize, if it were even possible, on the publication of material which less courageous publishers might have rejected.

This position of a publisher with courage relieving magazine peddlers from responsibility recalled to my mind a
decade of work done for the jewelry trade associations in
their pursuit of honest marking of gold, silver and platinum
jewelry. Gold trinkets, unlike ideas, can often be described in
definite terms. Obscenity is a vague and constantly changing
concept. But 14 K means an exact mathematical equation of
14 parts out of 24. There were, however, borderline descrip-
tions such as German silver, gold-filled, gold-plated, rolled
gold plate, and it was our function, working with the New
York City Bureau of Standards, to prosecute violators of
stamping and hallmark laws. Some of the legislation was fresh
on the statute books. After several years of work we had
reduced to statutory terminology the standards to be applied
to new popular precious metals: platinum, iridium and the
rest of the platinum group.

In the hallmark campaigns—which were necessary in order
that honest manufacturers could compete in the market
place—many small inconspicuous retailers were arrested. The
law gave no excuse to the seller just because he could prove
he didn't know that the ring was only 10 K although marked
14 K. Ignorance was no defense. The seller had to be on his
guard. Caveat emptor no longer applies to much of our commerce. If you brand at all, you must brand honestly.

Jewelry and magazines are not so unlike in the governmental sanctions and procedures which should be applied.
I drafted bills, which the Society for the Suppression of Vice
defeated at Albany, under which any retailer of a book would
be relieved from prosecution if on attack by the state he could
bring into the jurisdiction of the court the original producer
of the volume. Why should the newsstand seller even be
annoyed with a summons? Why should the bookstores of
Boston be disturbed by police threats against *Strange Fruit*
if they can produce the publisher of the volume to stand
trial? Wouldn't such procedure develop a commerce under
which retailers would refrain from buying from a jobber or

manufacturer who declined to come in and defend his own wares?

The same theory applies to jewelry because there also the retailer has no easy way of knowing whether the article contains obscenely little precious metal or deviates from the declaration which the manufacturer stamped on the article.

The forces of suppression are encouraged and invited to attack without caution so long as leading newspapers, book publishers, motion-picture producers refuse to step forward and let it be known that they will defend to the death or even up to bankruptcy not necessarily the ideas of other people—but rather the ideas which they themselves have sponsored. Every policeman in the nation must have been encouraged when constabulary of Providence, Rhode Island, banned Greta Garbo's film *Two-Faced Woman*, after an announcement that the cultured constable of the capital of Roger Williams's state had suppressed the film without ever bothering to see it. The author, the director, Garbo, the producing company, the Hays office abjectly submitted just as if we had no Bill of Rights.

THE SEX SIDE OF LIFE

An unexpected aftermath of the nasty job *Life* magazine did on me last year has brought me some joy. Dozens of men, many of them officers in the armed forces, wrote to ask me for the latest books on sex instruction for young married men. In a way, this is both amusing and pathetic. The letters came in because the article mentioned my defense in 1929 of Mary Ware Dennett on a criminal charge for publishing her pamphlet "The Sex Side of Life." That estimable little brochure, originally written for Mary's growing sons, was adopted for distribution by the Y.M.C.A. and Y.W.C.A. and many educational institutions. It was simply written and still is one of the best treatments in the field.

The censors, led by Canon Chase of Brooklyn, who sat with prosecutor Wilkinson all through the trial, objected to three main portions of the document. The author declared

[142]

that venereal disease was curable, and advised running to a doctor if in trouble. This, of course, cut under the fear motive for male virginity. In discussing masturbation, Mary Dennett told of the prevalence of the practice, among both males and females, and warned against the consciousness of guilt as well as against excessive indulgence in the habit. Such true appraisals were shocking to the censor, as truth so often is. And finally, she told her sons and the public that the sexual act was the greatest physical joy in life and should be handled with taste. That sexual behavior is a joy did not sit well with frigid, frustrated censorial groups, or, as I found out, with lusty, pious jurors.

Previous to this trial I had lost a case on John Herrmann's book *What Happens* in the Federal Court, and had learned a lesson, I thought, for after that book was condemned one of the jurors, who had been reading the *Graphic*, our then most common daily tabloid, tipped me off that the jury would have let the book get by if the word "masturbation" had been changed to "self-abuse" or "playing with himself." Another instance of the tawdry fear of words rather than concepts.

The Dennett jury went out, and while we were waiting for its return the prosecutor told me some dirty, ribald stories, to prove no doubt that he was no bluenose but merely arguing a cause in which he did not quite believe. The verdict—guilty. The judge called Mary to the bar. My heart sank. "Three hundred dollars fine or three hundred days in jail." And then great Mary said in part: "Judge, if I really am guilty of corrupting the children of the land, then three hundred days in jail is too little, and I certainly will refuse to pay a fine as a substitute." She is a tough, great fighter. She had little reason to hope that the Circuit Court of Appeals would reverse the conviction—as it did—with an opinion freeing for all time, I trust, the flow of sex information of dignity to the people of our land. But never again, so far as I know, has the Post Office Department tried to frame up another Mary Dennett. In her case the entrapment was ironically developed by a letter, written by the government on specially printed stationery, appropriately sent from the Vale of Shenandoah, Grottoes, Virginia, requesting a copy of the Dennett pamphlet. In answer to such request Mary Dennett sent her pamphlet through the mails.

In a gay, lucky and adventurous life at the Bar, probably the only causes for which I have fought and which have any enduring effect on human happiness are those like Mary Dennett's and Margaret Sanger's, and Joyce's *Ulysses* and the defense of *The Well of Loneliness* by Radclyffe Hall. Man's fear of ideas is probably the greatest dike holding back human knowledge and happiness. And in few cases have the great trustees, a euphemism, of the press—the newspaper owners— really pitched in to help. If the case were "juicy" it would be reported as a dirty cause célèbre. If the case involved contraceptives, fear of offending Catholics produced jitters and shame in most newspaper offices, unmindful of the fact that during our first century as a nation there was no statutory bar against the use of contraceptives. Over the years the New York *Post* and the *Herald Tribune* have been outstanding in support of this sector of freedom for the human mind. Special thanks go to Helen Reid of the *Tribune*, in the twenties and thirties when these battles culminated.

CHAPTER XXII

A BLACKLIST PARTY

GUY SHIPLER DROPPED ME A LINE. He is the great editor of The *Churchman*. I wish there were more like him and stout of spirit Harry L. Binsse, of the Catholic magazine *Commonweal*. Shipler reminds me of the amusing inclusion of Maggie as a Dangerous Red in the blacklists circulated by the then frightened Daughters of the American Revolution.

We had gone to Mexico in 1926 with Barnsie. We had never been near a revolution and it looked as if something were brewing in the land to our south. The great church versus state struggle was going on. Margaret wrote a piece for the *Churchman* comparing the clerical fight to industrial warfare. The priests were out of the churches; tender old women were leading vague services; peasants were staying away; their pesos were going for pulque or movies instead of treasures to place on altars. The situation was tense. Were the old women scabbing on the clergy? Maybe the public would learn to do without so much religious service? It was an amusing slant on the Mexican muss. For this, and as far as I know nothing else, Margaret was publicized as a dangerous radical.

This was so ridiculous that I decided to approach the black-list concept with humor. We ought not be too serious. A little spoofing might help. We organized a D.A.R. Blacklist party, thinking that only thirty or forty people would attend. Before we knew it five hundred men and women wrote in for tickets for the dinner. Senator Borah, on one of the lists, telegraphed regrets for his absence. Senator George Norris came through slugging. Dorothy Parker organized a picket line with banners declaring: "We are dangerous too. Why can't we get in?"

I don't think the party helped much but it gave a kind of temporary equilibrium to some liberals who take themselves far too seriously. Aside from Art Young, in the old days, and McAlister Coleman, I know of no top satirist of line or word waging war on reaction. The liberal papers seem to be afraid of the use of humor, and when they try it it's pretty heavy stuff. The *New Yorker* alone is effectively radical in the sense of cutting aside underbrush, whether it editorializes about oversized cars, airplane accidents, pacifism, fogs of religion or phonies of political propaganda.

In Mexico I saw my first bullfight and I couldn't take it

any more than I can enjoy a bloody prize fight. I left the bullfight to sip liquor at the peaceful Inn of San Angel all by myself, feeling a little cowardly and a trifle weak compared to tough Maggie and the thousands of young children who enjoyed the dangers and the grace of the performers and were not upset too much by watching the spilling of equine entrails.

I still prefer sailing.

CHAPTER XXIII

MORE DRAMATIC CRITICS

I SAW ETHEL WATERS, one of my favorite actresses, the other day up at the Savoy dance hall in Harlem. Some years ago she opened in *Mamba's Daughters*. At the opening night I saw many people who were thrilled by the play and particularly by Miss Waters's great performance. The next day the critics panned the show. It didn't have a chance to survive the rather unanimous adverse criticism.

Our theater suffers from a paucity in number of dramatic critics. Unless a backer has enough money to wait for the public to get informed about his play by word of mouth—a process that takes weeks if not months, and which few can afford—the sole method by which potential ticket buyers can get information is through about a dozen minds and pens known as dramatic critics. By and large they are top-notchers in their profession. But a dozen sources of advice are just too few, particularly since not many people read more than one critic's column.

After I read the reviews of *Mamba's Daughters*, I thought I would test a suggestion I had made in midnight chatter on many occasions. I was sure that thousands of people would enjoy the Waters performance, but unless we could break through the reviews carried in the papers, the show would close. Advertisements inserted and paid for by the producer of a play would do little good, because producers are no longer believed by the public which reads theatrical advertisements. Their puffing, exaggeration and less than completely honest "quotes" used in their paid advertisements are completely discounted by the reading public. A group of us inserted at our own expense the following advertisement, written by Carl Van Vechten:

The undersigned feel that **ETHEL WATERS'** superb performance in "Mamba's Daughters" at the Empire Theatre is a profound emotional experience which any playgoer would be the poorer for missing. It seems indeed to be such a magnificent example of great acting, simple, deeply felt, moving on a plane of complete reality, that we are glad to pay for the privilege of saying so.

Judith Anderson	Helen Hall
Tallulah Bankhead	Oscar Hammerstein
Norman Bel Geddes	Paul Kellogg
Cass Canfield	Edwin Knopf
John Emery	Ben H. Lehman
Morris L. Ernst	Fania Marinoff
John Farrar	Aline McMahon
Dorothy Gish	Burgess Meredith
Jules Glaenzer	Stanley Rinehart

Carl Van Vechten

January 6, 1939

The show ran for many weeks. Thousands of people had an opportunity to enjoy Ethel Waters, and *Mamba's Daughters*.

Some years ago, in *Hold Your Tongue*, my partner, Alexander Lindey, and I threw out a trial balloon for a method of cutting under the undue accent of power now residing in a few newspapers and a few dramatic or book critics. I still think it would be worth exploring.

Through the medium of criticism, the book reviewer may directly injure two, possibly three, persons—author, publisher, illustrator. The dramatic critic has a wider range of hurt-dealing. The playwright, the performers, the director, the impresario, the composer, the scenic artist, the costume designer, may all draw his fire. He can damage reputations by the score.

So, perhaps, the general suggestion that a more even balance of power be attempted between the critic and those he criticizes has greater persuasive force in the drama than in any other field. We are not concerned, of course, with a mathematical equalization. Any approximation would be acceptable if, on the one hand, it left the critic free to speak his mind and if, on the other, it afforded the disparaged person an opportunity to have his side presented.

For example, if a scheme could be devised whereby newspapers would permit some reputable and competent person, preferably an authority, to rebut in their columns the critic's condemnation of a play, not only would the public hear both sides of the discussion, but a great deal of the bitterness that sometimes leads to litigation could be drained off. And possibly the right to sue for defamation arising out of dramatic criticism could be done away with altogether.

The scheme would not mean that every time an adverse review appeared the press would become a vehicle for counter-gibes by the persons affected. Critics and producers would agree in advance upon a panel of, let us say, a hundred individuals, fairly prominent, well versed in matters of the stage, capable of stating their opinions simply and lucidly.

If a play drew an unfavorable notice in a paper, the producer could select any member of the panel, request him to witness the production and to set down his reactions; and if his opinion differed from that of the paper's critic, the paper would undertake to print it in its dramatic section, giving it as much space as the original notice received. The device of the panel, and the conceded integrity of the persons constituting it, would render corruption as between producers and the panel improbable and unlikely; at the same time, the newspaper would be called upon to publish reasoned dissents by qualified persons, not indignant squawks by outraged managers or fulsome ballyhoo by publicity men. The newspaper would have no cause for complaint; it would be dealing fairly with its readers and with the persons connected with the censured show; it would also be getting critical comment free of charge; it would be rendering itself practically immune to suit. The producers could no longer anathematize critics for ruining their enterprises, for they would have within their reach a means of counteracting such ruination. And the same scheme could be carried over into literary and art criticism.

To be sure, several objections may be raised against the suggested expedient.

First, the plan would work effectively only in newspapers; and to a much lesser extent in magazines and periodicals. It would afford no relief in connection with attacks on literature, art or drama contained in books, pamphlets, lectures or the like. This objection is not a serious one, since the great preponderance of criticism appears in newspapers.

Second, the cardinal principle of the plan is the balance of power. This presupposes that in every case, or in almost every case, there is adverse criticism which is to be offset by favorable comment, if obtainable. What if the criticism is laudatory in the first instance? The public must be protected no less than the artist. It may well be that fulsome praise on the part of the critic hoaxes the public. Should not there be, in such a case, a device whereby theatergoers might learn the other side of the story? If so, how will the other side be obtained and presented? The artist certainly will not go to the panel to secure adverse comment, nor is it likely that the newspaper will turn to the panel to confound and refute its own critic. In the case of a ballyhooing critic the panel plan will doubtless be of no benefit to the public. This objection presupposes that our critics are addicted to indiscriminate praise. Such is not the case. Moreover, the ballyhooing critic cannot be deemed a menace. His influence differs from the influence of his splenetic brother in that it is subject to the corrective of current opinion. If he renders undue praise, the community is not hoodwinked, because theatergoers soon find out that the critic's estimate was overgenerous, and undeserved praise is quickly and properly neutralized by opinion. The reverse, however, is not true. Where there is unwarrantedly caustic criticism, the public stays away; there is no opportunity for it to form a contrary conclusion.

Third, the plan may have a tendency to make the critic unduly cautious. He will be likely to pull his punches, knowing that if he slams too viciously the artist will go to the panel and probably secure favorable comment which will make the critic appear ridiculous. In this respect, the plan may operate as something more than a check; it may turn out to be a weapon of intimidation. This objection presupposes that most of our critics are cowards, and that the mere possibility of a difference of opinion will make them sheathe their claws. Since controversy is the very life of criticism, it may well be that our critics would welcome the publication of views differing from their own. And so, instead of rendering critics spineless and timorous, the plan may have the opposite result of creating a more vital school of criticism.

Fourth, the plan will be unfair to the critic. The critic, particularly the dramatic critic, is called upon to arrive at an opinion and to cast it into form in a very short period of time, possibly an hour and a half. This is true of the literary critic, who reads at least one, and possibly as many as two or three, books a day. A member of the panel who is called upon to contradict the critic will have ample time to write a deliberate, well-reasoned opinion. He will not labor under any stress of time. He will be in a position, without haste and at his leisure, to rip the critic's hasty judgment to pieces. In view of the assertion of numerous critics that they work best under pressure, this objection is not persuasive. But even if we concede its validity, we are not led necessarily to a condemnation of the plan. We might, as part of the plan, adopt the Continental system of dramatic criticism. Our critics would not be called upon to formulate their reactions immediately after the opening of a play, but would be allowed several days for the purpose.

Fifth, it might prove extremely difficult, if not wholly impossible, to assemble a panel. Any person requested to act would perceive that he might be called upon to refute a critic in a case where he, the member of the panel, might well agree with the critic's strictures. This would place the panel member in an embarrassing position. He would be faced with the choice of either impeaching his own integrity by rendering praise where he felt censure was due, or offending the artist by refusing to write a piece contradicting the critic. This objection presupposes that a sufficient number of courageous and disinterested persons could not be found in the community.

Whatever flaws may be picked in the plan, the underlying principle—that of the balancing of power—is sound. Regardless of the method employed to achieve it, it would mean the widest latitude for the critic and fairness for the producer and the performer. It would also mean freedom of discussion pro and con, without which truth is obscured and society grows stultified.

CHAPTER XXIV

TODAY I READ one of the Hearst papers. Every once in a while I pick one up. It is a press of phobias with great but dwindling influence. The Hearst empire was too big to be run from a palace out west. But in the building up of that chain a scar has been slashed on the press of America.

G. B. Shaw, a few months ago at his Welwyn Garden home near London, asked me if I liked Hearst. "By no means," was my answer. Whereupon Shaw said, "I like him. He must be all right because no government in the world, including his own, likes him." This has become my favorite non sequitur.

However, I like Hearst's sons and there may be some hope in the new generation, even though I watched the pathetic corruption of the soul of Arthur Brisbane. There is no telling what would have happened to him had he not tried to buy up all of Park Avenue. Once Brisbane tried to get Heywood Broun to go Hearst: $100,000 a year and they would let me draw the contract guaranteeing Broun complete freedom from censorship. Heywood said no and walking across Brisbane's room where the conference was being held, he happened to see a picture of an elderly man, sort of a Karl Marx type of head. "Who's that?" asked Broun. "He looks so serene and content." Brisbane came right back: "That was my father. He had inner calm and you can bet your last dollar he never worked for Hearst." That ended the negotiations.

Hearst's present prime hate is Russia. Influences like Hearst's are deep obstacles to sound relations with Russia after the war even though one of the greatest barriers to amicable dealing with the Soviet is of course the American Communist party. No doubt Stalin, having disbanded the Third International, will soon have to repudiate the Browder gang as appearing to speak for the people of Soviet Russia.

I have never seen any reason why the United States and the U.S.S.R. shouldn't get along peacefully and profitably. For more than a century, even when Russia was under the czars, we had more than satisfactory relationships although at one time our Congress went so far as to resolve against Russian pogroms. Today there is only one more step to be taken by Russia and then all will be easy. Russia has operated without free speech, free press and free religion. The latter was cleared up by President Roosevelt, I imagine. And today religion is "free" in Russia, at least as free as it ever was, remembering that the head of the church was always akin to a cabinet officer in the old days. But soon Russia should feel strong enough internally to allow a free and critical press; and maybe in time the people of Russia, without fear of being sent to Siberia, will be permitted to listen to foreign broadcasts. If we can once get at the minds of Russians, or any people for that matter, there can be no enduring ugly international problems. I recall that in 1921 a group of us urged Russian recognition, with just such a philosophical hope in mind.

Around this time I was flattered by a request from the Russian government. They wanted me to buy for their library the originals of the New York *Tribune* for a period during the early 1850's. With the co-operation of Helen Reid and others, I located most of what they wanted. The reason they wanted these original papers was that during that period a correspondent of the *Tribune*, writing from England, was sending over exciting reports. The name of the correspondent was Karl Marx. It was Marx who first pointed out that the future dilemma of the United States would stem from a flow of immigrants from Europe and Russia, which flow, he predicted, would mount as high as one million men and women in a single year—all of whom would be stupidly bottled up on our eastern shores. His prediction was sound. Immigration hit about one million at the turn of the century and as a nation we failed to appreciate this westward tide of mankind. Hence, the growth of our eastern seaboard slums.

For an odd reason I was kept out of Russia in 1937. We went to Italy instead. We wanted to live briefly in a dictatorship to get a feel of what a closed national mind means to a people. Everything had been arranged for a Russian visa, but when we got to London word came that Russia was afraid to allow me in. I was told that this exclusion was due to the fact that I believed in civil liberties and more particularly in political asylum, and still more particularly because I had been one of a large group who protested against the exclusion of Leon Trotsky from the United States when he was in personal danger in France. No doubt some bureaucrat in Russia thought I was a Trotskyite, whatever that is. In simple terms, I have always felt that we are a strong enough civilization to survive despite the entrance to our shores of the ideas of any man on earth. If perchance our great civilization cannot survive the ideas, not overt acts, of a man like Leon Trotsky, we might as well give up and resign. Fear of ideas as distinguished from deeds and acts is surely a confession of insecurity. I have a too great faith in our democracy to accept such a philosophy of fear.

On the other hand, I'm not inclined to think that the Russian governmental philosophy has changed as much as the industrial leaders of this country think it has. Maybe when tongues are hanging out for orders, business judgments as to forms of government are not unaffected. But we are essential to Russia. Credits we alone can afford to give for productive capital goods will make a difference of decades in the rehabilitation of Russia. And this will have a great influence on the Russian government's behavior. I'm hopeful that our government will not extend the credits direct. And because our industries can't afford to carry such long-term capital goods credits, maybe a government machinery for

[154]

rediscount, with guarantee of the top per cents, will give orders to our factories to keep our boys busy in the reconversion period. What Russia can pay back with, except fabulous gold, is not easy to see except in minor sums. Manganese, fur, platinum or caviar will help only a little to equalize credits. But that is our basic difficulty in trading with all nations and the curse of our economic position with all parts of the world.

Unfortunately, in a sense we suffer the penalty of plenty. We can, if we are smart enough, keep up our standard of living and still import only about $900 million of goods. That's chicken feed to an economy such as ours, capable of at least $250 billion income per annum, when the 12 million men of the armed forces get back into production, even though 5 million women may go back into their homes.

It's been exciting trying to work up a commodity budget vis-à-vis Russia or England. I play with it at times as I would with a jigsaw puzzle. The pieces must fit—even though some seem too small, too big or even missing. Naturally we want to buy from low-cost and sell to high-cost countries. Naturally each nation wants to sell goods with much labor in them and buy commodities with little labor content. I've been not too ambitious and so I have tried to figure out only duolateral budgets—U. S. and England, and U. S. and Russia, although Sir Harold Hartley, one of the great men of England, twits me whenever we are together about the need of working up a world multinational commodity budget. He says with justice that trade is planetary and not national.

OUR CURSE OF PLENTY

The need for working out some kind of commodity budget if we are to continue to trade with England after the war was brought home to me anew, recently, while I was making a survey of the British film industry. Like most adventures this one came to me in odd fashion. While I was in England in 1943 a friend asked what could be done about the censorship

[155]

by Will Hays of the Noel Coward picture *In Which We Serve*. The American censor, Mr. Hays, had banned the use of the word "bastard" in that great scene when the British sailors hanging to rafts are peppered by a Nazi plane. From what I know of our hard-hitting naval personnel, the phrase "You bastards" under such circumstances was less than accurate, for normally it would have contained a stout Anglo-Saxon adjective as well. Nothing could be accomplished to overcome Hollywood hypocrisy but through my efforts I came to know one of the driving personalities of British film production, oddly enough an Italian—Filippo del Guidice. As a footnote, it is interesting that most of the British producers of great films are not of British stock.

His great production organization, Two Cities Films, Limited, attained a position which has worried the American companies. He gave large shares of profits, approximately half, to the artists and directors who created the pictures for him, and now many of the American stars are asking for Two Cities contracts. Not only are the shares generous in this co-operative scheme but accountings can be made honestly and easily since in England there is no such device as block booking.

Films clearly could be the most effective medium for increased better understanding of British-American folkways. We, with our inventive genius, grabbed the world market in this basic industry of world language through the eye. The English audiences of necessity learned to interpret our gangster dialogue even though there was bewilderment in England when, during the blitz and thereafter, the American movies were still heavily loaded with gangster subjects. Furthermore, our movie industry has created a distorted concept of American life, since so many of the pictures portray our society as made up of glamorous $50,000 income families. On the other hand, English pictures have been difficult for us to translate because of accent and idiom. Naturally we commanded the market for we were creating million dollar pictures for a population three times that of England, with consumption power of five times that of England.

As a result, our major companies will take out of England in 1944 more than $80 million free of British tax. Practically no English pictures were distributed here for more than a year after the great Coward picture, which was well-handled by United Artists despite terrible difficulties. It is natural for our giant companies, which own the bulk of the box-office receipts of the nation through their control of theaters, not to handle English pictures. They will not even distribute, except under rare conditions, pictures produced by independents. Five major companies are all too few for a nation our size and in no event should producers of pictures be allowed to own theaters and distribution companies. It's high time the Department of Justice proceeded for a full divorce of studios and theaters. MGM or RKO or Paramount or Fox or Warner deems it irrational to distribute British pictures. It would be like asking General Motors to distribute Ford cars just because many people prefer Fords to Chevrolets. Every time any one of the five major companies takes on an independently made picture it means just so much loss of sale for its own product in its own theaters. Not only the five giants but the large theater circuits gang up against outsiders—as proved in court actions brought under our monopoly laws.

And so England will eventually have to come into this market with control of some American company which has distribution facilities or as a partner of independent American producers. It's too bad that on both sides of the Atlantic pictures are being bottlenecked. It's too bad we haven't divorced production from distribution.

I am deeply interested in the flow of movies, magazines and books between England and the United States. This merchandise is the most valuable commodity of man, the basis of Anglo-American good will. It's important that England and this country be constantly and increasingly in fullest communication with each other. Our surest bond is not

[157]

language or ancestry but rather that we pre-eminently have cultured and developed a joint heritage of freedom of thought. Hence England should abandon its stupid quota law for foreign movies and we should reduce our extreme tax burden on English pictures (five or six times the rate imposed in England on our product). All tariffs on books should be rescinded, both nations should jointly underwrite the free distribution to the colleges and libraries of all the professional scientific journals of both lands. Special subsidies might be designed for the postage of books and magazines and the Rhodes Scholar Exchange concept might be extended to students in greater numbers and to technically skilled government employees of both nations.

Exchange of examination papers, textbooks, school magazines and ultimately students and teachers is being contemplated by several schools in both countries and only recently, while lecturing at Exeter Academy, I found a fertile field for the expansion of such an exchange with a school at Exeter, England.

Our failure to join the international Berne copyright convention is one of the great barriers in the path of the spread of creative thinking. Unless we join an international agreement for protection of copyrights, our authors must suffer expense; complicated steps for world protection of their material must be pursued and without copyright protection great theft of their works results. I doubt if Congress will ever override the selfish lobby of the motion-picture companies which would rather pilfer than protect, as is natural to giants who control a field and are fairly immune from suit because of the expense of bringing actions against them in any court of justice. The ignorant resistance of printers' unions also must be evaporated. I was particularly happy when the President signed in March, 1944, a wartime copyright convention with England.

Our ordinary commerce with England will become even less important after the war than before and so there is a prime need for encouraging the knitting together of our folkways by exchange of thought. England, short of gold and securities, able to buy only to the extent that it can pay with goods, will have to devise a commodity import budget. It will not be able to afford all that its people may want to buy from other nations. In 1943 in London, I was given a dinner by England's leading bankers and the economic advisors to the Bank of England. It was on the same day that the movie *For Whom the Bell Tolls* opened in London. I pointed out that in exchange for that one picture we would take from England one million dollars, in dollars. I questioned if England could afford that kind of luxury purchase and drain on dollar exchange after the war when food and lumber and all kinds of essentials would be so badly needed by the people of Great Britain. I pointed out to my hosts that a choice would have to be made between eight million pounds of lard and a picture such as *For Whom the Bell Tolls*. Each would cost England about a cool million in dollar exchange.

And this simple exposition of England's industrial problem is our problem, but in reverse. We can't sell unless we will buy. Someday our great exporters—such as automobile makers—will realize that our tariffs kill their export business. We can't export if the other nations are excluded by tariffs from selling to us. In fact, it is the problem of each and every nation. Soon we will have to develop a world commodity budget; not every little item will have to be listed, but on a world-wide flow of the major raw materials and essential finished products and food depends the raising of world standards of living. By such flow each nation now without craftsmanship and work habits will find an invitation for the increased productivity of its people.

The essence of this philosophy is summarized in a story President Roosevelt once wrote out for me:

Some years ago the President of the United States was driving through Cartagena, the great seaport of Colombia, with the President of Colombia. The latter said "It is almost impossible to make our budget balance because we have practically no manufactures." The President said "Why do you all wear foreign-made shoes and shirts and cotton clothes? You grow plenty of cotton and you have many hides. It is very simple to make low-priced shoes and cotton goods." The President of Colombia replied "You must be jesting because that would decrease our purchases from the United States." President Roosevelt said "Oh, no, you go ahead and make your own shirts and shoes—raise your standard of living and this will enable you to buy from us more radios and automobiles and things you cannot manufacture down here." Soon Colombia started making shoes and cotton goods.

CHAPTER XXV

VARGA GIRLS AND FREEDOM

WHEN IN ENGLAND RECENTLY at one of the British bomber stations, watching the boys go off to Berlin and perchance return, I had plenty of time to sit and drink with those who did not go off on that night's mission.

In the dusk the American planes were coming home. One 24-trip British aviator said, "Look at those flying fools. Aren't they wonderful? They go out and fight Hitler in the daylight. I wouldn't dare do that. And see the formations they go out in. We could never learn to do that."

The next day at an American field a young Texas flier watched the English planes depart and said, "They sure are terrific—going up in the dark at night to fight the enemy. The nerve of them British. See, they go out one at a time— not even in protection. God—they have the stuff."

Out of such counterpoint does a new understanding world arise.

I sensed that another International bond impinged on the fame of *Esquire's* Varga Girl Calendar, which had spread overseas. I promised many of the boys, British and American, to send them Varga pictures and on my return wrote to Alfred Smart, one of the owners of *Esquire*, to send on to me a batch of the calendars. By the time I got back to New York, Frank Walker, as postmaster general, had ordered the taking away of cheap mailing privileges from *Esquire* magazine. These fliers about to die wanted those pictures. Who are we to deny them anything so trifling?

The Post Office Department should lose the case in the upper courts; and as associate counsel to the attorneys for *Esquire* we urged that it was high time the entire concept of precensorship of the mails be attacked as unconstitutional. Once more I hope we will find that Brandeis and Holmes pointed the path. To say that the use of the mails with cheap postage was merely a privilege and not a right of a magazine is mere legalism. Try to get national distribution of a magazine without the use of second-class mail privileges! The statute under which Frank Walker operates placed on him the responsibility of deciding which publications are "devoted to literature, the sciences, arts, or some special industry" and are "published for the dissemination of information of a public character." What an impossible job! What absurd legislation! It would have been far better for Frank Walker to have addressed a memorial to Congress posing his dilemma rather than to have reversed his own Board of Inquiry and barred *Esquire* from the second-class mails.

In 1929-1930, after trying many book cases, I began reappraising the definition of obscenity used by the Customs as compared to the Post Office. I interested a great senator, Bronson Cutting of New Mexico, in the absurdities of censorship by our custom officials. Lists of books banned from admission to our shores were prepared and compared with lists of material denied admission to our mailbags. There was no uniformity, no pattern, no consistent philosophy. Some sorry little people were told to look for dirt and very soon nearly everything looked dirty. But Treasury dirt didn't look like Post Office dirt.

As a result of the Cutting crusade, with Senator Reed

Smoot of Utah leading the opposition, and after a salacious secret session of the Senate, an amendment to our tariff laws was passed. I'm proud of that draft, Sec. 305 of the Tariff Act. It has worked with expedition and liberality. Under the procedure I worked out for Senator Cutting, the sender abroad and the receiver here of any book are both free of criminal prosecution. The suit is against the book itself and the trial is not unlike the Hitler-Mussolini burning of book trials except that here the volume gets a trial, and the ban is not by fiat alone. And still many a book is temporarily friendless, and the receiver at this end is without funds to fight the mighty government.

Under the Cutting amendment much progress has been made. An intelligent, cultured official, Huntington Cairns, gave a new approach to the Treasury's control of books at entry ports. The books of Dr. Marie Stopes were tried and even though previously condemned were found not to be corrupting. The titles of those cases are truly symbolic of the absurdity of all our censorship. "United States against 'Enduring Passion.'" *Enduring Passion* sneaked through. When I came up to argue the next case, a judge on the federal bench said that I would have tough sledding because the second book was entitled "United States versus 'Married Love.'" But *Married Love* won out, at least in court.

In one of these books the author had inserted prescriptions for aphrodisiacs. The Vice Society representatives objected, possibly thinking they were formulae for contraceptives. To which we made answer: Just the reverse; and surely the Comstock Academy should be made to elect which to oppose—contraceptives or aphrodisiacs.

Joyce's *Ulysses* was tested under this Cutting Law and the government was advised in advance that a test case would be conducted. The volume was sent in on the old *Olympic*—my favorite Atlantic vessel (several times I had the lone bachelor room on the very top deck)—and the port authorities were advised that this literary rocket would come to our shores on a certain day. But the rocket slipped through and in fact we returned it to Customs asking if its admission had been intended. We wanted a test, not the book.

For years some of us have been trying to persuade Congress to modify our postal laws so as to proceed against the writing rather than against the sender or receiver, if any tests are to be had at all. I'm weary of drafting bills, memoranda and briefs in support of such legislation. I'm bored with hearings and conferences in Washington. Maybe I'm just old and tired, for I find myself getting irritated because shouters for freedom of the press—Harry Luce, Colonel McCormick, Roy Howard and others who give fortunes to study the problem or fill their pages with theory about it—have failed to join that fanatical fringe of civil libertarians who with no funds and little access to publicity have tried so long to fight the government at every show of censorship. The most they do is defend themselves when under attack. That's just not enough in a society fighting for freedom.

CHAPTER XXVI

THERE OUGHT TO BE A LAW

TODAY A GREAT LEGISLATIVE DRAFTSMAN told me that all the laws of Sweden are contained in a coat-pocket volume. I doubt it. But in a nation of our size based on a federation of states we are probably in for decades of increasing numbers of statutes. Under Governor Dewey's guidance, 796 bills became law in the New York State Legislature during the session of 1944.

The only simple legislation is that without perception or nuance. Laws which make no attempt to distinguish between various groups, their income and the parts they play in society are brief in words but cruel. In a land of our dimensions, short declarations of principle in the law with wide latitudes for interpretation left to administrators create a folkway without uniformity. If Congress tries to legislate for each and every person and all situations, discriminations and frozen injustices result. If Congress gives only general directives, then the agencies interpreting the statutes take on by delegation much of the Congressional power.

The basic reason why laws are never simple should be evident to anyone. My first intimate education in this field arose in what seemed to be an ultra-simple situation. During the last war, when we were counsel for associations of jewelers, super-patriots were pressing for strict enforcement of an old statute which prohibited the use of an American flag on any article of merchandise. Flag fobs and coat-button emblems were to be banned. I started to draft a new statute legalizing flags on jewelry. Dennison and other paper decoration firms became interested. Patriotic societies frowned on flags printed on napkins. But what about writing paper, tablecloths, or ladies' blouses? Then also we faced the unforgivable foible of brassiere manufacturers who had printed flags on the shoulder straps of women's undergarments. Should the flag touch human skin? The new law we drafted had to draw a line between respect and disrespect for the flag. At one time this dilemma became a great national issue. A simple flag law is not so simple to all people and all interests.

Most legislative drafting is interesting because there can be no statute that does not hurt or restrict some portion of the citizenry. If it did not hurt there would be no need of a law, for the very absence of pain would spell public acceptance without the need of legislation.

Several decades ago Alexander Woollcott was banned from the Shubert theaters in New York because he had written unfavorable criticisms of plays produced by the Shubert management. The New York Court of Appeals decided that under the then existing law theaters were private affairs and the owner could exclude any person for any reason, save only race, creed or color. A few years ago Leonard Lyons, eager and alert columnist of the New York *Post*, was barred by the Shuberts because he had mentioned certain well-known Shubert idiosyncrasies. We drafted a bill to provide that theaters were a public utility to the extent that no one should be barred from entrance except for his own personal misconduct in the theater. Up to the Capitol at Albany came the great movie industry. An exemption was pushed through for movies. Theaters should be conducted without discrimination against critics, but Hollywood insisted on its right to ban whenever critics panned pictures. We had to give in to the Hays office even though Assemblyman David-son, the introducer of the measure, put up a brave fight. After the bill became law the Shuberts still continued their ban and even after a decision of the New York Court of Appeals upholding the statute they appealed to the United States Supreme Court. Now that the highest court of the nation has refused to listen to such appeal, Leonard Lyons enters Shubert theaters.

After the Bank Holiday our federal laws affecting stock exchanges were revamped. In representing a sector of the New York Stock Exchange, I found myself in the midst of a type of business which was understood at most by fifty people in the entire nation. Foreign arbitrage is a kind of Alice in Wonderland transaction, touching on world currencies, conducted by cable and radio in relation to the westward travel of the sun, a weird essential of international financing. Selling abroad and buying the same securities in our markets at the same time, or vice versa, has more than the difficulties of higher mathematics. All those government officials responsible for the drawing up of the legislation, including Landis, Pecora, Morgenthau, were frank enough to admit they didn't know enough about the interstices of foreign arbitrage to discuss our objections to the pending legislation. They sent us with our clients to an official at the Federal Reserve Bank in New York City. This expert, L. W. Knocke, grilled my clients for a day, and then we all sat down together and prepared those sections of the new Banking Bill which shocked the general counsel of the New York Stock Exchange. The arbitrage houses had been forthright and understanding and they got what they decently wanted. The Exchange itself puffed and shouted about brokers being put out of business by the new legislation. I'll never forget Richard Whitney and Roland Redmond, president and counsel to the New York Stock Exchange, on the way down to Washington, explaining to me that their strategy was to tell Congress that the new bill would put eight hundred members of the Exchange out of business. This in a period of eight million unemployed! I told them I was afraid the Congress might believe them and let forth a lusty cheer.

I don't know the synonym in the law for a family doctor. But business-family-run-of-the-mill law practice has a rich and satisfying variety: from flags on undies to helping Senator Hiram Johnson draft his foreign financing bill after the last war, from defining for legislatures "solid silver" to preparing for Senator Cutting procedures for appraising obscenity, from setting up public employment offices to working on reduced postage rates. It makes for fun—maybe at the cost of being too catholic and less than profound.

CHILDREN AND DIVORCE

There is another rewarding aspect to this kind of law practice. To sit in one's office and have a client bestow a confidence is a satisfying relationship. And then, on top of that, to be virtually asked to find out why partners are not getting along together, or why parents should disown or even prefer one child over another, is conceit-making work. Moreover, if clients have faith—faith to operate vis-à-vis life as advised—then in many cases it matters little if the advice is strictly correct according to the old lawbooks; it works nevertheless.

The most intimate of all confidences are handed to lawyers in criminal and divorce cases. In the former there are two fields—the polite business crimes which worry the clients but carry no shame or trace of moral turpitude. For example: agreeing with other milk dealers to raise the price of milk may create a few qualms, some disagreeable publicity usually easily controlled by their press agents calling the papers to set them straight, and possibly a fine which represents a tiny fraction of the pennies garnered through the increased price. In these cases all one gets from clients is a further insight into the less than honest dealings between businesses which have agreed, at least temporarily, on a united front. One of the great assets of trade unions is the inability of employers to trust each other enough to engage in any enduring joint battle. Thus unions can pick off the employers one by one. The bosses seldom stick together. The workers can attack the most vulnerable. But after a union has been recognized, and collective bargaining machinery is set up, then it's important to the union that the employers have a strong organization, with power of discipline. Thus the socially aware employers can create behavior standards for the sweatshops. This relieves the union of the need to use its own power to correct employer outrages.

The other class of criminal cases impinges on suffering caused by public discovery. An income tax indictment, an accusation of violating OPA, a blackmail claim by some woman—here the client is worried mainly about his social position. And this suffering is acute and pitiful. At first the client withholds some of the facts. But once he realizes that he is the loser if he fails to tell his counsel the entire truth he gets relief by confession and then looks longingly for help, whether on a plea of guilty or by reduction of sentence, or on some technique which will make the state prove every inch of its way "beyond a reasonable doubt."

Every person charged with a crime is entitled to an advocate who will press the prosecutor to the limit to prove the guilt. This is the essence of Anglo-Saxon jurisprudence. It is necessarily sound since all people are guilty of some violation, whether it be speeding, puffing a cigarette in a subway, or something more antisocial. Nearly every lawyer has certain personal limits solely to satisfy his own comfort. Some will not defend narcotic sellers. Some reject all but business crime clients. Some lawyers refused retainers offered during the war to defend persons who cheated our soldiers by manufacturing substandard munitions. In peacetime most leaders of the Bar feel disinclined to accept even large fees for defending trade unions, radical movements or unpopular causes. It was significant and helpful that fearless Emory Buckner, of Senator Root's office, represented the Amalgamated Clothing Workers' Union and that Charles Evans Hughes represented John L. Lewis's United Mine Workers in the Hitchman Coal case in the Supreme Court in 1931.

This question of types of crimes recalls a case of a man who wrote to me from jail. He had been sentenced to a long term for white slavery. While in jail he, like many convicts, studied the lawbooks. He discovered that when he was convicted the statutes provided ten days off for every thirty days of good behavior while incarcerated, and that while he was in jail the law was changed to provide only three days off for each thirty days of good behavior. Thus the state, he thought, had, after his conviction, illegally lessened his time off for good behavior. He wrote to say that this was an unconstitutional retroactive increase of punishment. He had sued in his own name to get out. He claimed he was illegally held. He sought the most sacred of writs—habeas corpus. Despite the less than sweetness of his crime, we believed in his cause because it seemed important that no warden should take upon himself a decision which added one single minute to any convicted person's prison term. The courts should have been allowed to determine the validity of this convict's plea. The Court wrote a ringing condemnation of the warden. Subsequently, under a state law, the client recovered some money from the warden. This money was repaid to the warden by a special act of the next legislature. Then the client wanted us to sue the Prison Board, claiming that all the high-minded respectable members of the state agency had supported the warden in his illegal refusal to release him. We declined and ventured the idea that it would be tough going before a jury, in view of his original crime.

He explained his relationship with his lady friend. He had worked when he found a job. When he was idle she worked at her trade—prostitution. But our client pointed out that his girl always told him of her adventures and turned the monetary gains into the joint account of the home. Then he hit with a haymaker: "Ain't that more ethical than the way your Fifth Avenue clients behave?"

Divorce cases are another type of matter where one learns much of the inner springs of human behavior. After about fifteen years of talking to husbands and wives and, at times, to their children, I decided to take stock. I wanted to look at the effect of our effort. Had I done a sensible job in the innumerable agreements written providing for custody and support? In the majority of situations I had represented both husband and wife in working out the separation agreements.

I wrote to dozens of former clients and asked them to review the years since their divorces or separations and to write me fully any suggestions or criticisms. There is no reason why lawyers should not check up with their consumers, just as do the wise manufacturers of cars or toothbrushes or sealing wax. The responses were exciting and illuminating. Many were so informative that I procured permission from the clients to have a series of the answers printed anonymously, in the Nation. I wrote a foreword to the series, a kind of footnoting and annotation of these reviews of human behavior. One fact stood out which gave me much satisfaction. For decades I had urged, and invariably with success, an arbitration clause. No person in such emotionally upset circumstances and certainly no lawyer can be farsighted enough to foresee all the pressures and changes to which life may subject the separated couple. Change in dollar values of alimony, effects of remarriage, shift in tax laws, illness of either spouse, effect of divided control over the education and health of the children, these and many other factors must be as flexible as life itself can and should be. Instead of running to a busy and usually not too perceptive judge, it was better for the parties to pick their own arbiter. The arbiter was usually a doctor, if a health problem was involved, a teacher, if a matter of the education of the child, etc. It turned out that only in a few cases was the arbitration clause actually used, but the mere existence of the provision had induced adjustments of the issues in controversy.

Of course the children are the only important "res" in a divorce. The adults concern me far less than does the emotional insecurity of the children. The adults must stew in their own juice. Sometimes they learn much by their previous marriages. Usually, in the generation to which I belong, the smashup was due to sexual ignorance, the use of words to argue out matters too subtle for language, and the all-pervading concept of ownership of another individual. The most that any person can acquire of another human being is a "hunk," small or large, but exclusive and noncompetitive as to that hunk. Bickering couples can often be saved for each other by looking back to the start of the "bicker era." I'm never much interested in the redheaded bitch who stole John. This lack of interest often disappoints the wife. I'm more concerned with the moment when the bloom went off the peach, and when love flew out of the bed, and hence out the door.

One other fact stood out in the documents written by my clients—rich, poor, Catholics for separations only, many children or few—and that was the invariable rule that the parent who knocked the other spouse in the presence of the child lost the child's affection in the long run, no matter how valid the criticism might have been. This is just as sure as that men who aren't much good with very young children put on a tremendous show with the kids—Coney Island, ice cream, electric trains, etc. But they just can't buy emotions. All they do is make it tough for the mothers, the holders of the disciplinary routines. Often boarding school saves the child and gives the new marriages a chance to take root, even though the new parent puts on a first-class effort with the child so as to get more love from the new spouse.

It's exciting work, revealing and enriching. It doesn't really touch on law or morals so much as it does on handling the infinite number of details which make up life.

In many of these cases my partner, Alexander Lindey, worked with me, and he, the most careful craftsman I know in this field, wrote, and dedicated to me, to my great joy, the definitive book for lawyers on separation and separation agreements.

I had promised at one time to do a book on this subject, a book for laymen. Too much has been written—mostly trite and uninspired—on "Why Divorce." The feminist movement, money, sex, et cetera. Little has been written on "After Divorce." Did it pay an emotional dividend? What of the child? Can our economy support a man with several homes? What of jealousies after remarriage? How far can divorced persons continue to adjust to each other in limited sectors after divorce? Such a work, I had thought, might be based on fifty of the answers I received from my clients, analyzed by each separate type of problem. For example: the guilty-feeling but generous male, who wants what he calls freedom, often wishes to provide that his "ex" should get thirty or forty per cent of all his future income. Does such bookkeeping partnership provide a sound basis for the future support of two homes? Should all support cease on the wife's remarriage? What about the divided control of a child in relation to the rights of parental visitation, choice of school or summer camp, religion or even medical care?

For some odd reason, the social aspects of this most important field of law have been untouched by the profession. The laws have been crooked and dishonest, and hence the use of them has put the entire subject matter into a frame of stealth and indecency. The opposition of the Catholic Church to civilized grounds for divorce has not reduced divorces but merely increased subterfuges and interstate competition for divorce business. The most precious relationship of life has been stultified by our jurisprudence, and the legal profession, so excited about taxes, railroad mortgages or reorganization of industrial companies, has been comparatively silent on the well-being of the home and the inner security of a new generation. The reorganization of homes finds scant comment in our legal writings. Nearly ten million men and women are living separate from spouse in the United States. A major problem faces my profession, which has in its files more data of value to these basic human relations than have doctors, ministers and teachers combined.

CHAPTER XXVII

THE RHYTHM OF BOWLING

AFTER A LONG HIATUS, WE went bowling again. It's still a great sport. It has advantages over tennis, golf or badminton. No equipment is required, even though experts like Marc Connolly carry their own ball. Women don't spoil the game. In fact, even with teams, out of deference to the American spirit of competition, the game is little hurt by varying degrees of skill.

Bowling is justly and increasingly popular. It's inexpensive, and first-class exercise. Of late years it's been difficult to get alleys. In the old days a gang of us used to meet a couple of times a week at Thum's Alleys at 31st Street and Broadway. And even before then, we had a Bowling and Breakfast Club, meeting at noon on Sundays at Teutonia Hall on lower Third Avenue. This informal club was named after a stern nonplayful divine, John Roach Stratton. Today we would no doubt call it the Little Flower LaGuardia Sporting and Gambling Association.

I know of no game which tells so much about the players. Co-ordination, rhythm, lack of tenseness, aim, and the effects of success or failure. When bowling regularly, I average 190 with big pins and over 105 with ducks. In fact, I still have in some trunk or drawer a silver medal bestowed on me by the *World-Telegram* in their annual Head-Pin Tournament. I'll never forget one evening when Henry Souvaine and I went into the big annual national tournament. Our wives sat in the visitors' gallery, or at least sat there until the first seven frames were finished, at which point they walked out making believe they didn't know either of us.

Win or lose, it's a great sport. At times the *New Yorker* crowd would make up a team and, as counsel to that essential weekly, I was allowed to play with Jim Thurber and Andy White and others who won a case of champagne at a Red Cross Bowling Tournament. Of course I never saw my share of the wine.

This bowling craze went so far that in the late twenties when we took our annual lecture trip to the New England colleges, Smith, Amherst, Trinity, Williams, Vassar, etc., we routed our lectures with a view to time between for bowling. McAlister and Elizabeth Coleman, Margaret and myself, with once in a while a ringer like Violet Thomas. Candle pins, duck pins, big pins, it made no difference. We were competing each against himself. In time professors at the colleges looked forward to our pilgrimages—not only because we took over their classes on economics or sociology, but rather for the tenpin spree.

And maybe psychologically the crash and noise when you hit between the number 1 and number 3 pins, and they all go down, has a significance beyond what we imagine. We used to name the King Pin; and then (this was Heywood Broun's idea) we would say: I'm after Nicholas Murray Butler, John S. Sumner, or nearly any member of that Supreme Court which threw out Minimum Wage, Child Labor and other social legislation. A rather innocuous kind of drainage of hate, even for Heywood, a not too good hater, and a bowler of form and surprisingly good scores. The worst bowlers we ever saw were Ben Stolberg, Steve Raushenbush and Norman Thomas (I make no connection between socialism and low bowling scores). Franchot Tone, Freddie March and that movie group were always pretty good (I make no connection between Hollywood and strikes).

When our old crowd broke up, with Gilbert Gabriel, Morrie Ryskind off to Hollywood and others shifting to badminton or bad movies, I tried to organize a bowling group from the office. It didn't work. So maybe a dozen times a year Maggie and I drop in at a neighborhood alley for an idle string or two.

CHAPTER XXVIII

OUR WORST BEST MAYOR

RECENTLY, DURING HIS REGULAR SUNDAY RADIO BROADCAST LaGuardia referred to a plan for a graded sales tax, about which I had written him. In doing so he labeled it as coming from "my friend, Morris Ernst." This was the reason so many people telephoned to me all afternoon, people who know how the Mayor has blasted and cursed me with great zest for many months.

Fiorello LaGuardia is an oddity in our political life. In many ways he is the most colorful American political figure. His entire life spent in public service, he has been a net force for better government and a better city. He's just too picturesque and photogenic for his own good. He talked himself out of a job in Italy at one time when he was bored with running New York City. He shouted himself out of the job of Civilian Defense chief for the nation. His boundless energy led him to grab innumerable jobs—so many that he made a full success of none and probably will never recover his former widespread enthusiastic following.

It's too bad he went sour. Never permitting any strong people to be near him, he suffered, as all tyrant types do, by being "yessed." I've seen Paul Kern, one of his law secretaries, bring papers into the Mayor's office; I saw the Mayor grab the papers, tear them up into little pieces, bawl the hell out of Kern—and Kern stood there and took it.

Too much of that kind of behavior affected not only the Kerns but LaGuardia himself. In a sense he is the worst best Mayor we have ever had. That he will leave little to build on is the prime regret of those who have loved and supported him. He's a one-man show, and too much of his success in the direction of clean government and more efficient administration has rested on arbitrary behavior, duress, bluster and threats.

Something happened to him about five years ago. A puritan streak took the upper hand. Unlike the old LaGuardia, he submitted to church pressure and banned Bertrand Russell as a lecturer in our city colleges. He ordered his overbearing and none too smart commissioner of licenses to bedevil newsdealers, theater owners, bowling alley operators. He sent his squads out to take magazines off the newsstands just because LaGuardia, or some unnamed mentors, deemed them to be obscene. No charges were filed. There were no trials. Impecunious newsdealers, whose economic life Commissioner Moss controlled, were afraid to fight back. The Mayor threatened with criminal libel arrest John Carter, who had written on the whole a complimentary life of him. This dictatorial Dewey-Hague type of action was occasioned because three pages in the volume referred to the young LaGuardia drinking to drown misery, and to his ineptness as a lawyer. He instructed his police to beat up "tinhorn gamblers." He dominated many of his appointed magistrates, and used such domination to demand excessive bail for defendants he didn't like. He begged children to squeal on their parents if the parents were betting on the horses. He caused raids on magazines carrying horse-track news. He put his political hand on the Board of Education and shoved that most important portion of city government back into politics in a subtle but direful sense. He never played completely fair with labor, for

[175]

he always straddled between the Communist leaders and the rank and file of labor. His bond with the fair-haired boy of the Communists—Marcantonio—led him into positions scarcely brave and honest. He stuck by Marcantonio even when that congressman supported a picket line against preparedness, voted against Lend-Lease, opposed the draft, and made political deals with Tammany district leaders.

I've known LaGuardia for many years. It's too bad that with his great capacity and high vision he should have stooped so often in recent years to short cuts, browbeating, threats and duress. In a sense he has taken on the Fascist-Communist approach—"the end justifies the means."

For years he liked me—during alternate weeks. At one time I acted for him as his personal counsel. This chore I had to withdraw from. I could not stand it. After I advised him to seek other counsel, he wrote me the following letter which is typical Fiorello and the kind of effusion which makes him so lovable at times:

Dear Morris:

I have your letter of February 26th. Don't be silly. I am not going to designate other counsel. Just because you are all wrong in one case and do not handle it in a lawyer-like manner is no indication you would do the same in my case.

You are infringing on my constitutional rights.

Sincerely yours

F. LaGuardia.

His next letter ended with the amusing suggestion: A flyer and a lawyer should never lose his head. Why don't you be calm like me. Lots of love. Sincerely your Fiorello.

The case referred to was my defense—unsuccessful in the lower court and never appealed because the clients could not afford it—of a burlesque show which Moss had called off. I've been beaten so often that I really do not resent for myself any defeat unless I attribute it to my own stupidity. But I was concerned about the pattern of the mayoralty established by Fiorello. In the burlesque case he made no bones about his intentions. If he couldn't win in court he would use his administrative powers, such as filing violations on buildings. There are few buildings in our city on which a violation cannot be laid, even though the violation might be removed by going up to our Court of Appeals. Few producers, however, can afford that kind of fight. LaGuardia has played very often on the power to wear people down by administrative duress. This is in essence the Hitler technique of throwing people into concentration camps because they fail to have a dog license.

In 1946 we in New York City will be faced with a great problem. The Republican party is dominated by the rich and those unaware of the desires of workingpeople; the city Democratic bosses are still on the make through politics, and lacking in vision. The vision and balance of power is held by the Liberal party. The American Labor party—the haven of Communists—will evaporate now that the 1944 election is over with. At the moment it would seem as if William O'Dwyer, now a brigadier general, who was defeated by LaGuardia by only a few votes in the mayoralty race of 1941 and who would have won out if the election had taken place after Pearl Harbor instead of a month before, is a possible hope of the city on a Liberal-Democratic party coalition slate. I never met O'Dwyer until after the last election but I've seen lots of him since. He is honest, independent and tough. He's the only Catholic I know of in political life who has publicly condemned the Christian Fronters and the rest of the bigotry boys. Whether the Democratic leaders will stand for him, or vice versa, is still an open question. But LaGuardia has left the city organization-wise in such a void that probably the Democrats could elect even another Hylan or O'Brien. This is a typical closing chapter for many movements in American political life that stem from the Judge Seabury type of parochial sanctimonious approach to politics employed in putting LaGuardia into office. Fiorello has thrown over his labor buddies who elected him. These leaders and the members of the Liberal party are probably more adverse to

[177]

him than are the Republicans or the Democrats. He did a great service to our city and it's just too bad that he ends it all with a tailspin. I wish him luck—he's too swell a guy to stay on his present bypath. I hope he bounces back to the LaGuardia of old. I see only slight hope. Unlike F.D.R., he doesn't like people who argue with him and tell him what they think, except for Bob Moses, our equally autocratic park commissioner, whom he would not dare fire.

I remember one evening before LaGuardia was mayor when Heywood Broun, LaGuardia and I went for some drinks to a little saloon opposite the theater where Heywood's *Shoot the Works* was running. There was a slot machine in the corner. LaGuardia ran to it, gleefully tried for the jackpot, with no apparent sense of guilt. Was he the same man who, less than a decade later, had slot machines dumped into the East River?

TAXIS FOR MORE PEOPLE

Riding in taxis was converted into a different kind of experience that day in 1934 when I dropped in at his office to chat about something, and the Mayor said, "What are you doing this afternoon?" I told him there was nothing special that I couldn't put off if I could help him in any way. I didn't get home for four days. He turned over to me the settling of the taxi strike of 1934.

It was a tough affair, cabs upset, tires and doors ripped off, violence prevalent and unpreventable. With 15,000 cabs in New York City, full police protection was out of the question, although Commissioner Valentine and his force did a magnificent job.

The drivers of cabs are not easy to unionize. They are independent contractors if they work for fleet owners, and if they own their own cabs they are small businessmen. The conflict between the two groups is quite irreconcilable. The fleets were controlled by two or three giant companies, interrelated in obvious or subtle ways with the manufacturers of the cabs. The drivers were paid no salaries, no minimum take

[178]

per day or week, but gambled on making a living by keeping about 40 per cent of what the meter showed, plus tips.

I was impressed by the wide variations in income of drivers working for the same boss. One quiet cabby never took in less than $60 a week, while the average was something less than $20 a week. This particular driver followed sport and society news in the daily papers. He knew the addresses of funerals and weddings and parties. He might have been an editor of Cue magazine.

By and large the men drove their cabs 100 miles a day, of which 70 miles was empty cruising, wasting oil and rubber and gas, riding without a passenger. Only 30 per cent of the mileage was productive—that is, with a passenger inside.

The organization of a union failed, due primarily to the Communist leadership, which held a monster rally at Madison Square Garden but had no real desire for agreement, progress or peace.

The companies were losing money, and the men were living on substandard wages. The largest fleets gave the best service. There were too many cabs on the streets in relation to consumer demand. At least one thousand cabs came out only at night to roll the drunks and work the market for clip joints.

Several points still stand out in my mind. All through the strike negotiations I kept in mind the first time I rode in a taxi—how my gaze was pinned to the meter, and how a piece of my heart was taken out after the clock went over $1. I assume this is a common experience. In any event, my studies led me to believe that not more than 1 per cent of the public ride a taxi more than once or twice a year. It's something like the theater, which because of high rates of admission caters to a negligible portion of the community except for a rare run like Life With Father or Abie's Irish Rose.

In settling the strike I urged the companies to reduce the rates, invite more people into taxis, and keep the cabs profitable not only for 30 miles a day, but 50 or 60 miles a day.

In that additional usage lies the profit for operators and decent incomes for the drivers.

But I found the same lack of vision in the taxi owners as exists in heads of railroads and utility companies and coal mines. When income shrinks, these merchants invariably want to raise rather than lower the rates. It took us several decades—and we are by no means finished—to get the gas and electric companies to learn that if they reduce rates they often make more money for stockholders. President Roosevelt before the war had to spank the railroads, all save one or two, into lower profitable rates.

I did persuade the operators into giving several trial bargain Mondays—at one-third off the meter price. I suggested that three or four people going home might bundle into a cab and share the cost at the lower rates. On those Mondays we had heavy snowstorms—welcomed but not arranged by the operators. So no real test was established.

With lighter cabs, such as those used in Washington, with sharing made legal, with lower rates, I'm quite sure that the taxi-riding public would more than double, and the pre- and postwar waste of 70 miles empty driving would be reduced, to the benefit of all concerned. The answer is not fewer cabs. Even though there is a great shortage of taxis at this time I'm sure that after the war we will look back with longing to the days when the streets of this city were usable by autos.

In the prewar days drivers lost their jobs if they didn't bring in certain minimum amounts every week, and one of the most pathetic economic events in our life was drivers riding around the parks empty so as to boost the meter readings, even though they were giving back to the boss the few dollars they had made that day for themselves and their families.

I've always continued my habit of cross-examining taxi drivers. They are my best Gallup poll. People who ride in taxis are normally Republicans, and the drivers are Democrats or followers of the new Liberal party. One of my pet drivers recently told me he drew up to the curb and asked two men to get out of his cab because one man had said, "If the war

[180]

will only last another year I'll have made an additional million dollars."

I told him, "Swell." Maybe he violated some law. Surely he has no right to be a censor of passenger conversations. Nevertheless, I'm for him.

CHAPTER XXIX

MY FRIEND FERBER

MAGGIE AND I HAD DINNER with the Edna Ferbers, the myriad different exteriors that make up our Edna. On the way uptown to meet her we sometimes guess which Edna will come out to see us, but the essence of my affection lies in the fact that even when she calls me "clay foot," or much worse, we both know that there is an understanding that nothing can really disturb. I can be comfortable with Edna because she knows how wrong I can be, she is aware of my weaknesses, yet she never tries to reform or change me.

How such a valuable touch of another personality comes into existence is never easy to figure out, but for more than twenty years we have been important to each other. She understands a Joan; she sees and hears all kinds of life more accurately and acutely than anyone else I know; she can brew a dish of conversation in her home with a flavor not found anywhere else I've ever been; and she has been sufficient in herself to be alone.

It was at Edna's that I first met my friend William Allen White of Emporia, Kansas. I had never met anyone like Will White, and to watch the Edna-Will banter was sheer joy. I have thought that maybe that deep bond between author and newspaper publisher arose because Will wanted to be a novelist like Edna and Edna never got out of her glands her early experience as a reporter. I was flattered when Will and Edna—people I truly admire—called on me for advice and help.

Will it was who first pointed out to me that Edna is truly an historian! Edna probably never reads much collegiate economics or sociology but she has written a panorama of the social life of our nation in economic folkway terms. She has a greater parish of listeners than the pedagogues of history. She has done in significant and apperceptive terms the story of our national mores and folkways. The misery and lushness of the great Mississippi; the sterilization of New England; the development of the rough lumber industry; the opening of the West; the conversion of industry for war; the birth of the economics of the feminist movement. These and others she has recorded for millions of people throughout the world to read and enjoy.

Her strong feeling of love for the United States compelled her to choose her material from our heroic patterns of hopes and failures. Students of this nation's development will learn more from Ferber than from many of the heavy tomes of the Adamses from Henry to James T. But of all Edna's writings the one she loves best is *Peculiar Treasure*, the one time she didn't need research or fictional imagination. For this story of her own life is also a cross section of the United States and of our land, one of the few spots on earth where the miracle of a Ferber could have happened during our lifetime.

The last time I saw Will White we were talking about the catastrophe of Harding's election in 1920 and the effect on the entire world when men like Will supported that handsome weakling for president after the last war. To my attack Will replied, "We were naïve. But this time we must look at a man's record in the past and his associates and supporters in the present. His campaign speeches you can throw aside. Man learns little and changes less during the time he runs for office."

He aroused my interest in the presidential campaign of

1920, which changed the history of our present lives. I recalled that many of my liberal friends of the *Nation* and the *New Republic* school, went to bed politically with Henry Cabot Lodge and the then isolationists. These liberals were perfectionists and not being able to get the exact kind of League they wanted, they refused to support the Cox-Wilson crowd and in effect aided in the election of Harding, and the isolationist Republican party.

My research brought to my attention the statement published October 15, 1920, and signed by William Allen White, Herbert Hoover, A. Lawrence Lowell, Henry L. Stimson, Charles Evans Hughes, all together by thirty-one then well-known liberal leaders. These were the elder liberal statesmen of that era. Hoover just back from feeding Europe, Lowell before Sacco-Vanzetti; Hughes, great New York governor. They had seen the candidate—Senator Harding; he had told them he was for international relationship and for world peace. A statement issued by these leaders and widely carried in our daily press called on the people of the nation to forget the Wilson ineffective idealism which would get us nothing. We should turn to Harding and the practical Republicans! That was the way to international peace and a world force to prevent war.

In 1943, I wrote Will about this published statement and asked whether he didn't want to issue a warning to the present generation of 1944. We must not make the same costly mistake all over again. I asked Will to write me that he had been naïve and wrong, and to let me publish his statement whenever I saw fit.

After some clarifications were exchanged in letters, he wrote me as follows:

Dear Morris:
Probably your letter was all right and probably I misread it. Anyway, we are not going to quarrel about that.

You and I agree exactly that it isn't a matter of men but of issues and unless the issues are definite and certain, any man is likely to slip out of his performance. But a man nominated by the

[183]

National Committee of either party is more likely to slip out of it because he will be motivated by the party desire to perpetuate hisself for Pap than a man who gets nominated on a battle for specific principles.

Harding's failure was ignorance. The man had plenty of courage but no intelligence and he would get first on one side of any proposal after listening to one side and get on the other side after listening to that side.

Enclosed find an editorial I wrote about Bricker. You may have seen part of it in the papers, but here is the whole thing.

I would be glad enough to sign the statement you suggest. Where do you want it to appear?

Will

Will agreed that I might make this statement public:

We who were violently and actively in favor of the League of Nations in 1920 were wrong in relying upon the mere declarations of public personages in favor of the League.

Many a time during the campaign of Dewey for president I thought of this warning, and felt sure that William Allen White of 1944 would have done penance for his admitted error of 1920. It was Will White who called Bricker an "honest Harding." The last time I saw him, he had no name for Tom Dewey, but I doubt if White would have repeated his 1920 mistake by supporting Tom Dewey.

CHAPTER XXX

WHY MINERS STRIKE

I'VE BEEN KIDDED AT TIMES because I introduced John L. Lewis to Wendell Willkie at Wendell's suggestion at a party I gave for Willkie at Jack and Charlie's in the spring of 1939. I used to see Lewis often as he passed through New York. Roger, when about twelve years old, was intrigued by

[184]

stolid, sure John. It was some time later that Roger met Earl Browder at our home. Browder is a meager, hick, stupid Kansas accountant. I asked my kid what he thought of Browder. Roger merely said, "Compared to Lewis, I think he's a sissy." Today Lewis is a synonym for wartime strikes.

We're still hearing the same old refrain about strikes. What a distorted picture has been planted in the American mind by newscasters relying on AP, UP and INS reports. If one could trust the press and the radio one would believe that nearly all workmen have been on strike at one time or another during the war and despite all "no strike" pledges. According to the President, in September, 1944, only 1 per cent of our workers had violated the strike pledge despite employer provocations, which increased in reliance on the pledge. Of course, the facts are to the contrary of what we hear or read and no doubt the dishonest weighting of strike news has led to further cynicism of the public toward daily newspapers and radio. Of course, strikes during war are shocking, nearly as shocking as the manufacture by some of our big corporations of fraudulent material for our troops in the field. And we ought never forget that the Anaconda Wire and Cable Company conviction for making fraudulent war material to be used by our troops at the fighting fronts appeared on the sports page of the great New York *Times* and was not even mentioned by much of our nation's press.

But workers on strike during war represent a psychological quandary seldom explained to the people of the land. I know the miners of Pennsylvania—good, stout, devoted Americans. I'll never forget the days of bootleg coal in 1937, when gay Governor George Earle who often bumped me for sheer joy in his private airplane, appointed me a member of a Pennsylvania State Anthracite Coal Industry Commission to look into those industrial troubles. The men had stolen four million tons of coal. They dug pits, without proper shoring up, risking their lives reaching for that black earth rather than go on relief. The operating companies, which for decades were owned by the coal-carrying railroads, were only a handful in numbers. Sixty-five per cent of the coal was in the control of a dozen or less old-line corporations. Dominated by the coal-carrying railway systems, this industry had relied on the power of monopoly rather than on the ingenuity of private enterprise. No by-products were used, no fight to reduce the price of coal to consumer, and hence complete surrender to the introduction of oil in the homes of the East. The automatic stoker was improvised too late.

The miners' union is the economic religion of the miners. In 1937 the men worked only about 168 days a year at a rate of about $7.70 a day. When I had John L. Lewis in one room and the operators in another, I suggested timidly to John that the price might be dropped to $7 a day in return—if I could get it—for a guarantee of at least 200 days' work a year. I knew that 200 times $7—$1,400 a year—was less than a decent annual wage. I knew how many years it took the union to establish the rate of $7.70 per day. Nevertheless, I urged a break in the rate in return for guaranteed jobs, cheaper coal to consumers and hence more work. To my surprise John quickly said he'd agree. I asked why he jumped at the proposal with so little hesitation. He merely said that the operators were too stupid to accept such a proposition which would cut the price of coal to consumers and give more wages and profits to all parts of the industry. He was right and the men continued to suffer in money, in work conditions, and above all, in indecencies of employer attitudes. By the last I mean, as an example, that thousands of men, working only two or three days a week, would go to the mine each and every day only to be told most of the time, "No work today." Few employers, among the large ones, had the vision to advise men in advance as to future days of work. A miner's heart-sinking meant little to the great directors sitting in Philadelphia or other fine large city office buildings.

And so in 1943 these miners, with sons dying on battlefields, were torn between love of the nation and their fighting sons, on the one hand, and, on the other hand, a fear that if the bosses rode tough and high, again as of old, then those of their boys who did return alive would come back to nothing worth while if there were no strong union.

I do not believe the men struck out of fear of John L. Lewis—although John is a man who can create fear rather than tenderness. Someday some student of human quandaries could profitably delve into the clash which sorely troubled every striking miner. As for John, it's just too bad. A tough labor leader of the old Gompers school—higher wages, shorter hours—came east and was subjected all too quickly to the "Ism Boys." He had never heard of Gitlowites, Socialists, Lovestonites and Communists. The Commies took him over. They surrounded him. Once I tried to make a date for an owner of a New York paper to see John L. Lewis in his vast swell offices in Washington. It couldn't be arranged without Lee Pressman, his counsel, being present and Pressman, at least at that time, was down the Communist line. John became a mental prisoner. They fanned his well of hates; they squelched that all-too-slight sense of humor and fun. And so John believed it was a Banker's War and that the "Yanks Aren't Coming," and all the rest of the American Communist propaganda finally symbolized by the paid picket line at the White House ($50,000 a year it cost and we have never found out who put up the money for "Peace Mobilization").

The minute Hitler attacked great Russia the Communist ferryboats and wreckers of unions, unlike those who merely followed the line, turned one of their most ridiculous mindsprings. They shouted for war, and John—poor John—just stayed put where the Commies had sent him. It's a pathetic story, for this tragic figure of a man of great capacity missed the tide of his time. He is a symbol of blindness through odd and costly hates.

On the employers' side, not all bosses are built in Westbrook Pegler's imagery—pure and altruistic and inevitably just and fair. However, distorted vision is inevitable as long as the misbehavior of large corporations is submerged in our press and as long as criticism is carried only in a few large papers or in little liberal weeklies of scant circulation. On rare occasions we get news of corporate antisocial acts on first pages, but usually only for a single flash, as in a case resulting in indictment of a financial empire like the Chase Bank.

I'M-THE-LAW HAGUE

As usual, in the last political campaign, the Republican press supporting Dewey started its annual riding of Mayor Frank Hague of Jersey City. I've never met him outside of the courtroom since the trial in 1938 when, in behalf of the C.I.O. and specifically John L. Lewis, I acted as counsel to prevent Hague's interference with picketing, parades, public assemblages and distribution of pamphlets. The Mayor of Jersey City had gone so far as to deport to New York City persons he deemed objectionable.

I'd like to chat with him, because he evidenced two characteristics rare in American political life. He was a fully honest witness. Secure, sure and safe (he thought) he brusquely came through with the truth when a little skirting might have let him evade the answer called for. Once, while he was on the witness stand, I asked him if he had not denied the right of a hall to Norman Thomas because he thought his speech, not read in advance, might be subversive, and also because "the building was not safe for such a meeting." I said, "The building is still used for halls?" "Yes." "They have pretty good-sized assemblages there, don't they, Mayor?" In justification of his ban Frank Hague replied, "Yes, any port in a storm, counselor."

Then on another day I pointed to the fact that out of twelve Democratic district leaders in his county, eleven held city or county jobs. One was city treasurer, others managed city parks or streets or other city bureaus. The Mayor said, "We take good care of them." Only one of all the political leaders held no public job. How come? I asked the Mayor. He quietly replied, "He is the contractor. I suppose he finds it more profitable without a position." All this, if you please, under oath in a federal court presided over by agile-minded, vibrant Judge William Clark.

Rarely did I feel that Hague tried to duck, and then only when my questions were quite wide of the mark, as when I was trying to lead him into discussing his personal tax returns, or a murder on the Pulaski Skyway.

This characteristic of openness was refreshing. He was so sure of himself that he deported people out of New Jersey to New York, broke up picket lines, closed parks and squares. He fomented riots against the C.I.O. and then deplored the danger of riots. His sureness was augmented by a similar case brought against him a year before our trial—a case which the Mayor won. No wonder he was "I'm the Law."

The other interesting tidbit growing out of this trial was the Mayor's full and frank desire to comply with the Supreme Court's mandate for civil liberties in Jersey City. His counsel called me up the day after our highest court had spoken. He said the Mayor wanted me to look over or prepare the kind of ordinance which the United States Supreme Court called for. It was drafted and, I add, passed by the Jersey City Fathers after less than five minutes of discussion. He was still "I'm the Law" in a sense. Mayor Hague wanted the best free-speech ordinance in the United States and he got it. No more trouble since then in the field of the Bill of Rights except the first week when I was called up by the Corporation Counsel of Jersey City to ask if it would be all right to delay speaking in certain parks for a time after sundown so that the baseball games could finish their seven innings as in the past. I told him that in my opinion batting out balls is a right of Americans just as surely as batting out ideas.

Imagine Tom Dewey getting a licking in court and then not trying to squirm between decision and facts. LaGuardia, of course, is a past master at devious court defiance.

One other incident of the "affair Hague" comes to my mind. We had used for the first time some old post-Civil War civil rights statutes. There was no use going into Hague's state courts, so we had to develop theories of going into the federal courts under federal statutes. When I say we, of course, that's really the brain kids in my office and Spaulding Frazer and David Stoffer, local associate counsel in Jersey City. After the lower court handed us a decision re-establishing civil liberties in Jersey City, I received a letter from counsel for the C.I.O. questioning whether they should go on with the case. I was heartbroken, and bewildered. I had been called in by John L. Lewis, head of the C.I.O., and the American Civil Liberties Union had joined in on the case. I still hold this letter saying the cost of the case made the worth of an appeal questionable. I was amazed. The case cost nothing for counsel fees to our office. Spaulding Frazer and his associates made a modest and totally inadequate charge for their services. Printing cost would be borne by Jersey City on the appeal. The reason for wanting the suit dropped should have been clear to me because from the very start the Communists had tried to mucker up the case. They attempted to block Dorothy Thompson from speaking in Jersey City. They sent out thousands of letters calling me a Fascist because I had asked and secured valuable support from Hugh Johnson, Dorothy Thompson and Walter Lippmann before I ever went near a courtroom. They got their stooges to obstruct with tactics and a brief during the trial. And now with victory in hand, they were afraid that with the right of free speech established by Judge Clark's opinion they could not corral enough people to go to the square to make even a show of a rally. I took the matter up with John L. Lewis. He overruled his counsel.

Frank Hague was and is right, that American Communists are dishonest, neurotic folk. He was wrong in being scared of them. He was pitiful in his tactics of suppression. He was unfair in calling everyone a Red. Which reminds me that Heywood Broun once said, "If they call me a Communist and I say I'm not a Communist, they don't believe me, and they are right not to believe me for they know that if I were a Communist I'd still say I'm not a Communist."

Disclosure rather than suppression is the only way of handling underground movements. Only slowly are we learning that lesson.

CHAPTER XXXI

TAKE YOUR CHOICE

Reader's *Digest* CALLED UP and wanted me to write an advisory article for them. I'm a pushover for such requests even though in this case as in many others the material is never printed. I guess this agreeableness on my part is due to the fact that I've represented for years a great number of writers including many of the leading columnists and commentators—Swing, Howe, Gunther, Shirer, Henderson, Harsch, Grafton, Pearson and others—and no doubt envied them all.

In 1931 I fell so low as to do a column for the Hearst *Journal-American*. Three days a week it appeared on the editorial page. They gave me a grand spot. My chore was a double spread called "Take Your Choice." I debated subjects then in the news. Do you favor baby parades? Should the Board of Aldermen in New York City be abolished? What about forgiving the war debts? Should we permit world fliers to get killed at the pace of their then self-destruction?

I wrote both sides to each debate; the side I agreed with was signed with my name and the opposition I signed "Patrick Stand," a rather feeble play on stand pat. After a very few weeks letters came in: "Who is this Pat Stand? He's putting it all over Ernst." In fact, years later Pat Stand was invited to speak in favor of Jail for Alimony Debtors at some forum at Des Moines, Iowa. I was tempted to put on a false beard and make the appearance. I've always thought there were too few unmalicious hoaxes.

It wasn't long before the column was dropped. I was inclined to believe that Hearst had read an attack I'd made on him in a book I wrote one summer for Earle Balch of Putnam's, *America's Primer*. But perhaps the column wasn't as exciting as my family told me it was.

Pat Stand, however, did not die. Around that time a well-known book critic going on vacation asked me to take over his book review column in his newspaper for a day. Which of the new books would I like to review? I worked up a silly little hoax with the critic. My *America's Primer* was reviewed by Patrick Stand. Of course I was honest, for I gave myself a generous break. If I had cracked down on my own creation it would have been bravado and less than honest.

I remember landing in New York from Nantucket the day after the review appeared. Bill Riis, a lovable troubled liberal, now brain trusting for *Reader's Digest*, ran into me on the street and said he had bought my book because he had read the rave notice in the newspaper. I said, "Bill, I can't take it. Here's your two dollars back." Although the book is still used in some schools, it never caught on or sold in any quantities.

And still Pat survived, for when Dave Stern of Philadelphia bought the New York *Post* in 1934 he asked me to do a column. I declined but suggested that if one of his top reporters such as Joe Cookman (an exciting editorial writer, who died the very day I wrote these lines) would interview me three or four days a week we might work up something amusing. Joe came to the office. He probably thought it was all a trifle irregular, but he was too kind to tell me so. Joe's column consisted of interviews with one Malachi Forsyte. Malachi commented on current events and looked into the future. The column was called "Ahead of the News." It wasn't too bad. On the last day we ran it Malachi Forsyte mentioned what Patrick Stand had to say about Morris Ernst's position on tax exemption of church property and the use of city armories in the evenings for all people and not only for polo players.

With this, the only triple literary hoax I know of, Patrick Stand died a peaceful, unheralded death. A babe all his life and too ambitious in his youth, he was never serious enough about his craft to work at it twenty-four hours a day.

Maggie, once a star reporter, and poet by the stick for New Orleans' then vigorous *Times-Picayune*, viewed all my reportorial foibles with tolerance. She really never was mean to me about these feeble expeditions. As a matter of fact she's never been mean anyway about anything.

However, I don't seem to be able to stop writing—one kind of thing or another. Ever so often I go off on a fiction rampage. All my friends laugh and tell me to stop such undignified nonsense. But I don't think I'm doing any great harm—not even to the magazines which buy—even though at times they pay and never publish. Incidentally, something should be done by authors to impress on magazines that authors sell for two purposes: one is money; the other, often equally important, is publication. Surely the publisher should return if he decides not to print; or at the least give an option to the author to sell elsewhere, upon return of at least half the purchase price. The same problem bobs up with newspapers where the practice of keeping a special writer sitting with salary and no assignment is so common as to be given a name: "They put him on ice."

I like a story I never could place in a magazine. Here's a chance to see it in print:

STATIC IMMORTAL

No one at this job ever bit a fingernail. There was no such emotion as suspense when all you did on eight-hour shifts day in and day out for twenty months was to analyze and tabulate "static." Of course, to normal folk on the mainland, static is little more than an inconvenient noise. Static on millions of radio sets creates human grumbles and as a direct reflex millions of human hands reach for little knobs and turn either to the right or to the left. Anything but static. But to our three shifts of four people each, static was a personality—not that we asked for the introduction or the nearly two years of intimacy. But no one can listen even to static for endless hours without feeling a warmth toward it that equals the friendly thrill of the amateur radio fiend when he first caught the waves from Byrd at the South or the North pole.

Twelve healthy Americans of varying degrees of collegiate and scientific training had been sent by the International Research Laboratories to Surfside, there to fathom static. We knew that the recording of the strange voices of static would take us into unknown regions of science but none suspected that the location of our station specially equipped for our studies would be as remote from life and people and dogs and fleas as that high cliff of sand rising forty feet above that tiny island shore far off in the Atlantic. Often did we think that the location was chosen because no decent reception had ever come over the air to this Isle. Seldom a day went by without soft baths of heavy fogs. From the porch surrounding our high tower we took down the pace of fogs just as regularly as sailors count the rise and fall of tides.

To the uninitiated let me say that static is just what the word meant before we had radio broadcasting. It's nothing but old friend Equilibrium. And of course to us men of science there can be no such thing. Just as nature abhors and fills a vacuum, it unbalances an equilibrium. For a few minutes a skillful acrobat can balance with his agile fan on a high tightrope. But that very artifice proves that it isn't right—I mean right to nature.

Without getting too scientific, let me tell what we were sent to look at and then tell you why all of us bit off nearly all our fingernails on that now famous night, exactly 26,482 full moons after an agile youth ran 26.4 miles in record time.

Big business, cursed as it is so often, in a weird way performs at times in its laboratories great service to mankind. To sell more radios it was necessary to get the jump on competitors and so our shop was organized to find out what static was and how to tune it out, as you would say. You can't watch a will-o'-the-wisp like static if you ever go to sleep on the job.

Twenty-four hours a day we made records. Charts covered the walls and filled the desks of our tower. Never less than three of us were there to adjust the phonograph records on which the strangest shrieks and sounds were recorded from the nowhere. These sounds were weighed and measured in sixteen different ways and then each of these results was paired off against wind records, tide climbs, barometer findings and temperature charts. Elaborate clocks were attached to the phonographs and the records showed the times when each set of noises entered or faded out.

For twenty months we didn't get a clue. Oh yes, there was some slight evidence that electric storms increased the volume of static, and snowstorms from the northeast reduced static so that even our sensitive sets, equipped always to find some static, could scarcely keep out the base orchestral notes from the larger 50,000-watt stations on the Continent.

You may think that our work was dreary but it wasn't. After the first few weeks when the statistics had started to pile up, each of us grabbed at the new phonograph interpretations and the corresponding weather tables just as millions of people eagerly reached for crossword puzzles in the evening newspapers back home. Then also we had two poets in our gang. I don't mean people who can rhyme words or scan phrases. I mean real poets—people who dream a decade or a century ahead of the rest of us. Madge was like Copernicus who, without a telescope, wrote about the distances and the coldness of the stars. Pete was more of the Icarus type—dreaming and doing. Pete it was who finally persuaded the bosses back home to equip the first underwater radio receiving set with timed phonographs attached. Forty fathoms down he sent his machines, remote from all direct contact with dirt and earth. Pete wouldn't rest until he could compare the records made underwater and those produced in our high aerialed tower.

It was this flight from solid earth which brought us fame. The first day's records were being run off for the preliminary tonal checks on static qualities. Ever so often words of human beings would creep into the records. Groucho Marx or Kate Smith would cut across the plates, even though we tried our best to eliminate any noises made by man at broadcasting studios. On this first sea haul we caught in the midst of swell static some foreign words.

Bill said, "Damn these foreign short-wave amateurs."

It wasn't until we were measuring the static pitches that Madge said, "Hold on— play that last half inch over again." The excitement in her tone showed that she was wandering from the pursuit of static. We played it.

"Don't you know your Greek?" she sang.

"Oh, bull," said Bill. "No one on this earth speaks your college kind of Greek nowadays. I've been in Greece and what they jabber there is more like a hash."

"That's it, you goof. Some college commencement exercises. Think of those dreary words being powerful enough to cut through static." Madge said no more.

We all went back to the charts, but after supper she snuggled up to the recorder and I saw her writing down that Greek sentence or two as the phonograph repeated the words at slow speed. She told me later that she had taken them down just for something to do and to see how much she had forgotten of her college Greek studied under old Pipi Clark.

Her labored translation she wrote on a slip of paper and put into her copy of Taggard's poems which she was rereading for the far from last time. The following day was the 15th of June. An electric storm had circled our tower and the Island most of the afternoon. The water recorder was brought to the surface at exactly five o'clock just as we dropped the duplicate machine off the stern of the double-ender which we used as our marine vehicle. Madge didn't go out in the dory but was waiting on the shore as we pulled the boat high up on the beach. She walked up to the recording room with us, I remember. At the time this made no particular impression on me but now I can scarcely understand her calmness.

The triple glass case was opened by burning off the wax.

Bill heaved out the instrument and Pete put the phonograph record on our reproducer. Halfway through, Madge jumped, and then sagged back into her place on the couch. Pete grabbed her. He thought she was suddenly taken sick. I started to turn off the record but as I reached out Madge shouted, "Stop it, no, not the record—you, I mean. Let her go—some more Greek. Don't you get it? It can't be a preacher at commencement. It's something real—it's not a speech. Bill, telephone over to the shop on the mainland. Get a complete check on all stations from exactly 3:25 to 3:32 o'clock. All stations, I said. All in the world. Don't forget to count out variations on time and crisscross the daylight-saving shifts. I've got something real and I'll go nuts if we can't check through at once."

Madge calmed down, as we all let her give orders just as if she had become captain of a ship. Between repeating the Greek portions of the record she would try to translate a word here or a word there. And ever again she would sing out, "It only has to be proven once to be proven forever."

We all caught some of her excitement. Without any knowledge of Greek we were not so greatly impressed. But Madge was surer as the record kept turning, but frightfully irritated as static whipped across the stern Greek words.

"Better give me some time alone on the Greek." Off she went to her room. Scarcely an hour later she came out with the most thrilling calm I have ever seen in a human being's eyes. "I don't care about that check on broadcasters. It can't be a theatrical performance; one talker is interrupting the other, and even in Greece a theatrical audience must come to listen. This is real talk. Don't you know how people, in direct conversation, seldom wait for the others to finish a sentence because each talker is thinking up his next sentence instead of listening. This is real talk. It's what we all have dreamed but always with a smile. Here underwater we have caught the first enveloping word waves that have gone on through history. Maybe the water retains. Maybe the electrical storm aggravated, maybe—oh, there are so many maybes."

We started to join with Madge. We caught her excitement, try as we would to be skeptical.

Bill started picking. "I guess you want us to believe that the box caught up a sound wave of more than a thousand years ago—that's about the time they stopped talking old-fashioned Greek."

"You're right," said Madge with great precision. "My guess, however, is that these noises started even more than two thousand years ago; let's see—they must have come out into the waves about 2,324 years ago, to be exact."

"To be exact," I snickered with a real attempt at meanness.

"To be exact," Madge repeated. "Or maybe I haven't clearly in mind the date of the battle of Marathon."

"490 B.C." chimed in Pete, as if to come to Madge's comfort.

"That's the time they are or were talking and there is no doubt about it," said Madge.

Then Bill joined with us. "So, you caught the archons in session working out a New Deal for Hellas? Did they call the roll for you?"

"No, but here we have three men probably sitting in a tent—"

"What do you mean 'probably'—maybe it's all probabilities," said Bill, and then, "Just read us your notes. Don't let's all go gaga as long as all of your evidence can be produced if you will be so kind as to end this . . ."

Madge turned on Bill without venom but with directness. "Bill, I wish you could read Greek. You'll surely doubt some of my translations. But all of you take my word for it, those parts which the machine caught can all be translated by a better scholar of the classics than yours truly, but I've got enough to tell you we have heard—heard is the word—the general in charge of the Grecian forces at the battle of Marathon. His name is something like Callimachus. Isn't it funny how unimportant his name has become, even though he thought he would be forever immortal just because he turned back the Medes and the Persians. He thinks he saved Grecian culture—forever."

Bill interjected to say, "They must have been turned back every year or so. Didn't a guy by the name of Miltiades do it too?"

Through my mind went the possibility of television, someday showing us that great battle of history and even the run of the Marathon Race, now better known than any part of the warfare.

In quiet tones as if he were listening to something far away Pete said:

"Wouldn't it be better if you just gave us your translations as you picked them up?"

"But, Pete, the sentences didn't flow without interruption. All your best brands of Island static cut across nearly every sentence."

"Well, let's have it as it came in anyway."

"No, I think I'll first read to you the only real big hunk that came in without any static interruptions. Then I'll give you some of the scattered sentences. Here goes—and you will soon see it's a general—Callimachus, making a report or sending a message.

You can report that our formation with a thin center brought all the success we had planned. With scant numbers of archmen or sumpter beasts but our crested helmets and ponderous shields overcame the thin shafts of the Persians. Our vows to Diana led us to attack our foe and the Medes, never heretofore last to attack, seeing us destitute of cavalry, attacked our thin center only to be led on into fierce and stubborn attacks from our right and left. The barbarians have retreated backward to the sea, to be pursued by us and hemmed in by our better and only ally, the great morass. We have won the day. The fields of Marathon . . .

For special mention, you may tell the people of Athens that a young man of the tribe of Leontis distinguished himself—his name is Themistocles. And with deep concern you may report the death of Cynegirus, brother of our famed poet

[199]

Aeschylus, who first before departing lost one hand—severed by a barbarian's ax—as he stood on the shore holding tight to the poop deck of one of the barbarian's ships. Our losses were heavy but the people of Athens have been saved. Go—fleet afoot as you were in the pacing to the Spartans. Tarry not—bring the tidings to mankind. Our culture has been saved forever.

And, boy, what is your name?

Pheidippides, O great Callimachus.

Then go . . .

"That's the end except for six scattered sentences or parts of them. Don't you remember the bit of Greek on yesterday's haul from the sea? Here is all there was to it. You, too, Aeschilles, need no Homer to sing your praises—you have established a perpetual reminder. That was all. You see, it could have been part of a valedictory, as one of you suggested yesterday."

Pete quietly interjected: "Maybe it was a valedictory of a man never to be remembered."

"The next bit," went on Madge, "is—

But, Callimachus, at home they should be apprised of your great feats and fame by the moon, for the moon foretells for those of Hellas and the sun for the Persians. So they will be needing long ere now some reports.

"And then—Your share, Aeschilles, only adds to the distinction long acquired by you through your great benefactions in the libraries and temples now saved forever from the barbarian destructions. Until men from the littleness of their souls stop praising your name your aid on this day will be added to the saving of the people of our famed—

"A new voice then comes in with—Cables of papyrus instead of white flax—static, and then—not less than a talent to a cubit which helped—

"I then get words like sumpter beasts and baggage bearers, then static and then three wings with a center."

We all sat in silence. Someone grabbed for Madge's notes. Bill slouched back in his chair. I don't recall what I did but

I'll never forget Pete—slowly he leaned toward the glass-encased machine ready to be dropped down into the sea the next day. He touched it fondly once or twice and then took the one step needed to go over and stroke Madge's cheek with the same kind of soft affection.

"Madge, don't you realize," said practical Bill, "you'll be famous now and forever. You're made, Madge."

Madge looked at him and at her notes and at the phonograph recorder. "It's too real to discuss now, isn't it, boys? This is more than research. Isn't it a little forbidding to reach along an unending wave into the past of great Greece and find that the men who lived and died thinking they were immortal are not even names to us today? Maybe no one gets immortality except along a sound or light ray or by an imprint left in the rocks like any distant fossil of history."

Pete tugged at Madge's hand. He pulled her over close to him on the couch. "A new world ahead, girl. Maybe we will find that it's all based on my pet theory of a twenty-eight day rhythm. We know that men and women and trees and water all flow in that deep rhythm of the returning moons. Why shouldn't sound and sight and even touch keep the same paces? If we find, Madge, that the battle of Marathon took place in the past on a day which is some multiple of twenty-eight days up to this day, then the tides of each part of the human race will start to run in new channels for us mortals."

"That's maybe true, Pete, but I can't help thinking how unimportant it makes us all. In this phonograph record that great general who turned back the Medes and the Persians, and that wealthy benefactor who endowed the culture of Greece, thought they would be known forever, but it turned out that the lad who raced to Athens from Marathon is the only one of the group who caught a little piece of immortality. He is the one who, never dreaming about it, is now remembered."

"That was true," said Pete, "until from the glass box undersea you picked them all back into now."

[201]

CHAPTER XXXII

THE VILLAGE OF CHELSEA

WE WALKED OVER ON SUNDAY through old Chelsea. During the war the water front seems different from the way it looked twenty-odd years ago when we lived on its edge. Chelsea, a neighborhood with sandy bottom, settled more than a century ago as a summer resort for old Manhattan, is still enough out of the way to have a flavor of its own. Before the pyramid for cliff dwellers known as London Terrace was erected, the houses on the 24th Street side had their little front lawns and gardens. Trees dotted the street. I'm sure that green grass and flowers and bushes do something to the people who live behind them. Chlorophyll, a mystery to man, may have some radioactive power that untenses him.

"The Chelsea Neighbors" was our version of a block friendliness which permeated the neighborhood. Mike (Boardman) Robinson, the artist, and Sally were a kind of rallying couple for the Welshes, the Joneses, the Blochs, and the rest of us. On only rare occasions did this small-town feeling erupt into noble and civic activity. When a cigarette factory a few blocks below was belching black smoke and cinders, Blanche Bloch and Margaret formed themselves into a committee of two and called on the august factory manager. They explained the law, the ease of prevention of the black clouds, and then, mild in manner, were peculiarly equipped to threaten the total and complete embargo of that brand of cigarettes by all the Chelsea Neighbors unless the nuisance was ended at once. And it was, thus giving us additional evidence of the power of consumer public opinion.

Above Chelsea, just a single block, one came upon one of the most dismal and despairing areas in all New York. Never a day went by but bug-ridden bed springs and mattresses were seen out in the gutter. Filth and hopelessness gave off a combined odor of resignation. The same families had lived there for years, never lifting up enough ambition to better their lives by moving to another street. The worst slums of the East Side had a twinkle compared to 25th Street between 9th and 10th avenues. The immigrants of our lower New York have an eye on the Bronx, and then the hope of moving down again to upper Broadway and eventually across Central Park to Park Avenue.

We live in an odd city. The river fronts should be the most popular and most expensive residential districts. Our island, which has lost its island flavor, has the Hudson, more beautiful than the Rhine, and the East River dotted with islands for vistas. But save for three or four courageous little sections the great East River is turned over to industry and slums and Riverside Drive is the avenue of boardinghouses. I'm delighted that cheap government housing developments are taking up the East River frontage.

Will we never learn that people will travel miles for decent living, to be near a tree or two? We still talk of further congesting Manhattan. If an insurance company or savings bank wants to go the Metropolitan Life one better, why not develop a truly large housing project on Staten Island? Beaches, bathing, woods, low rents, cheap land, green space between little houses, fashioned on the great English housing developments, are the potentials of Staten Island. Distance means nothing if people can get adequate living for low rents. Our middle class, with somewhat shorter work hours, is suburbanly proud of commuting for an hour into New Jersey or Westchester or Connecticut.

We made friends in the Chelsea Neighborhood, and permanent friends. Blanche and Allie Bloch, Marjorie Asch, the Robinsons and many others. Community or street friends are different from others. They bring to the relationship some-

[203]

thing of the value of a small town in the midst of all too big New York.

And now after two decades on 11th Street we know many neighbors. If their lights are on we ring and say hello. Few neighborhoods in New York have friendly lights.

Edna Ferber and many of our other friends wouldn't think of living downtown. They need Central Park for walking purposes. They are reservoir trampers.

I don't know why I never got the walking habit. Bowling and sailing give me my quota of muscle flexing, while shaving provides the equivalent daily minutes for contemplation. Even though I live within walking distance of my office, only once a year do I leg it up that mile and a half.

But in my youth I did my tramping. At the age of ten I walked from Keene, New Hampshire, across Vermont and back while summering at Camp Marienfeld, a near-nudist camp for boys. When sixteen, I walked from Connecticut across Massachusetts to Vermont. I can still feel the blisters on my feet. And then after freshman year at college, Art Mayer, a cousin in whose house I lived while my mother was sick out west, and I walked across Switzerland. With a rucksack we started at Zurich, climbed over the Rigi, the Furka-Grimsel Pass, the Simplon, and the Gemmi, all the way to Montreux where we swam off the Castle of Chillon. I remember much of this glamorous month of August in Switzerland, of lush honey and butter and rolls, and sunsets on glaciers, and simple people. At a cost of about $250 for ten weeks in Europe we lived less than extravagantly, except in Vienna, where we met my father, who without stating his reasons set us up with a room and *bath*. Vienna was sensitive and very unlike the way I saw it in 1922 during the peak of inflation. A memory of our tramp over the Semmering Pass also creates a mild nostalgia. While at Williams I climbed Greylock at least twice a year and once on snowshoes in winter. After college I canoed through the Adirondacks

[204]

before the days of cars on the portages. Yokes on shoulders and canoes on yokes made muscles and backs ache. But this was not tramping except between the lakes and rivers. And out in Yellowstone, Art and I again in the summer of 1910 rode horses through the park before autos were allowed on the roads. I had never ridden a horse before, and very little since. I never have learned the rhythm and my horseback riding still reminds me of some of the worst instruments of torture at Coney Island.

Just as perfumes have corrupted man's capacity to smell and so doomed one of the five senses, so also the automobile will have enduring effects on the development of man's leg muscles. What the radio will do to the ear of man no one can tell. It may well increase hearing capacity through mere interminable hours of use. And as for television, I can see the housewife of the future developing a normal wall-eyedness. How else can she clean pots and cook and sweep and still keep her eyes pinned on that portable television screen hung up in the kitchen every morning? What a field day the eye doctors will have as the human race departs from the matriculation period of movies once or twice a week to a doom of endless television in the home. Taste is also on the way out. Mass production of food, canned goods, and ultimately pills for sustenance.

Taste, smell, hearing and seeing, all will undergo revolutions—as part of the industrial revolution. Only touch will be kept in acute form and then man, overcompensating as usual, will develop more sensitive feelers.

Back to the old primitive, initial sense. It might still be fun. Let no one underestimate the sense of touch. Many foods are delectable, I think, because of texture rather than taste. Margaret likes the subtle ones, persimmon, alligator pear, palm salad. For my part I prefer baked potato peels, the heart of celery and the crisp outside of lamb or beef.

And as for feeling, my practice of the law in divorce cases alone convinces me that finger tips are far more important than words, on truly important occasions of life.

[205]

CHAPTER XXXIII

IT'S NO CRIME

I WAS LEAVING MY OFFICE. The night wire had been connected to my desk. The bell rang. On the other end was a troubled but tender woman's voice. It sounded past middle age. She would never tell me her name. She kept repeating that I would never know who she was. She wanted to see me. She was in trouble. Would I see her for a few minutes, and never try to find out who she was?

I thought, this is another one of the army of bedeviled people who constantly tramp toward every lawyer's office. But the voice was peculiarly soft and intriguing. I told her to come along.

Into my office walked with gentle step a gray-haired smallish lady, deep in her fifties or early sixties. In her hand she carried the current issue of *Harper's Magazine* and a neat uninitialed trim leather handbag. Her shoes were simple and sturdy. Her hat was a hat, not just a blossom or bow, becoming and uncostly.

She told me her troubles in rapid rhythm. Born in Russia, she had lived in New England for many years. A cultured happy existence, self-supporting, a schoolteacher in a private school, no wealth but no great desire for "things." First citizenship papers had been taken out. But now if there should be a war with Russia would she be put into a concentration camp or deported? She wanted an answer, yes or no.

It was a quite irrational inquiry. I tried to calm her down. There would be no such a war. Even if there were, the concentration camps would be clean and decent. There was nothing to worry about.

All my advice made no impression. She was deeply torn. I became increasingly inquisitive as to the real base for the profound disturbance in the gray-haired lady's mind.

To deflect the talk I picked up her magazine. There was an article on education. We discussed college entrance requirements and the default of our public school educational systems. After a long time I gained her confidence—or, at least, she was at ease.

"I don't want to know your name—but, tell me, why don't you complete your citizenship? You'll have no trouble in getting final papers. I'll be glad to help."

And then this poured out—poured in the sense of an overfull vessel gaining relief from pressure by overflow. Her cup of suffering rather than joy ran over.

"About a year ago I was leaving a department store in my home city. At the door a hand squeezed my arm. I still feel the finger tips. I looked down and saw that along with my purse I was carrying a small bottle of perfume. I must have taken it off the counter. I was arrested as a shoplifter. I went to jail. I gave another name. I've been in jail for months. I just got out. Not one of my friends knows anything about this. I've had to lie and lie and lie about where I've been. It's been horrible—even worse than the time I spent in prison.

"And so you see my problem. If I go to get my final citizenship papers they will ask me if I have ever been convicted of a crime. If I say yes, they will turn me down. If I say no, those same fingers will grab my arm again, and I'll be jailed for perjury. You never will see me again. You don't know my name or where I live. That's why I can tell all this to you. Please help."

The very telling had done her some good.

Some months previous to this talk I had represented a very rich woman who was accused of shoplifting. With a $90,000 a year income, she nevertheless had a habit of picking up vagrant little pieces of lace from store counters. She had bureau drawers stuffed with these samples and bits. At that time, I had made up my mind that this was no crime. It was a disease—an odd ailment. Surely our penologists and doctors must have the answer. There must be a wide medical distinction between the case of shoplifting for resale or use, and those other cases where there was lifting for no known purpose. I consulted my old friend, Dr. Menas Gregory, one of our leading psychiatrists in New York City. I went to Baltimore to interview the Johns Hopkins staff, and I read what literature I could find on the subject.

And so to this gray-haired stranger I could offer relief.

"You have had measles, haven't you?"

"Yes."

"You won't get it again, will you?"

I listed all the other infant diseases—chickenpox, mumps, whooping cough. I don't recall which she had experienced in her youth, but she got the point. She wouldn't get them again. She had had measles—once and for all. That was finished forever. This was my moment. "You have had shoplifting. You'll never get it again. It's a sickness."

I had learned enough from my rich lady's case to be sure and dogmatic. I explained how shoplifting, where people do not resell, is rather peculiar to women. We know little about this urge, but the established facts seem to indicate that it is often a concomitant of excessive masturbation or of menopause.

"You were going through change of life at the time, weren't you?" She cried tears of relaxation. She smiled through her tears. She opened her purse, took out two dollars, put them on my desk, puckered her lips as if she were throwing me a kiss. Her final handclasp was my real fee. I knew she was cured. She was whole and clean. Social stigma for a crime inexplicable was no longer scarring her mind and emotions.

Years later she dropped me a line without her name on it —signed: "Citizen of the U.S.A."

The gap between society's ignorant and cruel impact on citizens and the truths of science not yet divulged is the area of misery. And still we go on incarcerating shoplifters, homo-

[208]

sexuals, Lesbians and thousands of people whom we think of as deviators from the herd, people who need treatment and understanding instead of punishment and prison food.

It takes time for society to place in their proper pigeonholes the deviators from presumed mass behavior. It's too easy to condemn in big, broad, all-inclusive brackets. It's comfortable to feel superior by the condemnation of others. We boost ourselves by knocking others. It's less than respectable to delve too deeply into odd inner springs of human behavior, particularly if they relate to sexual mores. And the press—the great potential educator of us all—is timid and weak. Only recently was the word "syphilis" found in print or heard on the radio for the first time. Until these words are out in the open the mind of man seems incapable of tackling the problems which the taboo of the words relegates to ignorance. Venereal disease is not only curable but preventable—but we had no chance of doing much as long as the press enforced a silence on the subject. It's an insult for the newspapers still to use words like "statutory crime." It's a hopeful sign that in the recent filthy Lonergan scandal, spread out so fully in most newspapers, the word "homosexual" was actually set up in type for newspaper readers to read. Our defense of the Lesbian book, The Well of Loneliness, was a victory of some value, since the book was attacked not because of words but solely because it dealt with a theme which up to that time had been deemed obscene and corrupting.

The only essential obscenity in life is stealth, and cowardice and concealment. Life isn't black or white as Hollywood pictures it. Life is gray for most people. A girl in the pictures takes a drink—she must end up a sot. If she has an extra-marital or premarital affair she must be punished on the screen and converted into a whore. The penalty of sinning is suffering, says Hollywood. This just isn't true, thank God.

It's too easy to paint the two ends of the rainbow—leaving out the middle. But the films go still further, toying in tawdry fashion with the social borderlines of permissible sexual

[209]

behavior. Their test is: How close can we go without being jumped on by Will Hays? That, I submit, is filthy and obscene! To skirt up to the forbidden is childish indecency. It reduces the end product to the diet of a child, and develops an immature population inculcated with the idea that matters sexual are impure.

HAIRPINS AND NOSE-THUMBING

Hairpins. Those long-departed utensils of olden days now stand in this era of bobbed hair as horrible symbols of sexual misbehavior. Only recently a state board of movie censors ordered cuts in a film because hairpins were shown on the table of a bedroom. The sequence of the censor's mental stream that brought about the ban was naïve, dirty and simple. A girl with long hair should not take out her hairpins while boys are around. If the hairpins are on the table surely the hair is down, and no girl's hair is down with a male near by except for evil sexual purposes. Fantastic as this may seem, this was the basis of many movie cuts. Such are the hidden fears of censors.

Nose-thumbing—a practice not unknown to the youth of America—must carry connotations which were never explained to me, for sixteen elisions in movies were ordered in New York State alone in a single year for that type of communication.

In such fashion are our movies purified with the aid and connivance of the Hays office.

This kind of piffling control of movies goes on year after year in secret. No reports are made by state censors or by Will Hays of any details sufficient to let the public appraise the value of censorship of millions of feet of film each year. At times, in the rush of business, state troopers have been called in to doctor our movie diet. As long as censors operate in secrecy, there can be no public criticism of their efforts and hence no social corrections.

John Steinbeck had just received national praise for his

book and movie, *Grapes of Wrath*. With Burgess Meredith as commentator, and Herbert Kline as photographer, they created in 1941 a short semi-documentary film—*Forgotten Village*—a tale of the victory of modern medicine over witchcraft in a remote village of Mexico. The state censors in New York banned the picture. The great movie industry said nothing, and did nothing, having no interest in the principles of freedom from censorship.

The evil of the picture was supposed to lie in a short scene depicting a Mexican mother in the pains of childbirth, and another short shot showing a baby nursing at a mother's breast. Few cases are ever fought, because the big companies would rather trade with the censor than irritate him by a contest. Once in a while an independently produced picture raises a censorship controversy. In *Forgotten Village* the Board of Regents reversed the state censor. As far as I have been able to learn this is the only case in recent years in which this has happened.

To this day I don't know what was feared in this beautiful picture. Since when is a nursing baby an obscene sight? Does the censor never go to Coney Island Beach or see nursing mothers in our subways? Is it possible that scenes condoned in public places become so objectionable if put on celluloid film? For years female waist-up nudity has appeared in the movies. Pictures of the South Seas societies have had great kudos. The *National Geographic Magazine* does not put scarves on Pacific Island women. I had always thought that the censor was only worried about white breasts. Brown breasts—representing unreality—had previously raised no censor qualms. Was a Mexican woman too close to the Bowery? Maybe the censor wanted all breasts covered and why not start with this Mexican peasant woman? The childbirth scene showed no portion of the actual birth; the mother was fully clad in all her agony. Is it possible that this peculiarly human pain is more corrupting than all the torture shown in movies—torture often manufactured out of artificial, purposeful sadism?

Hundreds of educators and writers mailed violent protests to the censors. Steinbeck, a giant in our field of letters, was to be branded obscene, and a corrupter of youth.

After we left the hearing the state censor was charming and friendly. Steinbeck went into his private office. The kindly censor wanted a favor. Would Steinbeck enter his autograph in an album the censor owned? This pleasant fellow—the controller of our film diet—was collecting autographs of all authors of censored films. Of course he himself couldn't be corrupted by *Forgotten Village*. He was worrying about the rest of us. I never yet have met a person who would admit he was being hurt by a picture or a book. They are always concerned for the other fellow.

MASTER OF REVELS

Of all the titles given in history to a government official the one that delights me most is "Master of the Revels." In the days of Henry VIII of England when vagabond players were deemed little more than vehicles for the increase of the plague or as magnets for pickpockets, the king appointed a master of the revels to control the embryo circuit-riding theater.

But today we still have masters of the revels. Paul Moss, commissioner of licenses under Mayor LaGuardia, wields the guillotine in New York's theaters. It takes a certain amount of presumption to dictate to producers just how much leg or breast may be shown. This one-man jury has far greater power than a judge or a jury of twelve. He has the capacity to threaten, to frighten. He can cause expense to a producer. He can refuse to issue a permit for a play. He can darken a theater. Seldom does he dare issue a summons and complaint. That is too democratic. It gives the theater a trial and a chance to be heard.

For some odd reason Moss and the Mayor of New York are worried about the word "burlesque." They have issued a ukase that the word "burlesque" may not be used in New

[212]

York. Under any other name, gyrations, bumps and grinds may wend their weary paths on the stages of Broadway. And do.

I don't particularly enjoy burlesque—a continuous vaudeville playing on the sexual motifs, and usually in very trite, repetitious innuendoes and double-entendre. However, millions of people—mostly men—get fun at such shows. There is no evidence that these spectacles increase crime. In fact, certain studies would indicate that the closing down of such performances tends to increase public sexual misbehavior. Maybe our society needs vicarious outlets, the Greek notion of katharsis through drama.

In 1942 the Mayor and Moss jumped on burlesque. I've attended other improper bureaucratic hearings before government officials, but never did I believe that a quasi-judicial officer could tyrannize as does Paul Moss. He refused a license for Mr. Isidor Herk's burlesque show at the Gaiety Theater, on Broadway. The lower court sustained the Commissioner; and unfortunately the expense of an appeal—which Moss well understood—caused Herk to drop the case.

It was in this case that the great City of New York proffered the filthiest suggestion I have ever heard. "Let only one breast be bare" was the compromise offer—which Mr. Herk rejected.

True, the continuance of that particular show was not necessary for the people of our city; we could survive without it. But many of our leading writers and actors were outraged at the exercise of such power by a Commissioner of Licenses. Protests were filed. Great fighters for freedom such as Russel Crouse and Howard Lindsay of "Life With Father" fame gave a midnight dinner to the burlesque actors and actresses thrown out of work by Moss. It was a gay but pathetic evening. Only today I read that Herk died after spending some months in jail.

My main interest was in the hypocrisy of our administration of the law. The same sexually provocative material, dressed up in more expensive costumes, and portrayed by better-groomed female bodies, was being presented at $4.40 and up, in many theaters and night clubs in New York. Admission to burlesque was about 50 cents a ticket, so we had one law for the poor and another for the rich.

This pattern of snobbery shows up wherever there is a censor. Books selling at $10 a volume are seldom attacked, but let the same words and pictures be bound in paper at 35 cents, and down pounce the censors. Is the theory back of such deviation in policy that the rich can't be corrupted, or are they already so far gone that it's not worth-while trying to save them? Moreover, when the producers of entertainment for poor people are attacked, most of the respectable elements in the community take a little joy in turning up their noses and saying, "It's shabby. It's not art. It's not worth defending. It's bad taste."

In historic terms no single piece of suppressed material is worth defending for its own sacred self. Life would have gone on pretty much the same if Shaw's *Mrs. Warren's Profession* had remained closed, if *Huckleberry Finn* had been removed from all library shelves, or if Zorn's etchings of nude bathers had been finally denied admission to our shores.

The greatest difficulty I experience in defense of writings is the automatic reaction of newspaper owners and of many authors who refuse to dirty their pens by defending tawdry material. And still, unless each case is fought, there is no telling how much further the censor might go in his rampage. The mere existence of the ever-watchful Dramatists' Guild, for whom we have acted on many occasions, is not enough to cope with stage censors when little men are placed in too great positions of power. Indeed, the job of censor is too great for any man.

CHAPTER XXXIV

,

HE WANTED FACTS

I SPOKE TO MORGAN BRAINARD this morning. He is an anomaly as a president of an insurance company—Aetna Life. He has more humor than most big businessmen—simple, quixotic and truly a Peck's Bad Boy. I never hear from Morgan Brainard without thinking of Tim Westbrook, a very close friend of mine for thirty years. Tim affected both our lives. Tim—handsome, quiet, with an adventurous mind —was never in doubt about the Nazi peril even though he lived among many who thought we could stay out of the war. It was Tim who understood the New Deal whether he agreed with all of it or not. He had a real influence on the Aetna Life Insurance Company, of which he was a high official until his death last year.

It was five years after I had left college that I got to know Westbrook. In fact, he had only enough money for one year at Williams, but he kept up with the class at reunions and all other gatherings and in time became a permanent trustee of the college. As a freshman he was a big shot: president of the class, football player, and a member of a very swank fraternity —all of which created a gulf between us. My own fraternity at that time a local, later to become Phi Gamma Delta, was the home of rather serious and not too well-dressed young-sters. But in later years I was his closest friend from college days. Seldom did he come to New York from Hartford with-out dropping in for dinner. We worked many a night on the problem of the insurance companies' ownership of farms and mortgages at the time when the farmers of the nation were going bankrupt. Tim was the driving force in the vision which led to a policy of not selling farms which could not pay their way. Aetna pioneered in many respects in working its own farms. When a purchaser for a farm bobbed up, Tim would say, "There is no use in selling you this farm at any price. With all our advantageous buying of seed and cattle and machinery we haven't broken even on it as yet. If we sold it to you we would have to foreclose in a short time."

He had a subtle, student mind, of the kind that played with nuances, akin to his skill at the piano. I remember once I introduced him to Randolph Paul, then counsel to the Treasury Department and our leading socially minded tax expert. We were concerned about the insurance companies' stake in potential inflation and their seeming lack of philosophy or leadership to help stem a rising tide of cost of living. Tim had, like most heads of big business, favored the sales tax. Paul sent him some data on the subject and Tim promptly wrote back—how easy it was to take positions without objective facts and knowledge. He had changed his mind but also did what is so rare in the human race, admitted he had been wrong. This was typical of him.

I had one great avocation in common with Tim. He was an enthusiastic amateur carpenter. He built with his own hands a beautiful house way up in the wilds of the Salmon River, in Connecticut.

All through his life he was growing. His interests were expanding. Housing, taxation, health—in his own way he was working out a planned economy. I forgive him that he didn't like sailing as did Chan, his wife. His fear of water was like mine of precipices. But he had great physical courage. He had been a stout soldier. His volume of letters written when he was in the AEF in 1918, which I resented when it came out, was nearer right in its attitudes than was I in the late twenties. I had still too little imagination to foresee a Hitler and a paranoiac Germany. I had hoped we might spend money on schools instead of gunpowder.

During the last year of his life Margaret and I sensed that Tim was dying. I'm sure he was aware but never let on.

Modest, quiet in pain, he worked up to the end on the new science researches which would put an end to cancer, his own catastrophe.

CHAPTER XXXV

CHEAP INSURANCE

I PAID MY INSURANCE PREMIUM today for fire, theft and burglary on my home on 11th Street. It was twenty years ago that I first represented some of the Lloyd's Underwriting groups in England. At that time, I studied casualty and fire insurance rates and can't understand why any person who can get a policy at Lloyd's, London, should dream of insuring in any American company. The rates are at present just about one-third of the American rates, and you get more coverage and have it all in one simple policy which even a layman can understand.

Lloyd's is so efficient that a mere tariff wall does the American companies no good. They need a complete embargo in order to prevent Lloyd's competition. Hence in many states the American insurance companies pressed through legislation which makes it a crime to write a Lloyd's policy. The great argument made by American companies is that Lloyd's pays no taxes here, nor does it keep a fund on deposit with the superintendent of insurance in any state. Since the war, however, a fund of more than $30 million has been established, and as for the tax as a competitive factor, the argument is specious since the taxes in England have always been much higher than in the United States.

The absurdity of the American position is made clear when one realizes that much of the insurance written in the United States by our domestic companies is reinsured with British groups. The American companies would rather give up 90 per cent of their profit by reinsurance in England than face the competition of English companies going to American householders at rates one-third or one-half of theirs. It would appear that the British insurance companies are safe enough for American companies but not for American consumers.

The reason for the Lloyd's policy being so much better and cheaper lies in a direction far removed from taxes or deposits. It results from the fact that in England the Lloyd's Underwriters are interested primarily in insurance, while in our country the insurance companies are really investment trusts with the directors more concerned with investment of the premiums than in reducing the costs of insurance.

I'm always amused at the leading insurance officials when they urge the supreme values of competition, absence of government regulations, and the importance of unrestrained private enterprise. The truth is that they fear rather than relish competition, invoke governmental sanctions to wipe it out, and are for free enterprise only for others, not for themselves.

Some years ago while in England I bought a Burberry coat for about $50, or ten of those mythical guineas. When I came back I wore it down to the old Federal Court House one day when I was arguing some cause before the Circuit Court of Appeals. I hung the coat in the neat little outer coatroom of this great old court. When I came out it was missing. I wrote to Mr. Malyon, my gentle agent in England, explained the loss, and said I didn't know whether my policy covered such a loss, but if so, I thought $35 would be a fair adjustment since I had worn the garment a few months. The reply came promptly: "We also are not sure your policy covers this loss, but enclosed find $35 because such a loss could not happen in a British court room."

In the United States we are facing a period of reappraisal of all our insurance concepts. In 1906, Charles Evans Hughes, as counsel to a New York investigatory committee, urged that no life insurance company be permitted to have a worth of over half a billion dollars. Now the Metropolitan Life exceeds

$5 billion, and five companies together have assets in excess of $15 billion, and over 50 per cent of all life insurance company assets. This creates perils in many directions. Charles Evans Hughes warned of such "despotic powers." These funds crying for investment affect our basic theory of free enterprise in our financial markets and underwritings. One company collects as much money each year in New York alone as is required to run the governments of twenty states.

The evil of such power is not diminished because most of the life companies are co-operative—without stockholders. The mutualization of insurance companies is something of a snare and a delusion, particularly in the case of the giants, which are so big that the incumbent directors are virtually self-perpetuating. No outsiders could afford to circularize millions of policyholders for proxies. One company claims 28½ million policyholders. Moreover, the expansion of social security cuts into insurance concepts, and high inheritance tax rates will make million dollar policies unprofitable in the future. The complexities of forty-eight state regulatory bodies lead many to favor federal incorporation and controls, and the Supreme Court has recently written the introduction to much new thinking in this direction by Congress. The business of insurance at last is held to be within the monopoly laws of the nation. We are on the verge of new attitudes in regard to insurance of all types. Maybe insurance companies should be limited to areas of operations by carrying on into insurance the concept of Federal Reserve districts for banks. Then they would be less than giants.

Lloyd's Insurance has a warm spot in my affections, not only because of its glamorous historic background, and the unique structure which permits it to operate without vice-presidents sitting behind dozens of glass-topped desks. It was good to us, for during a period of nearly ten years I was asked to sail over to England for conferences on legal matters nearly every year. On a Thursday I'd get my cable to come over. I'd call up Maggie: "What are you doing this weekend?" No matter what the answer, I'd say, "Get ready.

We sail on the *Olympic* tomorrow night." We lived on 24th Street between 9th and 10th avenues in Old Chelsea, so it was practically like walking to the corner for a streetcar to go to the docks.

Off we'd go, usually in the late fall or winter. A week's work in London and then a spree of a week, driving down through the Wye Valley to Aberystwyth, Wales, or to Oban, Scotland, or, after a flight to Paris, a week along the Saint-Michel coast and on to Cherbourg.

I'm not much at sightseeing. I've had my fill of churches and museums and art galleries. A picture here or a statue there excites me. But what I'm keen for is a short automobile trip—small car, drive ourselves of course, charting a course as we go along—seeing the countryside, enjoying the alien foods and idioms and manners; getting a feel of another and different civilization.

Once on returning by plane from Puerto Rico to Miami in 1934, Roger was with us. We landed in Florida on a hot night. Seated at an outdoor sidewalk restaurant Roger, then about nine years old, looked over the menu and turning to the waitress said, "What is your native drink?"

It's a good question in any city of the world.

LETTERS FROM ROGER

Today two letters came from Roger; he's on his way, this summer of 1944, to England to join the great crusade. I never quite enjoyed my kids as babies. A bad upbringing, I imagine. Maybe the idea that it was sissy to enjoy babies. I'm sorry now. I missed something. Of Roger I was a trifle jealous. I didn't want to share Margaret. But when Roger first sailed a boat alone at the age of seven he was mine and I was his. We've had great fun together ever since. There are few people I'd rather dine and drink with. These two letters seem to me to have a neat quality for a kid of nineteen on a crowded transport, particularly for a lad who is tough, with good work habits and real ambition:

[220]

I'll try V-Mail and see how fast it is in relation to Air-Mail. We are still at sea, and pleasantly so. The weather is superb, clear, blue and windswept. I've finished "Lord Jim." Conrad comes closer to expressing reality (in feelings) than any author I can think of now. He is a master of the pattern. He winds and winds the thread of his plot within itself, he makes a simple statement on one page and picks it up, a hundred pages later. Do you remember the expression he has regarding the occasional lifting of the veil of obscurity which shrouds mankind? This is, next to Gibran's "Prophet," the most lucid explanation or description I've come across yet. We experience only a few hours a week (or a year) of true illumination, of true vision, of true understanding and appreciation. Conrad has seen this—which most people do not ever see, and has written about it convincingly. That in itself is a difficult task to accomplish. What would you suggest I read next of Conrad's? I'm quite impressed by him. He seems to have achieved something only a very few other authors have. W. H. Hudson, Virginia Woolf (perhaps) and maybe a couple of others have got the same quality he has.

Letters as a means of communication can be used in any number of ways. One can write only so much chit-chat at one time, and then must wait until more small things have passed before writing again. The letter has, as one of its qualities, the attributes of an essay. It should be complete and alone. It should produce a style effect. (The non-chit-chat letter, that is).

I've not seen many Italian soldiers, or 2nd generation Italians since Greensboro. There are some with us now. Their position is again impressed on my mind. In the confluence of personalities, I seem to be well liked by them (future political advantage), but they have such troubles, such conflicts; inferiority, superiority, bravado and bravura, warmth and steely coldness. Such unreasonableness and great cleverness. They are further complicated by the Church, which has done little to help them solve these problems. Of course, they alone can solve them for themselves. But the Church might have given guidance. If the American-Italians are carrying the psychological makeup of the Italian-Italians, I can understand the "on the fence" and two-faceted policy of Italy—Let me know what you think?

[221]

Only once did Roger and I ever get into a fight, and that was just as we left Northeast Harbor in Maine on the way down east toward Winter Harbor. A high sea was running. We both love rough weather sailing. It is a challenge. Deep down we know nature can always lick us. I don't remember what the argument was about. It probably was the question of who was running the ship—single authority or divided. Probably Roger was nearer right in wanting to come-about. At least I imagine I must have been wrong for I never get stiff unless I'm at fault. But, like most people, I seldom admit error at the time. Only long after, when all alone shaving, do I confess to myself. This by itself is ample reason for not growing a beard.

Now Roger is in London, getting tougher and angrier per robot. He's near enough to see Connie at the OWI station where she pumps short-wave broadcasts to the Continent. He's never been overseas before. He'll love the inner warmth and outer reserve of the British. He received in the Army Specialized Training Program a great education and will be further enriched abroad. He wanted to be a member of the Bar someday but the war may make it impossible, and he may shift to being a civil servant—helping run the government.

In the meanwhile, with Roger in the army, many of my friends are commenting on the fact that I look better dressed —gayer ties, sportier shirts, better-fashioned suits. I send all these compliments to Roger—who turned his wardrobe over to me.

CHAPTER XXXVI

HUM IT IN YOUR MOUTH

ENGINES ARE NO FRIENDS of mine. We just don't understand each other. Long ago I was tempted to buy an old Ford engine, take it apart and put it together again. Nothing short of that would reduce my heartbeats when an engine starts to die, sputters or fails to start. All I've learned is that engines on boats like to sleep late in the morning. They resent being toyed with before sunrise. They must be nursed and fondled before 8:00 A.M.

My heroes in life include the red-haired boy at the garage who looks at an engine, pulls out a wrench, touches a bolt and there she is, cured and wholesome. I beg him often to tell me how he diagnoses the ailment. He says he does not know, or at least he has not the language needed to let me in on the secret. Laurie Greenbaum has the same intuitions for anything made of metal—radiators, radios, pumps and engines. Sophie Buckner's garden in Sconset is the result of Sophie's finger magic. Other people with the same seeds and soil cannot do what she does. It's a kind of modern witchcraft of nature through finger tips.

Another object of envy is Leo Rosen's daughter, Elizabeth, who at the age of four could listen to several pieces of music played on the piano at her play school and then, on reaching home four hours later, sit down (without any instruction) and reproduce the tunes. At six she was able to add bass accompaniments. A classmate asked her one day, "How do you do it?" Elizabeth answered, "I hear it in my ear, then I hum it in my mouth. And then I play it with my fingers."

This reminds me that Margaret tells of a kid at school

who painted wonderful pictures of horses. When asked how he could remember details of horses' anatomy with such accuracy, he replied, pointing to his drawing paper, "There on the paper I see the horse, and all I do is paint around it."

These are the traits and people I envy. I find them all through life. Ted Husing senses a football play before the signal is given. He tells me it's simple—just mathematical probabilities. I don't believe him. Adolph Ochs, naïve and direct, "knew" the press, and Zeb Tilton the ocean currents, but they couldn't tell others the secret. Jim Farley had it for politics until his ambition got in the way and mussed up his judgment.

But of all the magicians I know, Jerome Frank, now a judge of the Circuit Court of Appeals, is the surest. He has the keenest, most exciting legal mind I've ever met. And yet, on top of all his knowledge of law, science, philosophy and economics, he has an intuitive feel for the solution of social problems. There may be other lawyers of more reading and greater factual accumulation, but none that I have met can jump over as many intermediate steps in thinking through a problem and plump right down on the conclusion. I'm quite sure that Jerry's selflessness reduces the infinite number of obstacles which block most of us in our thinking. His id, or whatever psychoanalysts call it this year, never stands in the way of his mental machine. Jerry's important book, *Law and the Modern Mind*, might well be followed by a volume interpreting judges, not only in relation to their past economic and environmental upbringing but touching on the relation of generosity of emotion to free wheeling in the field of thought.

Of course, the genius of our day is Franklin D. Roosevelt. Scarcely a week goes by without our witnessing some flash of his mind. His equipment is the essence of true invention. He creates more than political gadgets or exciting improvements. He improvises, leaping across mental gaps and emotional ravines which frighten most of us away from thought or emotion. Newton's deduction from a falling apple in the field of science is akin to the President's many concepts in the field of international political science such as "Lend-Lease." The greatest lawyers of the land would have shied off the idea. How can you lend a bullet that can't be returned? Who ever heard of leasing food which will be eaten?

Without such flashes we might have lost the war. We were a divided nation, subject to easy bogging down in the jetsam of old ideas of the last war's unpaid debts. Without aid to England, that island might have been overtaken, and with England gone, the Republican party, close to a majority in Congress, would no doubt have sat at a friendly table with Hitler and his gang.

These minds that flash are rare among sophisticated people, and few who have the knack are ever tense no matter how excited they become. Years ago I had the only dream I fully remember. It was in a dentist's chair, after imbibing some kind of gas. I dreamed of a contest between races or cultures or societies. They were mildly personified. The competition went on until the finals were being run off. Two top cultures were still in the race. One was far superior to the other in the quality which spells perfection. I have no recollection of the standards for prize winning which the vague judges established. But the more perfect of the two contestants lost out. The decision went to the other culture because, and only because, it did not consciously know that there was a competition going on. The merest knowledge of the competitive spirit was a defect so dire as to overbalance all other traits.

That's why sailing is swell for barristers and solicitors.

CHAPTER XXXVII

THE RIGHT OF PRIVACY

LOVE, FRIENDSHIP, DEVOTION, professional advice, even services of a public nature are usually shared experiences. Only those human relations touching in an impersonal way large groups of people or flows of society may with comfort be put on paper. This isn't a matter of shame or squeamishness. Even in the areas of public service, where I have been lucky enough to be called upon for legal chores and personal errands for people high in government, the tasks are not mine to write about, and the mere relating would often imperil the effectiveness of the efforts. Solitary anonymity may be a matter of taste or insecurity or lack of vanity, but the valuable memories of most people are far from hermitical.

Back in 1890, Louis D. Brandeis wrote with Samuel Warren an article in the *Harvard Law Review* on the Right of Privacy. This was in the days when newspapers still held strong editorial positions and had not yet abdicated to columns of personality dope stories. But Louis Brandeis was urging further impairment on the right to comment on personal lives, particularly of people who had not thrown themselves into the arena of public comment, and even of those who invite public kudos—an opera singer or an athlete, for example. Brandeis and Warren would have limited the right of the press in comment on personal, home and matrimonial lives. They preached the gospel of a right of privacy.

For my part I prefer a society where the snooping is less flagrant than in these days in the U.S.A. The New York *Daily News* ran about 3,000 column inches of photographs and the New York *Times* ran 528,300 words on the Hall-Mills murder case. Entire forests are cut down to run gossip stories of impending pregnancies andor divorces. But if there is a choice between restraining this kind of peekhole business, searching into the lives of people, or permitting outrages on privacy with no holds barred, I would favor no legal restraints whatever. Rather let innumerable people suffer by cruel and often malicious and untrue gossip columns than try to draw a line of freedom for the press, a line which inevitably would limit the pen of authors, and in turn the material out of which the social history of an era is recorded. Decent limits must be developed by a folkway, not imposed by the state. We cannot overlook the fact that the American public has chosen Walter Winchell as the commentator on air and in print with greatest popular acceptance.

I'm thankful that our libel laws are not so outrageously strict as those of the British. Despite the symbol of Hyde Park, London, we in the U.S.A. have far greater freedom of press than have the people in England, where libel threats put a check on all reporting and much creative writing. We also have drawn a cleaner line between libel and unlawful invasion of privacy.

Only recently a dramatic and pathetic case involving privacy came to my desk. A couple of parents had nearly ruined the life of their child by giving publicity to all his attainments. It was an interesting story of our times, of some value to educators but painful to the youngster. Years later a writer was interested in what had become of this lad. A checkup was made, and the result of the inquiry printed. Once more the object of inquiry was caused discomfort. For decades he had tried to forget his limelighted youth. He wanted desperately to get out of the goldfish bowl into which his parents had tossed him. He sued, entirely apart from libel, or the truth or falsity of the article, on the ground that he had a personal right to privacy. Society had no right to write about him. Here was a case of emotional hurt of an individual who wanted to be let alone. But this hurt must be weighed against the right of society to read, to learn, to know. And who is brash enough to think he can draw the line between valuable and valueless information? As long as enough different people own printing presses and have access to the public mind, the public choice of values is a wiser criterion than the judgment of any transient judge or temporary postal official or political state movie censor.

Another force of society in the direction of limiting the right of people to read is the hangover of the idea that an author's letters belong to the sender and not to the receiver. The receiver may read the letter, he may donate it to a library, he may even sell the autograph, but he may never publish. It's high time that this conception of the receiver's rights be redefined. What if I discover a letter written by Oliver Cromwell or George Washington? Must I search out their heirs to get permission to publish?

A most important and acute case of this nature involves the Emily Dickinson poems and letters which have been withheld for decades from public enjoyment. Thought by many to be the greatest of American poets, this recluse from Amherst is still an intriguing enigma for all those who are excited about the deft symbolism of this woman who lived alone but was never lonely. Emily Dickinson was first introduced to me by the poet Genevieve Taggard and I'm thankful for the introduction. I've read the biographies of Dickinson written by Taggard, Whicher and Pollett. I'm persuaded that George Whicher comes nearest the truth. But with much material withheld from publication by heirs, the story is not yet fully told. I've long believed that the property right of Emily Dickinson's descendants, the profit motive of her distant heirs, will be brushed aside by courts in favor of an overriding public interest. This must develop to be the law, at least in cases where the author is dead and has left no instructions for publication or caveat against publication. And then by statute or judge-made law we will have to put limits even on material prohibited from publication by the original authors. For my part, I would give no rights of privacy to the writings of any person, since an author should take the risk that those to whom he sends his material will respect his wishes. Moreover, authors always have the privilege not to write and mail letters. There is no law which insists that they write, or that they may not destroy.

DON'T WRITE THAT

For years I have been concerned with our libel laws. They are far more than a technique of society for preventing false and hurtful statements from being issued. They represent the constant pinpricking of boundaries between protecting a single human being and the desire of society as a whole for knowledge, whether true or false.

An appraisal, in anthropological terms, might be made of various societies by tracing the statements thought at any one time to be gratuitously hurtful without any compensations for society as a whole. "He is the head of a family" might cause ostracism in a matriarchal land, and still a particular state may think it wise to allow such accusations to be fully made in order that the mouths of the people shall not be frozen tight in the necessary appraisals of men who try to rule the roost.

In our own land, as crimes and misdemeanors changed, our area of libel shifted concurrently. At the time of the formation of the nation, there were dozens of antisocial acts punishable by death and many then crimes have literally evaporated entirely.

Years ago I helped get out a pamphlet entitled lugubriously: "Blue Laws and Fool Laws—Anile and Senile." I thought it about time that our legislature repealed outdated criminal statutes, even though in our mores we seem to prefer nullification and disregard to reappraisal and revision. Ralph Waldo Emerson urged nullification. It's still the people's reluctant but inescapable answer to the social lag created by legislators.

In 1931, when our study was published, it was a crime to discover, without reporting it, Captain Kidd's treasure, and in 1944 it still is. Of course to have horse races within one mile of a court calls for a dire sentence.

To accuse one falsely of a crime is said by lawyers to be libelous per se. In reality, the rule of law that accusations of crime untruthfully made are libelous no longer stands up. Accusations of having committed crimes are not always hurtful. Our so-called list of crimes is so fantastic that people are at times even proud of being law violators. At this period in our social growth it is scarcely hurtful to say of a woman, "She overhead a conversation on a bus," even though to eavesdrop in a public place at times is a crime in certain states.

My partner, Alexander Lindey, and I wrote a layman's book on libel and slander addressed particularly to editors and publishers, called *Hold Your Tongue*. It had a small but admiring group of users as judged by letters, many years after publication, from lawyers, writers, teachers and jurists. The fashions in libel change as do women's hats.

Recently a most perplexing additional area of possible libel has arisen in cases where persons are called Communist, Fascist, or pre-war Nazi—that is, where the libel concerns a state of mind. When a prominent labor leader wanted to sue because he was unjustly called a Communist I was tempted to take on his cause because a labor leader might lose his job or be unable to get another if the rank and file of workers believed such a charge. On the other hand, the Communist party being a secret and underground movement, wider latitude must of necessity be allowed for labeling people as members thereof. This secrecy of membership rolls, in fact, is one of the great advantages of totalitarian movements. Thus can decent people be tainted and democracy be stained and confused. There is no easy and sure way of proving or disproving membership in a secret organization, since the records of such an entity would not be believed, and Earl Browder or Gerald L. K. Smith, under oath, would not be persuasive to a jury. If membership is difficult to prove, what about an accu-

[230]

sation of mere "state of mind" as a basis of prohibited libelous writings?

This problem of the labeling of people's mental states came to acute attention in connection with the accusation, in Pearson and Allen's "Washington Merry-Go-Round" column, that Congressman Sweeney, of Ohio, was in effect anti-Semitic. This wasn't the charge, but the Congressman so interpreted the column. The Congressman could show no hurt. Even if he lost his seat in Congress, as he did, it's scarcely good proof to ascribe the fact to the spread of that belief; for in this odd land he may even pick up votes from bigots. In most states—for libel is ordinarily a state behavior problem—it was held to be nonlibelous to call a man anti-Semitic or anti-Catholic, or pro-Fascist or anti-Fascist. If untrue, of course, it could cause pain, but certainly in the case of public officials who have put themselves forward for approval or disapproval, the public need of wide freedom of comment overbalances the possible offsetting hurt to individual officeholders. Moreover, legislators have the franking privilege and immunity from libel charges. They can attack without danger of being sued. They should be tough-skinned.

Not originally associated with the Sweeney cases—about fifty cases were brought in the lower courts of many states —I was asked to argue the case in the United States Supreme Court on the constitutional ground implicit in the throttling of such comment. I had tough sledding, particularly when I urged that, since there was no protection for minority groups, such as Jews, Catholics and the like, there being no suit permissible for a libel of a large group, these minorities should have preserved for them the right to slug back in verbal terms. Otherwise they were defenseless against the onslaughts of bigots.

It was said by some that it might even be hurtful in certain areas to be untruthfully called a Jew or Catholic or atheist, as it is when a white person is called a Negro in southern communities. This analogy confused the issue still further. In an adult society there should be no such thing as hurt or benefit by being a Jew or Catholic or nonbeliever in any religion. Those personal ways of life, however, still carry absurd significance in elections, appointments to office, and in cases of employment. A hangover, I suppose, from the days when the church was the state and heresy the historical ancestor of present-day sedition and treason.

In the Sweeney case the highest court came down with a tie vote, 4 to 4, as if it were a baseball game called on account of darkness. This problem of tie votes and failure even to get quorums on the Supreme Court bench has been increasingly accented since so many former attorney generals now sitting as judges have felt it necessary to disqualify themselves in cases they had previously touched while in office. Although less than a dozen cases are so affected in any year, nevertheless there are several methods now being considered for resolving this blind alley of our jurisprudence.

We should not overlook the great service Pearson and Allen rendered by defending these wholesale suits, brought, mostly, on a contingency basis by lawyers for Congressman Sweeney against innumerable papers in many states. It was much like the libel disease of James Fenimore Cooper, who brought more than a dozen suits, won all but one, and ended up out of pocket.

But the possibility of putting some paper or columnist out of business by this kind of mass libel suit financial burden is not to be laughed off. There are forces in our society to whom the funds are available, and this technique of annoyance—even if all cases by the plaintiffs are lost—is not without value to those who fear the press.

For years I have urged the adoption of a minor reform in the field of libel. If a newspaper or magazine, for example, prints a statement believed to be libelous and untrue, the injured person should have the right to demand retraction in the same space and with the same emphasis as the original article. If such retraction is published, then no libel suit should lie unless malice can be proved as to the original charge. If no retraction is made, then malice should be presumed. The paper should get ample time, say thirty days, to check up its error, if any.

Something along these lines would increase the protection for individuals, provide a corrective machinery, and relieve the press of many suits. At least one state has adopted a program of this nature.

Now that our press is in the hands of very few men, who in turn have increasingly wide circulation for their properties, no adequate relief is found in a money judgment rendered in a court many years later. This is peculiarly true because practically the entire press refuses to run stories of libel cases except those involving such important persons that it cannot be avoided. But if a magazine with a circulation of millions libels a person, the best cure seems to me to have the same paper run the correction promptly and not sandwiched in with some ads in the back pages of a much later issue.

The press has shown no evidence of leadership or social concern with the problem. I wish more owners of papers would study the life pattern of old man Scripps. When he was arrested for drunken driving, or blackmailed by some dame, he saw to it that, under his concept of a free press, meaning a brave press, the stories were run in his own paper. I wish I had known Scripps.

CHAPTER XXXVIII

G-MAN

AN OFFICIAL WHO HAS ACUTELY AFFECTED our way of life, through the kids growing up, is J. Edgar Hoover. I've known him for less than ten years but have had an increasing admiration for him and his staff. I started with suspicions. I listened to the blank, indiscriminate attacks on him by my Civil Liberties friends. It was fitting that that fringe should be on guard. A national police force carries implicit dangers within itself. But after listening to repeated assaults on the FBI at meetings of liberals, I took the time to look into the facts. Since 1926 the FBI has recorded more than 100,000 convictions, with a record of over 95 per cent of all cases brought to trial—a higher percentage by far than that of the headlined crime-buster Tom Dewey. In all these cases the record of protecting civil liberties is most significant. No duress, no holding incommunicado, no rubber hose, no third degree—practices common to the police of most big cities.

At the time when there was agitation for permitting wire tapping despite the Holmes-Brandeis opinions in the Olmstead and other cases in the Supreme Court, Hoover suggested to Attorney General Robert Jackson that Judge Ferdinand Pecora or I should make an investigation and report. As early as 1928 the regulations of the FBI specifically prohibited wire tapping, but the old Prohibition Bureau of Investigation had permitted it. Hoover believed that, given the power of indiscriminate wire tapping, investigators would ultimately stoop to the level of the crooks themselves. If Dewey had only learned that much, New York City would be relieved not only of wire tapping but of a recent and more threatening development—public disclosure of information procured over tapped wires as practiced by District Attorney Hogan, Dewey's chosen successor.

I am convinced that wire tapping other than by federal officials is unconstitutional and in violation of federal statutes, since the Congress included interstate communication within the federal field of control, and since telephone lines have been declared to be interstate in essence. Someday soon this issue will be tested in the Supreme Court by a person indicted or convicted as a result of the invasion of his privacy by wire tapping.

Hoover has been properly concerned about American Communists and Fascists, and has to stand silent while reporters, disregarding the facts—as did I. F. Stone so recently

—continue to spread less than the truth about the FBI. Invariably such critics confuse the record of the FBI with that of other government agencies. Stupid questions about reading the *Nation*, membership in the A.C.L.U. and the like are asked about persons desiring government jobs, but I have yet to see documented and proved a single case where such nonsense was asked by Hoover's men. Liberals can't procure reforms by attacking, under pseudonyms, the wrong governmental agencies. It reminds me of George Seldes' attack on Dorothy Thompson, based on a newspaper column which careless Seldes thought was written by Thompson, but in fact was written by Walter Lippmann. Seldes did not even apologize for, as he said, the Lippmann and Thompson columns were both printed in the *Herald Tribune* and hence easily confused!!

The assaults on Hoover, which became most violent at the time of the simultaneous arrests in Detroit in the Spanish Loyalist Communist passport mill conspiracy case, do not stand up in the eyes of anyone desirous of looking at the complete record. In all the kidnaping cases only one charge of violation was made, and that was disproved by the phonograph records, taken at the time, of interviews with the indicted and subsequently convicted kidnaper. In only two or three cases of federal-local police jobs are some doubts created as to error committed either by Hoover's boys or the local constabulary. This is a great record for any police, especially in a land this vast, with a buccaneer people.

Hoover is a great constable. He knew Holmes and Brandeis and their philosophic interpretations of the value of our Bill of Rights. He supplements their philosophy out of the daily administration as head of 13,000 employees whose work last year resulted in the conviction of 13,616 criminals. In addition, the FBI conducted thousands of investigations primarily to determine the loyalty of individuals and had custody of the fingerprints of over 50 million Americans.

Of course his greatest accomplishment is evidenced by the unbelievable control and limiting of sabotage before and during the war. Few people know that the FBI investigations resulted in over one thousand convictions for technical sabotage. Before the war all potentially subversive people were carefully watched, and the resulting guarding of the plants of the nation is one of the outstanding accomplishments of governmental controls. That the Nazis had plans there is no doubt, and that Hoover spiked them is true, and that the story of his efforts cannot now be told to our public adds still more credit to Hoover's devotion to effectiveness rather than to popularity through headlines.

Some years ago when Connie came to Washington to hear me argue a case in the high court she dropped in to see Edgar Hoover. He was out of town. She saw his crime exhibit and left him a note: "I've seen your exhibit and I've decided to give up my life of crime." A reply came: "Dear Connie: It is encouraging to know that you were impressed by what you saw, except that I do wish you would reconsider your noble intention of including the Stork Club among the petty vices which you are about to give up. I should indeed miss seeing you there."

CHAPTER XXXIX

MY FAVORITE BANKER

I HAD LUNCH TODAY with Russell Leffingwell of Morgan's down at his office. I haven't known him for many years. In fact, I met him as recently as the last reorganization of Paramount Pictures in 1935 when I served as a member of the Vanderlip Bondholders Committee. Lansing Reed, one of the truly distinguished members of the Bar, a partner of John W. Davis, was counsel to the committee. He had his troubles, what with conflicts of interest of banking groups, undisclosed sources of power, and the general improbable economic babel built of celluloid and called Paramount.

I found Lansing Reed to be in agreement with my desire to keep an eye on the new directors to be selected to run the reorganized company. Picture companies usually go broke but always find it easy to ensnare fresh capital from the investors of the land. It should be a foolproof bread-and-butter business, but as yet it is scarcely a business. It is still a first-generation undertaking. Lansing Reed had to act the strictly impartial lawyer for the entire committee but he gave me much comfort and advice. At one stage of the preparation of the new plan of reorganization I proposed that it might be wise and profitable to put on the Board of Directors at least a few people who knew something about the use of the leisure time of America. I suggested Arthur Sulzberger of the New York *Times*, Henry Luce of *Time*, President Conant of Harvard University and at least one outstanding author. The bankers agreed to Luce, who went on the Board and off like a shot. An educator was pooh-poohed, for what have films to do with education, particularly since Will Hays has told many, as he did me, that he is against pictures in the schools for this would reduce the pennies spent at theaters at night. To which I replied, "Why not take books out of the schools, also?"

But one sultry day the bankers agreed to take the president of the Authors' League on the Board of Paramount Pictures. It was Marc Connolly at that time. His recent production of *Green Pastures* had been a great success. I had urged that with Connolly or Robert Sherwood or some other creative author of distinction on the Board all authors, actors and directors would prefer working for Paramount, rather than any other company, for that would be the one company where in case of a dispute the creative group would have an understanding friend at court.

Late one evening Percy Johnston, president of the Chemical Bank and an aware member of the committee, told me all was agreed to for Connolly. The next day the financial

[237]

pages of some daily papers carried a story: "Ernst urges Groucho Marx for president of Paramount." I knew that they had done me in, but I went to the next bankers' meeting with a very straight face and said, "That wasn't my suggestion but it's a good one. Groucho is a first-rate clever businessman." But of course I knew I was licked. On returning to my office I found a telegram: "Please send me the name of a good lawyer. I want to sue Ernst. Why shouldn't *I* be president of Paramount? Signed Harpo Marx." Lansing enjoyed it all with me. Of course the Paramount reorganized Board was of the old type, little social vision, interlocking of interests with supposed competitors, and no evidence of the growing power of the screen over the development of man.

I have always been thankful to Lansing for having me at his home with Russell that warm shirt-sleeve evening. This was a start of a relationship of great spiritual value to me. We are, as Russell once wrote me, "fast friends."

I wish I could be more like Russell but I can't. It's background, glands—probably many intangibles. His wisdom and sureness about even his unsurenesses, his conscious disciplined reach for truth and fairness act as a refresher to me on many occasions. I remember no more gracious moments than the time Russell and I had a long talk with President Roosevelt. They were old friends but Russell had voted against the third term. The President knew it. We talked about the two functions of an executive—running the government and leading the people. And then later at lunch with Jerome Frank, who was then the chairman of the Securities and Exchange Commission, I listened to Jerry, the most exciting mind I know, and Russell, analyze the finance problems of our nation.

Russell Leffingwell once wrote me a 24-page letter, a detailed criticism of the manuscript of my *Too Big*. He agreed with me in essence but was also most helpful in his adverse criticism of places where he thought I had overstated. It's a source of constant wonderment that Russell and I click so well. Civil liberties, too-big business (which I think he learned with some heartaches), too-big government which he came to appreciate while he was the active head running the Treasury Department of the United States in the last war, the value of intimacy with people and problems, on all these fundamentals we see eye to eye. I think I shock him once in a while but he never really scolds me although he does jump on me when I favor a tax program for social purposes. On this score, it seems to me that he belongs to the outgrown school—of taxes solely for revenue. As far as my vision goes, I can't imagine a tax without some social effects, and hence I want to choose the best combination of revenue and social impact I can devise. And by "best" I mean the one that coincides most acutely with my prejudices.

It was at Leffingwell's offices that I first fully saw the potentialities of banking as a profession. I failed to sense it while a bank director or during some years as member of the New York State Banking Board. I don't think it was possible during those lush years when banking and brokering and underwriting were confusedly interlocked, but now I should imagine that any corporation is less than wise if it can get J. P. Morgan & Co. to take its deposits and doesn't bank there. I know this sounds overenthusiastic but I've watched Leffingwell's associates operate: George Whitney, on industrial problems, and Henry Alexander, who in comparison to a dozen leading bankers seemingly also concerned with the dangers of cancellation day for government contracts, could act as counsel and teacher to them all; and Gordon Wasson, whose liberal imagination helped me so keenly in some work I was doing on cultural ties between England and the United States.

But this doesn't mean that I don't wade in against the partners at the directors' table at Morgan's in favor of F.D.R. and the New Deal; the need of greater vision of management in relation to trade unions; the rather blind spots I seem to see among industrialists and bankers on questions of social security; and the dire need for annual contracts of employment for all workers in order to boost our national income. In fact, I rather think that crowd likes me as a sort of odd whipping boy who can take it from them with a smile and sling back within the limits of a luncheon guest.

What that group needs, having been spanked plenty during the past decade, is to build up some new courage, for as a whole they are still the leading craftsmen in their field. Moreover, a little mixing with the other 99 per cent of the population wouldn't hurt. They have been penned up in their own self-satisfied circles. Recently I took Leon Henderson there for lunch. It did them no harm. And Leon and I were both surprised at the wide areas of agreement we found on after-war prognoses—with respect to potential inflation, unemployment and pace of reconversion.

BANKERS, NOT SO RUGGED

One of my own most rewarding connections with the banking world has come to an end, I'm afraid, for I'm about to be retired from the New York State Banking Board. Retired is a euphemism for nonreappointment by Governor Dewey. I have some regrets. I've been a member since the inception of the Board, but Governor Dewey has impressed his policy of making new personal appointments on nearly all boards and commissions—not only of Democrats but even of Republicans appointed by Democratic governors.

Before the Bank Holiday of 1933 I had worked with Governor Roosevelt, and later with Governor Lehman, on banking legislation. The New York State Banking Board was a fairly new concept, originally of nine members, four nominated by banks of various types, size and districts and four appointed from the so-called public by the Governor. The chairman is the active superintendent of the department. This Board was a necessary, flexible and valuable instrument during the closing and reopening of the banks in 1933, and since then. Its success is in part due in a subtle way to the fact that it has shunned publicity; in fact, there has never been a picture taken of the Board.

To me it has been a rich experience—not only during

1933, when we slept at the Banking Department offices, but since then at the temperate monthly meetings. For some years I sat next to the tall sailor-banker and entrepreneur, Mortimer Buckner; opposite Perry Wurst, hard-hitting upstate Republican, and alongside of the wise and selfless professor from Cornell, Harold Reed, or the farmer Henry Talmadge from the tip of Long Island. These men and others were conscientious and good craftsmen. The savings banks were most fortunate of all groups, as they were represented by Harry Kinsey, a banker and only a banker. He favored the New Deal philosophy of divorcing banking from all other businesses such as security or brokerage business. He knew that a man had a full-time job if he ran just his bank.

And looking back, the meetings brought out one significant and constant stream: the clash between individual rights and the responsibility toward society. The Board has greater power than any Public Service Commission of any type in any state, or in fact far more than the SEC. Of course we could close an unsafe bank. But that was an awkward power because the remedy was usually out of proportion to the needs of the situation. We could fire a president of a bank even though he was the majority stockholder. We did virtually that on two occasions and I remember twitting these rugged individualists on the Board about how corrupting it is to have power! What would they have done to Charles Mitchell, president of the National City Bank, or President Wiggin of the Chase? We also fixed the rates of interest which savings banks and other institutions were permitted to pay to their depositors. This again is a frightening power. A small bank, conservative and well managed, never did fall for that 5 per cent rate to suck in depositors. But now it says: "We can pay 3½ per cent; that's more than the other banks in the neighborhood are allowed to pay or could with safety pay."

Question—for those bankers who reject in theory all governmental "interferences": Should the depositors of this bank be deprived of this higher interest rate just because, if this

[241]

bank pays 3½ per cent, it will invite the deposits out of other banks in the neighborhood and such other banks may go broke, and in turn the applicant bank might be hurt? It was surprising how readily, in their own fields, the banker representatives repudiated free enterprise, the values of competition, the profit motive and the theory of "keep the government out of business." I'm not saying they weren't right but I honestly believe I was more worried about exercising these vast powers than were these men of the finance profession itself.

One of the most interesting aspects of the banking profession is its lack of adventure in ideas as opposed to adventure in a gambling sense with money. There was a time, for example, when the bonds of only three railroad companies were lawful for investment by savings banks in New York State. A century ago, for very valid reasons, bonds were considered safer than stock, but corporations became so vast in size that foreclosing on a bond created a fiction because there were no bidders for the mortgaged property. Hence the courts had to guess at what the market value was so as to protect other classes of investors. Bankers should know that the only difference between a bond and a properly written preferred stock is that in the case of a bond bankruptcy usually results, whereas in the case of a preferred stock bankruptcy is practically impossible. I cannot for the life of me see why railroads should issue bonds in the future. Everything that is in a bond issue as to a priority claim on interest or assets can be written into a piece of paper called a preferred stock. If the railroad's earnings fall down and interest cannot be paid on the bond, a receivership results. This means millions of dollars of expense for lawyers and accountants, and obviously just because a railroad is run by a gentleman called a receiver appointed by the courts, no additional railroad fares flow into the railroad treasuries. The purpose of a receivership is solely to reshuffle the interests of the various security-holding groups. All this can be accomplished in advance by what would be in effect anticipatory intercompany reorganizations without the aid of court, by setting forth in the preferred stock shares the terms of reorganization in the event of defaults. The great obstacles to this simplification of railroad reorganizations are the legal profession—or at least that part of it which makes fortunes every year out of railroad reorganizations—and a few bankers, who likewise have prospered thereby. But above all we must reappraise the outworn idea of practically every state in the union, as to what is a "chancery security." Surely we should have learned by now that widows are not safeguarded from loss because their investments are called bonds. Some years ago we were able to break through this rigid prohibition in the state of New York, and debentures and other kinds of securities other than bonds can now be purchased by savings banks and others, whose funds are considered particularly sacred. This door must be opened wide enough to stop coercing rate-regulated utilities into issuance of bonds. What we need is an adventurous new deal within the banking profession, with new ideas and new blood and new attitudes.

I was once for a short period collaterally in the profession. As director of a clean little bank, the Murray Hill Trust Company, I was learning much from the inside. But I was called upon to sue, in behalf of a client, the great George F. Baker's First National Bank. I was right in my suit. That bank had established a security affiliate with stock illegally trusteed, and with a definite rule never to issue a statement. Morgan, Baker and Gary owned more than 50 per cent of the stock of this powerful institution. A foundation of which I was treasurer owned about one thousand shares of the stock selling at $900 a share. Naïvely I walked in on Jackson Reynolds, the president of the First National Bank, and asked his advice. Should we sell? Would he show me the balance sheet? The first question he properly rejected, the second he took as a personal insult. No total balance sheet or full disclosure would ever be made public. I attended a stockholders' meeting with our thousand shares. Seward Prosser, president of the Bankers Trust Company, incidentally a great sailor, his *Constance*, a one-sticker used to beat the steamer from Woods

[243]

Hole to Nantucket, and he sailed without auxiliary engine, voted some seventy thousand shares. I raised a little fuss in a dignified way. Big bankers are timid and easily scared people, and this was even before the Treasury Department moved from Wall Street to Washington in 1933. To my surprise, shortly after the meeting, a statement of the First National Security Company was published. This was a front-page story in the leading newspapers. But what wasn't run in the press was the inadequacy of the statement. Thirty-four millions of assets were not decently disclosed in the figures given to the public. I sued. The Murray Hill Trust Company asked me to resign as a director because our little trust company would be ruined by the big bankers downtown. I did resign and in writing stated the alleged reason for the request of my with-drawal—that the big banks would otherwise ruin the little trust company. Parenthetically, I did not then nor do I now believe any such dire punishment would have been meted out, and I so stated in my letter of resignation. Years later I kidded Russell Leffingwell, of Morgan's, about this episode and I'm convinced Morgan's would probably not have known about my little foray.

The result of my suit was the disclosure, at least to my client, of the unpublished data. Whenever the client wanted to sell some of its shares it showed a part of this secret in-formation to bank stock specialists in Wall Street. The shares would climb up hundreds of points at a time. And I sold the stock for the client all the way up to $8,200 a share. The client made about a million dollars profit.

As a bit of Americana it is worth-while recording that the client was a foundation known as the American Fund for Public Service. Selfless Charles Garland had inherited more wealth than he wanted to bother with, and gave a group of us about one million dollars—most of it in First National Bank shares. He said, "Give it away, it will corrupt you. There is need in the world for it today." The directors were Norman Thomas, Roger Baldwin, Sidney Hillman, Robert Morss

Lovett, James Weldon Johnson, William Z. Foster and others. I was elected treasurer.

It did corrupt us even as we tried our best to give it away. At least it corrupted everybody but me, for I was already corrupted. I knew the cumulative geometric growing power of money. An applicant for a new labor school would be asked: What have you in the way of collateral endorsers? A liberal magazine would be rejected on a loan because of interest rates. No tougher man at a bank cage exists than Roger Baldwin, one of America's great liberal fighters, who having lived a life framed in by Puritan observance of farthings, was the secretary and driving force of the American Fund. We dished out this fortune, plus dividends and profit. It went, in the main in dribbles—never quite enough to put a venture of novelty and unpopularity on its feet.

But this foundation made a fortune out of George F. Baker. If that isn't cockeyed, glamorous and unbelievable United States, what is? The Fund board, composed of men of modest wants, and heading in the main starving liberal organizations, never did learn that $10,000 can do fifteen times more good than $1,000. The Fund was afraid that easy money would corrupt the organizations seeking aid, never realizing the countervailing fact that most liberal groups spend most of their energy and vitality on money-raising and that alone.

Brookwood Labor College, which we financed, came near to being a landmark, but the Communists set out to wreck it. And did so. Incidentally, my friend Clinton Golden, one of the great present statesmen of organized labor, was a tower of strength at Brookwood. We helped the Scopes monkey case in Tennessee, the Sacco-Vanzetti fight in Boston, and lost fortunes in labor and liberal press and magazine ventures. I made many friends during that period among the sacrificial crusading sections of our national life. It was exciting and fun.

CHAPTER XL

WHO KILLED PARMENTER?

ON APRIL 15, 1920, AT 3:00 P.M., a paymaster, Parmenter and his guard, Berardelli, were robbed and killed at South Braintree, Massachusetts. Witnesses testified at the trial that the occupants of the murder car looked like Italians. The departing car, with a flapping awning, was seen by various witnesses over a dash of about twenty miles where it seemed to turn around. The testimony indicated that there were two cars on the job and a change of cars took place at a little wooded triangle. The murder car was found the next day.

A shoe company had been robbed of its payroll boxes—tin boxes 2 feet long, 1 foot high, and 8 inches wide, in which wooden boxes were placed—containing $15,766. A traveling salesman named Gould was so close to the car that a shot went through his clothing. Gould went to the prosecuting authorities and told them that if they ever picked up suspects he could identify the murderers with certainty. The authorities charged two Italians with the crime but never called upon Gould to identify the defendants. Presumably Gould would not have thought that the right people had been arrested.

The trial proceeded, reported on the back pages of the local papers. Years later Roy Gould, a razor paste salesman, learned of the arrest of Sacco and Vanzetti. He saw their pictures. He came forward voluntarily to swear he had seen the shooting and that the wrong men had been tried and convicted. Mr. Katzmann, the prosecutor, had concealed Gould's evidence of innocence. I wrote an article for the *Nation* on the ethics of a district attorney concealing evidence of innocence. I asked leading lawyers to comment on this phase of our jurisprudence. Emory Buckner, United States attorney in New York City, was shocked at Katzmann's concealment. The chairman of one of the Ethics Committees of our lawyers' associations, wrote that Katzmann was under no duty to produce evidence save that pointing to guilt, and Max Steuer went overboard in declaring that a prosecutor should always introduce evidence of innocence just as an attorney for defense should produce any evidence he possesses of guilt.

The Sacco-Vanzetti case became a cause célèbre.

I was not professionally active in the Sacco-Vanzetti case, nor did I go to Boston with Ruth Hale, Robert Benchley, Dorothy Parker and others for the final curtain. After reading Felix Frankfurter's brave and concise analysis, I made up my mind that the defendants had received less than a fair trial. As a matter of fact, in a busy world most of us make up our minds on important issues by pegging our faith on the judgment of others.

After the Rockefellers financed the publication in six volumes of the entire record of the S-V case, with a foreword by John W. Davis, Elihu Root and others, I read every word of the entire record of trials, motions and appeals. I became convinced of the innocence of the fish peddler and the shoemaker. A world-wide protest followed their electrocution. By such public indignation does the process of law receive correction.

From that time on I engaged in an elaborate and exciting inquiry. Through underworld creatures I ran onto a trail, explored by others to be sure, but as a boy detective I kept up the pursuit for nearly twenty years.

I am sure I know the gang who did the job. Sacco and Vanzetti had nothing to do with it. In the thirties, the bad boy of the gang was at Auburn jail in New York State. He had been given about fifteen years for killing a cop in open daylight on Mulberry Street, New York City, not far from police headquarters, and at the time of his arrest had in his possession a rare Steyer gun. Back at the trial of Sacco and Vanzetti there was evidence about a bullet fired through a "Star" gun said by ballistic experts to be a Steyer. With the aid of Paul Kellogg, editor of *Survey Magazine*, I persuaded the head of our state prisons to transfer the gunman to Wall-kill Prison, the best of our state jails and much desired by all prisoners. Wallkill grants many freedoms, there are few guards, many privileges. The Superintendent made it clear that he understood our intention to talk to the prisoner about the Sacco-Vanzetti case but that he, as a state official, would not lift a finger to persuade him to see us.

Confident that out of curiosity and gratitude, if nothing else, we would be granted an audience by this killer, we waited for a decent time and then I wrote to him. I told him why I wanted to see him. I told him of the evidence I had from interviews with another member of the gang. He never replied. I wonder if he really ever had curiosity about his benefactors? I would still like to chat with him. He should feel very safe. He could go on the courthouse steps in Boston and tell the entire story. Nobody would proceed against him. It would be like proceeding against former President Lowell of Harvard, former Judge Thayer, the convicting jurist, and former Governor Fuller. Society cannot afford to convict the memory of such personages, even for the sake of historic truth.

While reaching for this criminal, I had arranged through an attorney in Providence, a conference with the head of the gang. I had complete familiarity with all the details of testimony at the original trial so it was fairly easy to pick up the talk of the gang leader to see if he was bluffing. Where did you get the second license plate for that other car described by the state in the evidence against Sacco and Vanzetti? Why did you turn the car around and double back at Matfield after the murder? Did you change cars? If so, where? Describe both cars? Where were the cars stolen? Where did you get the license plates? Describe the curtains of the car. (The evidence mentioned a flapping curtain—could he tell me which one?) How much money was in the box? Tell us the size of the box? Where is the box?

No person of this man's make-up would have read the minutes of the trial with enough precision to fit all his answers into the known facts, down to the description of the flapping of the side curtain on the murder car. Nor could any human being have guessed the answers as to time and place of the many details of the shooting day about which I confronted him. I left completely satisfied that the gang chieftain was in the murder car and knew all the details of the planning of the robbery, the details of the shooting, and the technique of escape.

I had something hot. At a meeting at the home of Oswald Garrison Villard, the great editor of the *Nation*, whose counsel we had been for years, a fund was raised to pay for checking up this statement if reduced to writing, and to pay money to the gangman and his counsel if it checked. Obviously the criminal's word was worthless, but after he had sworn to a statement the facts could be checked up by outside independent evidence and his statement thrown away. Money would be paid over if the statement was accepted as true by some reputable disinterested attorneys.

With $10,000 underwritten I had increased hope. I then went to many of the leaders of the New York Bar. Would they help? Hughes's firm was disinclined to let Charles E. Hughes, Jr., prejudice his judicial career; George Z. Medalie and others wanted retainers of $25,000 or more. In brief, I could not induce any of the leading lawyers to take on this chore. They were afraid that their respectable clients would object. I know enough leading bankers and industrialists so that I am persuaded these fears were invalid and only another case of legalistic jitters.

My correspondence with the gangster revealed him as an aspiring writer. Part of one of his letters follows:

My manuscript contains of 574 pages. Now if you are interested to put my story on the market I'm sure the book would sell like hot cakes. Have you read Al Capone's book, his book would not compare with my. You must remember that I been in the racket 40 years and still live, therefore I must have something to tell. If you were to read the history of my life your hair would stand straight up under your hat.

I went back to my underworld contact. I remember sitting in the lawyer's office with the leader gazing out the window, and after a few minutes giving a signal to someone on the street below. I asked what that was for. He had merely signaled to some of his boys that I was "jake." Nothing to fear.

We got along swimmingly. Only through sheer stupidity did I fail. I disclosed that I had promised one of my underworld intermediaries $1,500 or some such sum. He was burned up. Why should that guy get so much when he was to give the story?

I shifted. Would he deliver to me for $2,500 the money boxes stolen from the shoe factory? To this he said, "You couldn't get them out of Canapa Pond at this time."

That was the end of our talk. He took me to a taxi-driver friend of his to drive me to New Bedford for the Nantucket boat. Years later I saw him once more with Robert Lamont, editor of Little, Brown. By that time the gunman had settled down, got religion and wanted to sell an illustrated book he had just finished.

We checked up the pond he had mentioned. It was on the exact route of the escaping murder car. The name he used for the pond was the local name for that bit of water. I checked with metallurgists to see if the American Express Company numbers would still be discernible on the stolen metal payroll boxes. But then, bringing up the boxes would prove little, for he might have heard from others where the boxes were thrown.

It's now more than twenty years since the murder of the paymasters and the murder of Sacco and Vanzetti. It would have been wholesome as a bit of social catharsis to have brought out the true story, to which hoped-for end the Rockefellers had published the record.

Except for Herbert Ehrmann of Boston, a great lawyer for

the defendants in the case, most of the main participants have died. I found few of my friends to encourage me. This was dead fish. New problems took their energy. I didn't exactly lose interest. I just gave up. But I suggest that it would be dangerous for anyone to egg me on to take up the clues, no matter how stale. Truth can still win out even if slapped down for several decades.

CHAPTER XLI

PLANNED PARENTHOOD

THE POLITICAL MURDER of my friend Carlo Tresca about two years ago on Fifth Avenue in New York City remains unsolved, while the press of the city keeps headlining all kinds of unimportant misbehavior of petty racketeers, with scarcely a mention of this dramatic unsolved assault on our democracy.

Tresca, a philosophical anarchist and fighting editor of *Il Martello*, was a softy at heart despite his bitter hate of Fascists and Communists. He identified both groups together as movements desiring more, rather than less, power in the state.

In years gone by Carlo was feared by many who didn't know him. Bomb throwing was associated with his name rather than the rum cakes he would bring to our children and others, or spaghetti parties which he threw with gay bravado and merry cheer.

Carlo was the kind of man who, when he was indicted for running a one-inch advertisement of a birth control book and was offered, during the time when Charles Evans Hughes was secretary of state, a deal whereby the case would be dropped if he would return to Italy, rejected the offer without a quiver.

He went to Atlanta Prison as a result, this being the only prison sentence I know of for the mere publication of an advertisement of contraceptives. What our then administration wanted, under pressure from Fascist Italy, was to have Tresca brought back to Italy for the guillotine.

In celebration of the old days of the Lawrence strike, an important step toward the liberation of the textile workers of America, in which Tresca was a leader, he gave a party for a crowd of us including Margaret Sanger, another fighter in another field.

At that party I tried to start a campaign to get the Nobel Peace Prize for Margaret Sanger. It seemed to me, with population problems acting as valid or invalid causes for war, that this crusader in her fight for voluntary birth control had made a truly significant contribution to world peace. Maybe after the war she will be thus honored. Lucky gal, Margaret Sanger. To have started and seen near completion, in one's own lifetime, one's own crusade, is a rare experience for any human being.

For a quarter of a century it has been a joy and privilege for me to be an errand boy for Margaret Sanger and her great medical associates, the late Dr. Hannah Stone and Dr. Abraham Stone. Their little clinic was raided by Policeman Grover Whalen in April, 1929. Medical cards were stolen by the police from the doctors' files and the doctors themselves were huddled into Black Marias like dangerous criminals. This was startling even to the timid and overdignified medical profession, which at that time, fortunately for us, was under great suspicion for the sale of liquor in violation of prohibition laws. Only a handful of doctors had been honest and courageous in the controversy raging over contraceptives during the previous decades. Doctors such as Arthur Holden, Foster Kennedy, Eric Matsner, Alfred Hellman, and of course, Robert Dickinson, were our main support in the public fights. But after the raid the bulk of the profession was outraged that cops should be allowed to seize medical records taken down by doctors and historically deemed, at least in our state, as sacred and as privileged as confessions are to a priest.

The day after the clinic raid hundreds of women of position and wealth telephoned to our office to inquire if the New York police force had seized the records of their medical conditions. Doctors likewise got many panicky calls.

This error of Whalen's police was the turning point in the legal battles for the legalization of contraceptives. A not too smart but altogether agreeable lady detective had been sent into the clinic as an agent provocateur to get evidence. The lady detective had gone to the clinic, been examined, found wanting and ailing and had received a prescription. She had told the doctor that she had three children, ages 5, 3 and 1. It was simple to prove to the court, from the survey made by our Federal Health Service, the greatly increased mortality rates which result from inadequate spacing of births. The clinic doctors won the case, and the lady detective, being informed in the court testimony of the condition of her insides, later came to the clinic to find out if it was really true and what to do about it.

When this case came up for trial in the Magistrates Court, hundreds of young people were sitting in the back rows of the courtroom. I was at a loss to understand why, so early in the morning, in the Jefferson Market Magistrates Court, this flock of youngsters should be present. I asked the clerk to account for it, and he wryly answered, "That's just a bunch of workers arrested for picketing a cafeteria and here they are in luck getting reserved seats for a birth-control trial."

While Margaret Sanger was in New York and in command of strategy, a series of further clarifying cases were brought into court. Pessaries were imported from Holland. They were stopped at the Customs. We tried the case under the Cutting Law. Federal Judge Grover Moskowitz rendered a brave opinion which was fully sustained by the Circuit Court of Appeals. Gradually all the courts took the position that Congress could not be presumed to have meant to impair the health of the nation, no matter what a literal mind might read into the old Comstockian antibirth-control statutes.

After a few years it was apparent that under all federal legislation—postal, importation, interstate transportation, etc.—contraceptives could be lawfully handled in interstate commerce unless the purpose was other than the prevention of disease of parents or offspring. All states came in line with this policy save only Massachusetts and Connecticut, and in New York a wise chief justice of our highest court, Judge Frederick Crane, had taken down his most generous dictionary to define "prevention of disease," and happily selected the phrase "any threatened ailment."

But Massachusetts and Connecticut continue as areas of darkness. There the powerful Catholic Church, having endorsed the unfortunate Rhythm Method of family limitation, still puts up an expensive and, to date, successful fight. The medical profession of both states continues its bootlegging of contraceptives, and the Catholic Church condones and encourages the selling by mail of thousands of pamphlets, dials and other contraptions which pretend to advise married and unmarried women when to have intercourse without danger of pregnancy.

An editor of one of the liberal Catholic magazines took me to lunch one day to ask what the Church could do about the terrible spot in which it found itself. He said they knew that the Rhythm Method did not work, that it brought on untold misery, that thousands of Catholic women became pregnant, were too chagrined to go to Catholic doctors, and that the Protestant doctors were being consulted instead. Shades of the old theory of the economic interpretation of history!

Only last year I had a most uncomfortable day in the Supreme Court in arguing a case, originally brought by other attorneys, to test the constitutionality of the Connecticut prohibition vis-à-vis the Federal Constitution. The Supreme Court went medieval on us. They picked on a most technical point in the original pleadings and refused to hear the case on the merits. Thus, because of form of complaint, thousands of women are still condemned in Connecticut to pain and misery, and innumerable babies will be born dead. At least that will be the case for the poor and friendless. The rich and sophisticated will be able to procure pessaries from leading physicians in true bootleg fashion.

In other districts, however, vast progress is being made. North Carolina actually operates fifty clinics where its Public Health Department dispenses contraceptives. In overpopulated Puerto Rico we helped brief the law leading to a decision which allows that most thickly peopled spot on earth to gain relief, if desired, from unwanted children. And before long, I'm sure the United States Supreme Court will be compelled to spank Connecticut and Massachusetts for violating the right of a doctor to practice his profession as his medical judgments dictate, and the right of the children and mothers to enjoy the life and joy now denied them by statutes in violation of due process.

The Catholic Church is already making a shift in its theology. Originally it opposed Margaret Sanger's program on grounds of morality. It urged that with contraceptive information available women would become more loose in their sexual morals. But as soon as the Church realized that at least one-third of all patients seeking birth-control devices at the clinics admitted to being Catholics, the attack shifted its stance. Rhythm Method, unworkable, psychologically cruel, and indiscriminately dispensed, was made available to millions of women, married and unmarried. In effect, the Church said: Here is a calendar which will tell you how to select the sterile days in each menstrual month. That the calendar does not work seemed to make little difference to the dispensers. The theological point was urged that there was a distinction between natural and unnatural contraceptive techniques and the Rhythm Method taught people presumably how to defeat nature.

The ultimate birth-control case which I have long said I would love to try is a case based on sound present medical knowledge not inconsistent with the sociological purpose of the Rhythm Method,—a case which frankly would be predicated on evidence indicating that married couples, particularly young ones, could not live in healthy marriage without joy, and that sexual relations were a necessary part of wholesome joy. I firmly believe that the health of many married couples, young and old, calls for the use of contraceptives whether for economic or for other reasons. A life without sexual relations develops into a distorted relationship. The Catholic answer, the Rhythm Method, is inadequate to meet such a situation, and is at best only a device inadequate to give full answer to the exigencies of the situation.

Leadership of doctors is needed. But cowardice of the medical profession reached its peak in 1943, when the St. Elizabeth's Hospital (at Elizabeth, New Jersey) issued a ukase to the effect that all doctors on the staff must pledge themselves not to prescribe contraceptives in the hospital and also in their private practice. This being virtually the only hospital of the neighborhood, the doctors—Protestants, Jews or non-believers, as well as Catholics—were compelled through economic duress to take this pledge. There might be possible debate as to the right of a hospital to lay down such a rule as to advice within the hospital, but it seems to me there can be little dispute as to the outrage practiced on the medical profession when this institution, through economic power, enforced its prejudices on the private professional ethics of staff doctors while practicing outside the hospital. I followed this situation with some care, and as far as I know not a single member of the medical profession uttered a protest although the event was much discussed and was bound to have, as it did have, repercussions in other hospitals.

Maybe contraceptive advice is the most important need of mankind. Overpopulation of various lands—that is, a population ineluctably unable to live off its own soil—is the root of much of the world's illness. That and illiteracy are the focal points crying for man's attack. Maybe the new league of nations should have as an admission requirement an insist-

[256]

ence that some small percentum of a nation's income be spent on free public education, and that there be no ban on voluntary parenthood.

I've never been impressed with fears of falling population. This land of ours, endowed by nature and made rich by our skills and work habits, could carry a happy people if there were one hundred, two hundred or only fifty millions. Population in quantity is essential only for the purpose of killing and fighting enemies. But above all other arguments, the fact stands out that in a comprehensive program aimed even at increasing a population, planned parenthood through contraceptive dispensation is a necessary integral element.

CHAPTER XLII

LETTERS TO A BABY

IF I WERE A STUTTERER, this would have been my big moment. A young lawyer, the kind of lawyer I envy—legal training, ingenuity and scholarship—wanted, out of his reticent self, to return to me some of the affection I hold for him. Married, and now with an heir, he and his wife wrote to tell me I was godfather to their child.

All through my life I've heard friends talk of their godfathers and godmothers. I never could put my finger on just what the relationship meant in terms of affection, obligation or discomfort. I'm not much on relative relationships. Aunt Ray, who brought me up during high school years when my mother was ill and out west, a brother and a sister with whom I have a devoted but not the usual constant relationship, are the beginning and end of close family feeling. I've never paid enough attention to babies. I'm a little afraid of them. I never can forget that I tower above them and that they in turn must be awed by the mere size of adults. I don't even like young dogs or cats.

So I sat me down and wrote:

Dear Jimmy:

Your old man and your old lady have done everything they could to destroy our relationship. This giving of degrees like Godfather is as silly as getting an honorary degree from college. I must confess to you that I have always wanted an honorary college degree, particularly if a red tam-o-shanter goes with it, which even you, in a couple of weeks, would enjoy. You will understand, but your old folks won't, that I never did like babies and that they scare the bejesus out of me. As a matter of fact, I was even a lousy father until my kids were old enough to sail a boat alone and hold their liquor. I don't like this kind of relationship by title and the chances are I will treat you as badly as I treat cousins and aunts and uncles.

The only purpose of education is that children shall lick their parents and stand up against adults, and I take it if we ever meet in later years that the only obligation I have taken on is to help you fight the old folks. Young people are always nearer right than us old cockers, because as you grow older you compromise all through life in order to live. You are probably nearer right today than you will ever be again on every important issue, and, when I talk about issues, I am talking about real things such as mom and pop would not understand. You've got a brazen mother and a timid father which is a very good combination because more people are ruined by the overwhelming affection of parents than by any amount of disregard. Maybe after you have imitated older folks long enough and by mimicry have learned to talk, you will persuade the old folks to drop this nonsense of title. Relationship by certificate or title is usually worthless and universally stilted. Always remember that mom and pop were married by the church and the church does not keep them together. If you will only listen to what they say to each other when they are having orange juice for breakfast, you will learn nearly everything there is to learn about human relationships.

In any event, you need not expect any presents or what is called social attention from me. I only sent one flower in my life and I don't ever remember sending a box of candy. As for toys,

I think that kids ought to make their own toys. At least we grown-ups do if we are smart. There is more mystery in a piece of string if you really look at it than there is in the biggest electric train to be found in a toy store.

Just one piece of advice—keep away from books for many years. As soon as you start reading books you are drinking in what adults have thought instead of creating your own ideas. Eventually you will have to read some books so as to be invited out to dinner in the evening, when people talk about books they have not read and seldom understand.

Some time we will have a conference and see if we can break through this nonsense.

Yours,

P.S. Ask your Dad some time to tell you the difference between mortmain and livemain and tell him I think that livemain is really more disastrous than mortmain.

I want to warn you about the stupidity of adults once more. Practically the first thing you throw at them is a yawn and they have no idea what you mean. The more they read books, the more they are stupid, because the more they know, the less they feel. Of course you and I know that you were living in water for a longer time than you have lived in air. You and I know that your yawn has nothing to do with your stomach. You are just bragging. You want to show off because you have thrown away your gill slits which you had to have or you could not have lived. I'll bet you the old folks did not even notice that you had no tears until a few days ago; maybe you haven't got them yet.

People are all so busy with what they call big things, like global democracy, that they don't know that wet tears come very late. We know that this means that it is a new stunt that we have acquired. Don't you remember that about a million years ago human beings could not cry? And so all your newest tricks are really new in terms of millions of years. I guess you took a look around at other babies in the hospital, and if so, I think you must have noticed that at the minute of birth there was no such thing as a black-skinned baby. This thing called pigment also comes very late and often after birth. This is really a lead for stopping this nonsense about liking or not liking people because of the color of the skin.

Have you made up your mind whether you are going to be left-handed? My own guess is that it depends on which side of the bed your mother or nurse is standing. If they stand on the right side, you are going to be left-handed.* This is very natural, although we old people don't know it. Take a look at your eyes, and remember that the hand you use will be just the opposite of the side of the brain which is most dominant. I saw some sparrows in our yard this morning and there was not a left-handed one among them, although my favorite robin in Nantucket is left-handed and neurotic. There is a lot of other ignorance in your old man's letter.

Yours for tremendous trifles,

* P.S. or vice-versa. As a matter of fact, a crib in the middle of the room usually spells ambidexterity or leads to stuttering. Keep that a secret from the old folks. Of course they use language and words and they don't even know that the world might be better off without language because animals communicate very well without language and don't really hurt each other much compared to the way human beings treat each other. I just learned this from a girl I love.

CHAPTER XLIII

THE SCHOOL

SCHOOL STARTS FOR ANOTHER YEAR. School has a special quality in a schoolteacher's family. Margaret, after helping out Fola LaFollette as a volunteer for a year at the City and Country School fifteen years ago, has been teaching there ever since. Connie had gone to "C. and C." several years before Maggie took over the library, started to adjust the kids with reading difficulties, and taught etymology.

It's been gay every evening swapping law office and daily school episodes. Of the two, of course a school is more important, particularly a school aware of new techniques and changing times. Modernity in the practice of law is not so easy to attain.

Connie and Roger both went through this school and, much as I resisted several decades ago the approach of Caroline Pratt, pioneer in modern schooling, I know she has been right. Work habits are not impossible of attainment as a part of true excitement in the pupil's mind. Only recently have our public education authorities called on this great school to revamp portions of the public school system, which in New York City is of such vast proportions that any innovation is as risky and difficult as a change of method in U.S. Steel or the Chase Bank. Maybe the public school units are so big that real education can never reside there.

The teachers of the City and Country School own the school. They are the corporation. But this doesn't mean that the teachers don't belong to the Teachers Guild, although a kind of Gilbert and Sullivan effect results when the union of teachers at this co-operatively owned school deals with the "C. and C." corporation. But it all works out fairly well, particularly since the teachers, in a sense, have the souls of missionaries and hence many a year cut their own salaries to make the budget balance.

Of course parents make the school the center of many of their social activities. The Fair each spring elicits hundreds of volunteer hours of parents' co-operative time; the gym is open evenings for badminton, basketball, or other indoor sports. In the future I should think that cities should be built around the schools. To each school there should be attached a playground, a park, a swimming pool, the health center, the Federal Employment Office. For the area around Washington Square, "City and Country" goes far in this direction. Do you need a nurse, do you want to rent an apartment, exchange rubbers? The school will act as clearinghouse.

One day I walked into Maggie's classroom at word-study

period. She was asking the twelve-year-old kids to make up a word that means "seeing and hearing over the water at a distance." That was a cinch for children who had played with roots and parts of words. Aqua, audio, video, tele. Each child made up a different word—telaqua-audiovision and telmar-audioscope are two that I remember. It's more than a game. It enriches the use of English. It makes for subtlety and nuance of speech. It permits refinement of feelings and ideas. Historic proportions are visible in the life of man through the development of speech as a tool of the mind. And some kids at thirteen years of age really ask, for valid realistic reasons, to study Latin or Greek. Incidentally, Maggie's books, particularly In a Word, the one with the great Thurber drawings, keep on selling, and enviously I see her open her semiannual royalty check envelopes.

My education was never tied up with life itself. I remember only one touch of reality in nearly twenty years of education. Ted Lewis, a professor of English at Williams, had grown up in a poor Welsh town. In 1906 he told me about Workmen's Compensation Laws then being discussed by the Lloyd George Liberal party. Professor Lewis made theory live and touch the emotions of masses of people. That next summer when I worked my way to Liverpool on a cattle ship —tending cattle and peeling potatoes—I met a batch of professional cattle "stiffs." Thanks to this professor I came to know what such year-round boat cattle tenders sought in life. Without his eye openers these men would have appeared to be nothing more than vulgarity and ignorance.

At "C. and C." the seven-year-old kids dictate stories which the Elevens set up in type and print, from which the Sevens in turn learn to read. The Nines run a store, buying, at wholesale, pencil and paper and ink, which are sold to the other kids at a price sufficient to cover the service item. Thus arithmetic has a function. Percentage, overhead, interest on investment, division of gross profit in the form of wages, all tie in to a process of work and fun. And the Eights run the school post office.

I wish I had a good education. Even Williams College, at which I was lucky from start to finish, and which gave me much, had as I look back on it little of what today appears to be education. Roger learned more in five months in the language division of ASTP than I ever got in four years of college.

But maybe it was my fault and not that of Williams, for Maggie got richness of mind and knowledge at Wellesley. And how I envy her that Phi Beta Kappa key!

I WISH I'D LEARNED

Today I received two knocks. I was told that I had a meager aesthetic sense and that my diction was none too good. It is little cracks like those that hurt most. The old saying—the greater the truth the greater the libel—is no mere paradox. Only the probable is believable. To be called a murderer would seem to me to be a quip, if anything.

But all through life there are errors of ignorance or worse, and all major mistakes I devour and digest within myself. I've been wrong in myriad situations, so wrong that I wouldn't tell a soul, either an intimate or a stranger. But from time to time I have taken stock and made a kind of current inventory. This was the game I learned from my mother. With a very negligible memory of my early youth, one of my clearest recollections is the time I was chased home by the kids on the street, yelling at me, "We told you so, we told you so." In near tears I explained to my mother that I had changed my mind about something in some game which I do not remember. My mother taught me at that moment the joy of admission of error and the satisfaction of recognizing change of mind. Seldom since has my ego been much in the way when I had to shift my thinking or conclusion. Of course at times I've given my ego a first-class fight and often came to the knockout only after being all alone with the door closed.

As samples of regret, and errors and stupidities of the kind that touch no one else and represent only a surface group of currently recognized defeats:

I should have studied at college. I might have learned much that passed me by. I was unimaginative enough in the 1920's to oppose preparedness appropriations by Congress, hoping that war could be prevented by not participating in the preparedness race of nations. I was foolish in overplaying the argument in the defense of a nudist magazine before the Court of Appeals. This because the female relatives of the judges filled the courtroom's public seats. I should not have argued with Judge Pierce Butler in the Frank Hague case in the Supreme Court. What a beating I took from him. I'm still bruised. I need never have been shy and afraid of F.P.A. just because I couldn't match wits with him. Maybe I should have run for the Assembly in 1911 when urged to do so by the Congressman of my district. And why didn't I learn celestial navigation so that I could understand George Roosevelt's articles in *Yachting*? I have such admiration for George Roosevelt's seamanship that I know I'm missing much. Of course I'm sorry I voted for LaGuardia in the last election when he ran against Bill O'Dwyer. I knew better but went with the tide around me. To grow to my great age and not be fluent in Spanish and French is little less than a sin. It has cut me short at times from considerable joy. I'm sorry I didn't represent some of the Christian Front groups when they were indicted, and when I was urged to do so by high Catholic prelates who thought I could be of help in a kind of lego-analytic catharsis.

The Christian Front case would have been an exciting chore. I sat with several priests and one friend, a high prelate, then in Washington and now in the Pacific, and discussed whether it would not be wise to approach the case from the point of view of the underlying social implications. Take nearly any flat in New York, and isn't it merely a question of fate whether the man on the third floor back turns out to be a Communist, a Christian Fronter, a Nazi or a believer in democracy? We do not solve problems impinging on anti-

[264]

American influences merely by convicting a few leaders. Our democracy is inept if it fails to get at the underlying causes. In this particular case, I met a man and his wife and got the feel of his problems. The man had a good job, had never been unemployed, and had led an exemplary youth. He was the kind of lad who was never even arrested for throwing a base-ball through the glass of a lamppost. He was frugal and considerate in his home. He had children. One afternoon he had the radio turned on and he heard the voice of Father Coughlin. Being a devout Catholic, he believed without any questioning the words of Father Coughlin. He was scared that Communism would take over the Catholic Church. He had no evidence but he soon found himself at meetings of Coughlinites at Columbus Circle, and in not too gradual stages joined the movement, became an official; and before he knew it, he was wrapped up with a group of people who were planning the destruction of Communist properties.

It might have been illuminating to have placed into the record of the case the background and the resistance and submission of such a lad. He came in to me through relatives, also devout Catholics. They are still my friends.

If I believe all my best friends then I've been excited about too much and too many. No doubt I've spread my efforts thin. In terms of effectiveness, if any one person can be importantly effective, it may have been an error. In terms of happiness I don't know. In any event it probably could not have been otherwise.

And so forth, and so forth ad nauseam. This category if complete could be a book in itself, and what a bore, and how inadequate it would be.

GOD BLESS

Probably the greatest spiritual education of my life was experienced during my trips to England during the past year or so. I knew England fairly well from many short visits before the war. In a little sensible Morris Oxford car Maggie and I had driven through Scotland and Wales. My recent air trips—Africa, South America, Ireland, Newfoundland, Iceland—all added up into a rich travel. Each time I came home perfectly at ease, describing flights at night, oxygen jags, my unstinted admiration of the crews. But always I've been at a total dead end when I tried to tell what war had done to the souls of British people. We in our land will suffer from the deaths of tens of thousands of our boys but, fortunately and unfortunately, we will never be enriched by a blitz. Thus will we be isolated from other civilian peoples, for imagination and language together are insufficient tools to describe what a blitz does to the spirit of free human beings. The blitz does something to synthesize a community. It creates homogeneity. It increases kinship. Casualty lists ring at separate doorbells, but rocket planes ring the communal doorbell of a city. Solidarity and human parity rise with each ton of explosives. Ordinary common denominators such as wealth, education, and background diminish and in their place are found the essence of the democratic ideal. Property, accumulation of possessions, shift into clearer perspectives. Blood from a single wound, frayed nerves of a lone scar, become the joint possession of the saved and the maimed. A dead soldier is more than a son or husband or father. He is part of the group. He belongs to all the people. Thus is individual sufficiency reduced by division.

When I was a kid we had in our city a well-known house wrecker—maybe still carrying on—named A. A. Volk. When a solitary rare building was being torn down A. A. Volk put up a sign to advertise the firm. Before I went to London at the time of the African invasion I had studied our pictorial magazines. I thought I'd be prepared for the destruction I would see. Rather did the pictures in Life and Look and the Sunday rotogravures remind me of A. A. Volk—the specialist in tearing down a single building.

The scene is not two-dimensional. Nor does a stereopticon adding a third dimension depict it all. Here we have a fourth dimension. Talented authors have tried to tell the story of England. But I have yet to meet a single person who was really prepared for what he was to see, by reading the most succinct of words or seeing the clearest of photographs. A spirit of a community probably can't be depicted, and least of all by me. No grumbling, no cheating except for a few rich people; acceptance of all and everything to preserve freedom. New values took the place of comfort. There was mutual security in individual insecurity. We in the United States might behave that way under similar circumstances. But we should not only deplore but envy England's experiences of misery and suffering. They have learned during war some of the moral equivalents for peace. Russia had created effective homogeneity, but with sacrifice of freedom of thought and criticism. England, living in a siege economy, has reached what seems to me to be the highest peak of mankind's efforts at joinder of lives and effort without the lessening of the joy of being a distinct individual. The English possess identity—but on the level of human freedom.

False standards have been pierced. Empty prides have given way to proud upstanding humility. No one is humble. Wealthy solicitors, learning that I gave away all my extra clothes before returning each trip, did not hesitate to ask for a shirt or pair of socks. When I divided up my last few garments between two retired aviators who ran the airport of departure, one turned to the other and said, "But it isn't Christmas." The garments, their value or their acquisition, were irrelevant compared to the unashamed frankness of the gratitude. It's not always easy to receive. Only an adult people can take as well as give.

Some Americans preach sacrifice to the British. They say: Only by sacrifice can we make a new world. This is unwise and insulting. England needs no Jeremiahs from afar. With the coming of peace English housewives will raise their shades, eat eggs and see bananas, for the first time in years. Out of the elimination of waste will the world be healed. In England, I estimate, no less than 20 per cent of the waste of the economy has been cut away. Without that, the island could scarcely have survived. And we with our passion for

[267]

production, we who have invented invention, will have much to learn from the British war experience.

Early in the war we pondered whether we could afford to send tractors when bullets and guns were in dire shortage. We did ship tractors for British farms and now we learn that for every ton of tractors shipped we have saved 4½ tons of food shipments, for the British use our tractors 1,500 hours a year on the average while we use them about 300 hours.

I've sat with many of the British war ministers in efforts to weld Anglo-American understanding through a great number of tremendous trifles. I have an idea that after the war dreamboys like Harold Laski will suffer great disappointments. I should wager that Churchill under the influence of the labor pressures and through intelligent co-operation of labor leaders will come through on an after-war program of such dimensions as to drive the intellectuals, as distinguished from the labor leaders, into shame. A Beveridge plan will be adopted without a doubt. But Churchill and the labor leaders in his Cabinet know that it is nothing but what the author claims for it. It is insurance against the stupidity of the government. If employment is full, the benefits will be negligible and not much needed. If there be extensive unemployment, the working portion of the island won't be able to afford the premiums necessary to pay the benefits. Hence Lord Woolton, heading up Reconstruction, and others, I surmise, will come forward with a planned economy for work and productivity for all. We in America, I think, will owe much to the vigilant intelligent influence of Morrison, Bevin and the other great labor leaders, and the mass of liberals in the Labor party, to whom the present coalition government owes most of its domestic direction and its primary feel of the average man. England out of island necessities has experienced the destructive effects of laissez-faire—an instrument for the destruction of free market places and the regimentation of small business under the overwhelming power of monopolistic giants.

I'm happy Connie and Roger have lived in England during a period of pain and misery. They will be enriched. They will understand. They will never be able to forget. They won't ever want to forget. They won't know that they know. It will be a part of them forever. As the English people say: God Bless.

CHAPTER XLIV

THE FLAME

GAY, EFFECTIVE CONNIE is on her way to Normandy, She probably will get into Brittany for a day or so. I have written her to look for a candle and a priest in a small town in Brittany. I have sent her the name of the village, the description of the church and the name of the priest—though I am not at liberty to make these public. Not at liberty only because that part of the story isn't mine. It belongs to F.D.R. and the priest.

Here's the story as the President wrote it to me:

"Early in August 1918, the Assistant Secretary of the Navy was making an inspection of U.S. Naval Air Stations on the Coast of Brittany. As he was proceeding from one station to another, his pilot car most unfortunately knocked down an elderly priest, injuring him slightly. When the Assistant Secretary of the Navy got there a few minutes later, he extended the apology of the Navy to him and offered compensation for the injury.

"The old priest, who of course spoke Breton, but had apparently forgotten most of his French, replied that he most certainly did not want to accept any compensation from his friends of the American Navy which was doing so much in the cause of saving France.

"The Assistant Secretary asked him if there was something that the American Navy could do for his church—a very lovely old church on a promontory. The church dated from the fourteenth century. The old priest's eyes filled with tears and he said:

'Oh, if I could have even a little contribution toward the fund I have been gathering all my life to have the stained glass windows re-leaded, it would mean more to me than anything else in the world.'

"The stained glass windows were among the earliest in France and had not been re-leaded since about 1750.

"The Assistant Secretary asked the old man how much it would cost and he said, with tears in his eyes: '1000 francs—a sum far greater than we could possibly raise.'

"The Assistant Secretary thereupon wrote out a Navy requisition for $200.00 and gave it to the old priest.

"Several months later, an officer reported to the Assistant Secretary that he had been in the church and that the work of re-leading the stained glass windows was nearly completed and that in one of the bays of the church a perpetual candle had been lighted by the old priest in honor of the American Navy.

"Six or eight years later, it was still burning and I have no doubt that now, in 1942, it is still burning—unless the Germans have put it out."

CHAPTER XLV

AN EAR OF CORN

HENRY WALLACE CAME TO OUR HOUSE late one afternoon, in fact that December 6th Saturday before Pearl Harbor. He had recently returned from his South American trip where, unlike most American good-will ambassadors, he was able to converse and make speeches in Spanish.

[270]

The Vice-President was in grand form. I had invited a dozen or so friends to cross-examine him. Harry Scherman of Book-of-the-Month and Russell Leffingwell, opposites on gold theories which I don't understand at all; John Royal of NBC, just back from South America; Frank Case of the Algonquin, the last of the personal innkeepers, perceptive and wise; and then also William Shirer, Dorothy Thompson, and a group of commentators and editors. Our neighbor, Dorothy Stickney, came in and her garden-laden hat nearly broke up the party.

Before we could pick on Henry Wallace he had a question or two to ask us. He said the agriculturists had about licked the germ which had caused rubber to move from Brazil to the Far East. Henry Ford had spent millions trying to bring rubber back to Brazil—this before our adventures in synthetic rubber. Ford had failed but now we could plant enough rubber trees in South America to supply the world in about seven years, the time it takes for fruition. Question: How many people should we allow to live in Borneo and the rest of the rubber islands of the Pacific? For when we plant in South America are we not determining the economy of those distant islands?

Another one: In the middle of South America there are about 15 million Indians, a century or more remote from what we call modern civilization. I imagine they are not un-like the natives I saw last year in Liberia and Portuguese Guinea, illiterate and as yet with no concept of counting beyond the number four. The death rate of these Indians is about 50 per cent up to the age of six. Henry Wallace made clear that we could go down there and in a decade, with our great health machinery, cut the mortality rate in half. Do we favor that?

Wallace, one of the greatest realists of our day, gave his answer. We should not go in with our health service any-where unless at the same time we are prepared to teach people to live off their own land. Otherwise we are increasing their misery and in time we would have one vast Puerto Rico

[271]

or India in the middle of South America, with periodic famines again decimating the grownups we had saved as babies.

In Wallace's office in the Senate Office Building there stands in a glass case the Wallace-bred ear of corn. I know little of corn, except that when I first went to Williams College I cut corn for a few weeks late afternoons on a farm near by. But I'm told by people I believe that this corn developed by Wallace has proved to be one of the major contributions to winning the war. It stands up in dust and rain and has substantially aided the feeding of our armies and others on this planet.

We are now feeding our 130 million people and the equivalent of 30 million others. Without affecting our national health one bit we could feed an additional 30 or 40 million people at our high standard by mere change of diet and reduction of waste. This would not be easy to sell to the American people because it would mean a change of folkways at a time when the press would emphasize the difficulties—and there are many—of policing such a shift. But I can't forget that the 300 million slaves of Hitler, after they are freed, will live at a lower standard of diet during the first year of liberation than during the last year of servitude. The Nazi scorched earth policy will add to the European shortages. But I'd trust Wallace in preference to anyone else in the world to cope with and conquer this problem.

I'm reminded of a story, probably apocryphal but still most probable. Harry Luce was supposed to be in conversation with capable charming David Bowes-Lyons, who ably acted for England in the United States on psychological warfare problems. The talk supposedly took place on a boat coming from England to New York.

Luce was raising hell with the British in India. This was long before Gandhi betrayed our American Freedom for India agitators by conceding the necessity of governmental racial states. Quiet Bowes-Lyons demurred to Luce's absolutism with factual evidence of population troubles, racial problems, dangers of Moslems and Hindus killing each other off, and the unspeakable problem of the untouchables. All to no avail. Luce insisted we would smash the Empire and free India.

Bowes-Lyons is supposed to have said, "You know, if I weren't the Queen's brother I would be tempted to give lectures in the United States, particularly on the problems of Puerto Rico and the American Negro."

To which Luce, quite typically, is said to have replied, "You'd better shut your mouth, it's none of your damn business."

Wallace, far from being doctrinaire, sticks to his business, is informed, sure, quiet and strong. The opposition has tried to discredit him by picturing him as a man of ideals or even as a dreamer, as if that were anathema. But the labor unions, farmers and middle-class people are no longer fooled by the phony slanting of much of our press. They know he ran Agriculture, a department with over 80,000 employees, and ran it efficiently and with no slightest rumor of corruption or maladministration.

He has never had around him any glamour builders-up, but there is glamour inside of Henry. Something blocks him from showing it. A kind of personal humility—that greatest of all human traits.

Sometime ago he sent me a picture of himself. The inscription read: "To Morris L. Ernst." I hapened to remark to a mutual friend that the inscription typified one of the differences between F.D.R. or Al Smith and Henry Wallace. The former, when writing to even a casual acquaintance, made the recipient feel a close kinship. This criticism got back to the Vice-President. Another picture came along with a lush and flattering inscription. As with most flattery, I like that which is furthest from the truth. I wrote Henry Wallace to thank him, said my face was red, but that it was about time he stopped being afraid to show personal affection by word or writing. I think Wallace is a great person, and an invaluable selfless public servant.

That he failed to obtain party political support for renomi-
nation for the Vice-Presidency might mean merely that he is
closer to the idealism of the people of our nation than to the
lower vision of some political chieftains. I would bet on him
as an important leader of our nation in years to come. His
selfless fortitude in behalf of Roosevelt and Truman in the
campaign added to his stature. Out of his defeat for the vice-
presidential nomination he will experience, I believe, an
enriching suffering; a suffering which will add to his gaiety,
personal warmth and even wider popular acclaim.

FERTILIZER FOR THE FARMS OF EUROPE

One of my own little tidbits is coming through. Today I
got a cable from England to gather material about fertilizing
the farms of liberated Europe. I have long felt that the
farmers of Europe will find more hope in nitrate or phosphate
for their starved soil than in imported bread and milk and
food. Those farmers were rich and proud. The Nazis have
sterilized the land of Europe. They have robbed the soil so
that it may take years to bring it back to old-time fertility.

I do hope we will soon announce to the people of Europe
that we are coming with fertilizer. Men can tighten belts if
grain is in sight. Having wasted our own soil—profligate in
acres as we were, we moved west leaving rich lands eroded
and denuded of life-giving powers—we have learned our
lesson. The TVA has written our present great gospel of the
soil. It would be a fitting declaration of our new knowledge
and faith to go on the radio and say to liberated Europe:

The Nazis have withdrawn on a scorched earth policy. We
are coming with the means of life. For a short time after
liberation you will be worse off than under Nazi slavery. But
we are bringing you seed and medicine for your soil. This
is your golden sunrise. Two-thirds of the people of this planet
are engaged solely in growing food—even though a century
has gone by since the start of the industrial revolution. Pick
up the meager soil in your hands. Let it sift through your

[274]

fingers. Look at its lifeless shreds, for soon hope comes to you to grow food and prosper once more. Never again will bandits starve your soil.

It occurs to me that this interest of mine dates back to the time I represented the farmers of Long Island during the improbable regime of Mayor John F. Hylan. Our big city—so dependent on the daily intake of food—had no concern for those long lines of trucks that brought us life. Into the jaws of racketeers at our market places they drove. Since that time we started certain minor reforms, but probably one of the greatest preventable wastes of our city and nation is connected with needless expenditure of manpower and money in bringing food from farms to the mouths of our people.

CHAPTER XLVI

NO MORE KROCKING

RECENTLY I GAVE MY FIRST and, I hope, my last big party. It was a dinner to Sumner Welles.

I happened to be with Welles in his office when the "Krock" piece on the front page of the *Times* started the final drive to get Welles out of government service. I detest the cheap use of news stories to level charges which, if they belong anywhere at all, should be found in editorial columns. Here was a devoted public servant needlessly lost to the nation, at least temporarily. I leave aside entirely any alleged differences in personal relationship or in international attitudes between Welles and Mr. Hull. My ire is directed at the use of so-called news reports to drive men out of office. I had lived through a similar episode with Leon Henderson, when he headed the OPA.

In talking to Swing, Thompson, Gunther, Shirer and many

other friends, I came to realize that the Krocks of the press were intent on doing a job of no dissimilar proportions on Stettinius of Lend-Lease and Elmer Davis of OWI. Incidentally, I have never met Krock as far as I can remember, but I abhor his type of attack. I even prefer nasty hard-hitting Pegler with whom, of course, I disagree on practically all his tactics as well as on matters of taste. I just don't like one-sided snipers. I like my opponents tough and direct.

With the Krock episode in mind I gave Sumner a party and invited about forty people, owners of radio, press—leaders of public opinion. All those present admired Welles. We deplored his departure from present political usefulness. And I knew it was our own fault. I was ashamed. We just hadn't been in there pitching against the anti-Welles forces. Had we stood up and made ourselves heard we would not have had to do special honor to Welles on that evening. And I said with complete sincerity that I gave the dinner in the hope that I would save the expense of giving further valedictory parties for Stettinius, Davis and others.

We can't develop a trained group of devoted selfless public servants with a shabby element riding so much of the press. If the snipers would state alleged facts, then debates could reach the truth. If they dared state sources and name names, the man to be "done in" would have a chance to make a defense. It's easy to say: "Why pay attention to the Krocks? Why not treat them with disdain?" But life doesn't work that way. That front-page gossip story—emanating from a still unnamed source, resting on anonymity, the tool of cowards, was to be used as tinder for all the nonheterogeneous opponents of Welles. Anti-Russians, isolationists, and others took up the fire. The Washington office of the *Times* would not have given the same amount of front-page space to answer the attack, even if an anonymous rumor could ever be answered.

I'm told by some that Krock disclaims the discredit for the job and I'm confident his great paper regrets the episode. But Krock is head of the Washington Bureau from which the piece emanated and on his own theory of resting responsibility on the men at the top, he might well have resigned if he applied to himself the sanctimonious standards he applies so glibly to his political opponents.

I pick on Krock particularly because he writes for our most significant and greatest daily newspaper, and his attacks on nearly all the followers of the President are usually of the same snide quality. Years ago at a dinner in Washington, called to discuss the impropriety of Krock's use of power, one of the leading officials of the nation ended the evening by saying: "I'm truly embarrassed because every week or so Krock commends me and my confreres."

Some say that the answer to this kind of journalism should be for those under attack to write answering letters to the papers. But that is less than feasible. A letter snucked away in a letter column is no answer. Moreover, for Krock's prey to rise up and hit back at innuendo would be playing into Krock's hands. In the old days of the press, papers debated with each other and editors felt strongly enough on issues to horsewhip each other at times. Today that corrective is considered impolite. I know that conscientious, informed Anne O'Hare McCormick does not see eye to eye with Krock. I see the brave New York *Post* taking up, through Grafton and in editorials, answers to Krock and others by name. But in general a class loyalty pervades our press where few papers permit criticism of so-called competitors. In fact, the press is in the "after you, Gaston" doldrums. The better papers should remember the effect on the decent utility companies when they were staying in bed with H. C. Hopson of the Associated Gas and other really evil light and power influences. Unless that portion of the press which has integrity slaps down the antisocial news publishers, the entire press will be tainted as a single unit by a disgusted public. Maybe the revitalization of the press will be delayed until all columnists and editors who disagree with a Krock (including his own editors perchance) will answer back, point by point. Maybe such criticism of the Krocks of the press would persuade them to rely on facts, creditable and from disclosed public sources.

I'm not a softie in the field of criticism of public servants. I think it wholesome that they be kept on their toes by a vigilant press. I'm in favor of the pushing around of our officials. But must we keep on tripping them up with concealed strings? Must we continue to have sneaky nudges from hidden corners? The press should stop krocking. A new verb should be added to our language—"to krock"—example: Stop krocking me.

HEROES UNSUNG

At least two other great public servants have been concealed from the American public. I don't mean that their names are unknown, nor that much space has not been given to their undertakings. I do mean that they have been depicted primarily from the opposition angle, since most of the press was opposed to their efforts.

I met Congressman Warren Magnuson (now U.S. senator) of Seattle, Washington, at Drew Pearson's one night recently. It was a gay evening with Senator Kilgore, Edgar Hoover, Roald Dahl of gremlin fame, Walter Winchell and some others—a bantering stag group. In chatting with Congressman Magnuson, a member of the original Cox (now Lee) Committee of the House to investigate the Federal Communications Commission, I twitted him about the recent front-page story (March 8, 1944) in the New York Times. Here was a diatribe taken down from a speech by Congressman Miller of Missouri, attacking Jim Fly, chairman of the FCC. It was the usual anti-administration type of criticism—unsupported by the evidence, with sole reliance on surmise and innuendo—a krockish speech. Why did tough Congressman Magnuson let Congressman Miller get away with that kind of stuff? I am not naïve, but Magnuson's reply shocked me. He told me that for several days he had known of the impending Miller attack on the floor of the House. He remained patiently at his seat in the House so as not to miss the chance to answer promptly. He did so. Plaintively Congressman Magnuson told me the outline of his answer, deliberate and nondemagogic. And then he added that he didn't expect a break from Krock, columnist and manager of the *Times* Washington office, but he added, "Don't you think, no matter how anti-Fly they are, they might have put a footnote at the bottom of Congressman Miller's long reported speech 'Magnuson also spoke'?"

No, he had no right to expect it. Calling names is news. Defense of decent public service gets no headlines. And in so far as men like Krock hold power, that is just what we are in for. What happened to Sumner Welles, a great public servant, is another example of the same kind of use of the press.

James L. Fly, head of the FCC, and David Lilienthal, of TVA, hold two of the toughest jobs in our body politic. Lilienthal, quiet, unassuming, selfless, heads the TVA which in centuries to come may be appraised as the most significant domestic adventure of our generation. Fly is the fighting attorney who beat the entire utility crowd, including its spearhead, Wendell Willkie of Commonwealth and Southern, in the five years of court battle waged to prevent TVA's coming into existence.

It took both types of men to convert the blueprints of the TVA into a reality for the 4½ million people whose soil and spirit have been fertilized by the dams and their wide-flowing benefits. In TVA there is no placard giving immortality to Lilienthal or Fly, even though every mayor of any big city gets his name tableted on airports, incinerators and school buildings.

Lilienthal's reputation is greater outside the United States than here at home. Sir Harold Hartley, England's great power expert, truly believes that TVA as run by Lilienthal is one of the most hopeful answers to raising the standard of living of peoples of the world. For my part I am convinced that a few TVA dams on the Danube would do more for Balkan confederation than all the conventions and agreements prepared by statesmen and lawyers. Peoples' lives are built on

[279]

economic realities rather than on printed phrases. Cheap power reduces the need of costly powder.

Jim Fly is the advocate type, heading a commission which regulates those very interests which can turn public opinion against him and his commission. Moreover, one-third of our radio stations are dominated by newspapers and it is no wonder that Fly seldom gets a fair break on the radio or in the press which owns the radio. Radio stations at least must by law make a pretense of impartiality in discussing controversial election subjects.

After I testified at hearings condemning the peril of having an increasing number of our radio stations owned by the press, I took occasion to check on the reports in those papers which owned broadcasting stations. I don't refer only to reports of my own testimony. I found that the hearings were disregarded by many radio-owning papers save on those days when a pro-paper-radio witness testified. I discovered that only a handful of papers had the decency to tell their readers to discount the possible prejudices of the paper because it owned a station and might be less than objective.

What a job Fly has done. Congressmen are timid in opposing the networks, because they want to get on the air. Religious groups are bought off the path of objectivity by getting free time. In the monopoly suit against the three networks, a kindly, innocent divine such as the Reverend Harry Emerson Fosdick attacked the FCC. I wrote him. He wrote me he had never read the commission's Monopoly Report! We have a long way to go before the owners of air monopolies learn that their franchises are public trusts. William Paley, head of CBS, and David Sarnoff, head of NBC, have taken a long while to get under their skins the idea that radio is the people's instrument and that their companies, making at times much over 100 per cent annual profits before taxes on their depreciated investment, are deeply affected with a public interest. These two dominating characters, despite their great contributions, have stupidly planted in the public mind, by repeatedly shouting government ownership, the concept of government ownership of radio. They must know that Fly and the entire commission and administration oppose government ownership. Their tactics are creating a public demand for government radio. I am confident that government radio would be a real calamity for us, although in England it works. I much prefer all the evils of advertising impact to the danger of our government's running our radio programs, except for foreign short-wave, which is in a way a branch of our foreign services. Fly has prevented the networks from completely owning the air of America, and he has done it without the least trace of government censorship. Not unlike the press, these radio magnates are shouting freedom of the air when they really mean freedom to dominate the air for their own attitudes and profits.

During the contest in the courts over the efforts—ultimately successful—of the FCC to prevent the major networks from restricting, by contracts with associated stations, the use of the ether, not a single network would allow even a forum discussion of the problem. The American Civil Liberties Union telegraphed to CBS, NBC and Mutual to suggest radio debates on the issues involved, issues which the first two networks thought of sufficient significance to warrant gathering an army of high-paid lawyers to contest. Not a chance! NBC went so far as to telegraph in reply:

May 19, 1941.

THANK YOU VERY MUCH FOR YOUR TELEGRAM OFFERING TO BE OF ASSISTANCE TO US IN ARRANGING A PROGRAM IN CONNECTION WITH THE RECENT REGULATIONS ADOPTED BY THE FEDERAL COMMUNICATIONS COMMISSION. WE RECEIVED NOTICE TODAY THAT THE SENATE INTERSTATE COMMERCE COMMITTEE HAS CALLED A HEARING BEGINNING MAY 31ST TO CONSIDER THE RESOLUTION INTRODUCED BY SENATOR WHITE OF MAINE. I FEEL THAT PRIOR TO THAT TIME IT WOULD BE BETTER TO DEFER ANY RADIO FORUM DISCUSSIONS ON THE SUBJECT.

To which I answered in effect: "I suppose you would not allow discussion of Lend-Lease legislation at a time when a

Committee of Congress was considering that ingenious product of the President's mind!!"

This same pattern of silence was evident in the reporting of the government monopoly suit against the Associated Press, although any violent speech by any congressman attacking the government's position got full coverage. An article supporting the government, such as the great statement of Professor Zechariah Chafee of Harvard, found scant space in our press. Three great New York papers and syndicates refused it. The stories carried by the press on the day when the Circuit Court of Appeals spanked the AP and decided for the government must have seemed unintelligible to the judges themselves. The news reports in the papers, in many cases, led readers to believe that the AP had won the case.

With our press in its present mood, it is simple to drive out of office practically any public servant. A well-recognized technique is to "resign" an official. Constant and repeated reports of an impending resignation can undermine the ablest officeholder, although a few like Frances Perkins ride out the storms. It is ironic that as soon as certain officials are driven out of office the attacking interests compete for their services. Leon Henderson, our leading over-all economist and the type of tough official I like, no sooner had left OPA in 1943, after being vilified by much of the press, than utilities which had opposed him, investment trusts he had laid bare in the great monopoly investigation, TNEC, and bankers galore wanted to buy his brain and ingenuity. Likewise for Milo Perkins, and many other great public servants.

The more the opposition derided Roosevelt and his family the more I found great numbers of these same "haters" making fabulous financial proffers to the President's sons to take employment with them. It doesn't add up to anything decent. Some frank critic of the young prewar Roosevelt sons should do an apologia and relate in simple terms what each of these four Americans has done in this war. He will find four stirring tales well worth telling, but the papers which rode them at every turn seem to think there is no story in

F.D.R. Jr. at Salerno, or in Jimmy on the commando raids in the Pacific, or in Elliott flying 18,000 miles to take pictures of African Nazi airports, or in quiet John, wangling out of safe shore duty to ride the seas.

CHAPTER XLVII

THE ROOSEVELTS

MUCH OF THE PAST FIFTEEN YEARS of my life has been colored and enriched by Franklin and Eleanor Roosevelt. I confess that whenever I have been with either I came away feeling that life can be made good for all people. As Margaret says to Roosevelt-haters—a species bitter and unpersuadable: "We pity you. You are missing so much—living in these days without affection for the President and Mrs. R."

Not the least of my great good fortune has been my opportunities to add in minor untitled ways to the Roosevelt stream —a stream rich and exciting. The President's pursuit for our nation has been varied in dimensions and in pace. Its direction has been constant, enriching ever-wider fields and touching ever-greater numbers of our people. Being without public responsibility, never holding an elective mandate, I have at times thought the pace too slow, but on looking back I am unable to find a single Roosevelt objective which the people, or any political party, would cancel or deny. Financially secure, the President approaches aggregation of wealth without the latent envies or the bitterness which is the habit of ordinary reformers, most of whom have never had the feel of a checkbook. Not Hoover, Landon, Willkie or Dewey— the four counterspokesmen of the nation—has ever fallen into the folly of attacking the F.D.R. program now firmly embedded in our folkway and articulated by legislation. The President's objectives have convenient tags and initials—SEC, NLRB, AAA, etc. In their living reality they touch cheating of security buyers, rights of workers to choose their leaders, pensions for the aged, relief for those who are excluded from work through no fault of their own, and such a myriad of human needs as to represent the single greatest era in our nation's social growth.

In its essence, this program deals with power—the balances of power. To many it seemed violent and paced too fast. I suggest that increased pace was made necessary by the social lag of the Harding-Hoover-Coolidge era. President Roosevelt saw that a buyer of a share of stock had no power to use judgment against organized concealment of truth. He knew that few men and women had the power to save enough to live an old age in freedom from want. He sensed the power of employers operating against unorganized workers in a market place full of surplus, hungry people.

I have often pondered the source of this Rooseveltian appraisal of undue power. It became clear to me one bright afternoon at Hyde Park. I crashed a party through Connie, who had been working on the 1940 Roosevelt radio broadcasts—and more particularly the election eve program which, at least to a proud father, seemed to touch new spiritual fibers in our body politic. I recall that the next day—even though election day—I happened to be at my desk. The phone rang. The President on the phone. He didn't want to talk to me. He called to tell Connie how much he had enjoyed the broadcast.

At Hyde Park I concluded that the extra quality—that last bit of spice—which distinguishes him—stems from his infirmity. Out of that calamity he has accepted life—including his handicap. Vile lies about his illness, circulated with peculiar volume and venom every four years, fail to embitter him. His finger tips touched the scythe, his eyes must have seen the river. Compassion and understanding took the place of hate. Man can be gayer and more objective to the extent that he has suffered or neared death. At times my friends have complained that F.D.R. hates too little and too few. Whether asset or not, it is the fact. I can think of only two people whom the President has deeply disparaged for years.

He is no proletarian in the revolutionary use of the term. But with a feeling of kinship with the small shopkeepers of his district, Hyde Park, he felt intuitively the dangers of giants—a danger which Louis D. Brandeis discerned only after years of research. Like Brandeis, he never resents power which rests on imagination or work habits. Power for power's sake is the evil force to be opposed. Thus he fought the Stock Exchange, the utility tycoons, the National Association of Manufacturers, with a twinkle in his eye, because he knew that Richard Whitney, H. C. Hopson and Samuel Insull were just a little ridiculous in the United States of the 1930's. As a lawyer, he early agreed with old Judge Holmes that "the true grounds of decision are considerations of policy and of social advantage, and it is vain to suppose that solutions can be attained merely by logic and the general propositions of law which nobody disputes."

Leaders of the Bar disparage Roosevelt the lawyer, but I suggest that the Roosevelt prognosis of the constitutionality of minimum wage, child labor legislation, TVA, the Utility Holding Act and all his legislation was better advice for clients to follow than the panicked protests of unconstitutionality uttered by most of the leading lawyers of the land. He guessed the old Supreme Court wrong on NRA, the mechanism used by the giants to negate the antitrust laws.

But if I am right in my feeling that his objectives are quite free from criticism, if it is true that he operated within the frames of our constitution—a fluid instrument, to be sure—critics then shift to their final plea that the President is less than a good executive. This is no place to debate that issue —for which I have never seen a bill of particulars. But when all the evidence is in I probably would rely on Quentin Reynolds's answer when returning from distant battlefields and confronted with grumblings as to breakdown of our government: "Somebody did a hell of a job back here. Somebody did a hell of a job. Could it have been F.D.R.?"

Franklin Roosevelt has been accused inconsistently of being both a dictator and a weakling. He is neither. His glands deny the former; his zest for life the latter.

This zest has caused gaps in some of his relationships. Essentially humorless people like Robert Moses and John L. Lewis never could meet the Roosevelt mind, a mind which picks other brains by jests, by quips, by needling. Since F.D.R. is less than laconic or taciturn, it is not easy to gauge how he learns so much from others. To him every query is a challenge to a mental joust.

Eleanor Roosevelt is essential to Franklin Roosevelt, entirely apart from her own generous and substantial contribution to our way of life. As a roving reporter she is used as a foil by the man in the chair. She stands up to him—no meager chore, for he is the most agile of all our social engineers. Knowing her slants and predilections, he can discount as he sees fit. But stand up she does, as few of the liberal adventurous people around the President have been willing to do. I know that he likes best those who are tough with him, although this judgment of mine is not easy to prove against the record of Henry A. Wallace, Sumner Welles and Milo Perkins—temporarily outside the immediate circle. As to these great public servants, I suggest that history might write each episode in terms of choice of immediate desires. Who can be sure that the resignation of Mr. Hull would have been less of a loss in terms of attaining international agreements than the resignation of Welles?

In an inconsequential way I've been on the slugger side. Too often those who have deplored as a weakness of F.D.R. his letting down of a Henderson or other devoted public servant were the very snipers who brought them to earth. Some of those who cried the most bitter crocodile tears at Wallace's defeat in Chicago were pitching for some other candidate for vice-president up to the last moment of the final ballot.

In the main, the President is a softie only in the sense that he hates to fire anyone. Kicking upstairs, promoting, changing titles—nearly anything rather than discharge an honest selfless devoted public servant. It's a tender fault, not too costly, and due above all to the usually divided and confused liberal support for the President against the demands of the press and reactionaries for someone's hide.

Of course I'm prejudiced. My judgment may play me a trick because I have seen that great man pull victory gaily out of despair; compromise, if that's the word, in his fight for greater democracy at home in order not to imperil international democracy. I have never met anyone who, having left the President, is not amazed at his agility of mind and his grasp of the boring details of the daily operation of our government. It may be that too much of his energy is consumed by details, but even that conclusion can only survive against proof of his desertion of larger problems, proof which I fail to see in any indictment. The answer might be in his excess energy. Like Mrs. R., he wastes no energy on indecision or regret, the two greatest consumers of human libido. He is comfortable with himself. He can sleep at night—a capacity essential for survival in these less than calm days. He can wait, have patience, pick his moments. As a skipper of small sailboats he must have learned that to stop going forward is to go backward. He knows that unless you move ahead you soon find yourself clawing off a lee shore. He can be casual in a calm or in a blow—knowing that life never depends on the isolated choice of a single moment. Moments and choices are seldom isolated in time or effect. This sense of timing irritates both his impatient friends and all his enemies eagerly ready to pounce on premature moves. His daily immobility must have increased his sense of the nearness of distance and his feeling of the historic flow of years.

After I have explored the President's programs, faced his easy charm, I still find myself most impressed by his ability to pore over millions of words of reports each year, reports from each and every little bureau and agency of our too-big government. Among those who live life as an adventure, few develop the craftsmanship needed to cope with day-by-day decisions. It's too easy to dismiss a dream with a generality, although without the solution of the implements of the dream it easily becomes a nightmare.

If I had my choice as to one book which should be compulsory reading for all our people, it would be the debates of the Constitutional Convention—May to September, 1787. Thirteen little nations, after a war fought on a vague united nations basis, faced all the difficulties of today in working out an international relationship, desirable in peace.

And as I reread those debates of 1787 I have concluded that Franklin Roosevelt combines within himself the most desirable attributes of James Madison and of Benjamin Franklin, without whom, and for very different reasons, we would not have organized our nation.

Benjamin Franklin acquired his breadth of approach, his disarming gaiety, from the security of old age. Living could do nothing more to him—of hurt or harm. F.D.R. learned all this in that split second at Campobello, Maine, in August, 1921.

When I reread the record of the Convention, June 28, 1787, I can think of no other American save F.D.R. who would have chosen the path old Ben used to hold the Convention together and assure us a nation. The last great Setting Sun speech of gay loquacious Ben, declaring faith in our future, might still find its counterpart over the air waves of the entire world as a warming fireplace chat of F.D.R.

And as I relive 1787—my favorite period of history—I see James Madison, not officially the secretary of the Convention, nevertheless sitting under the dais on which George Washington presided, taking down with a quill pen every word spoken during those four trying months of secret meetings. It was Madison who checked every detail, every plan, every proposal, every word. No comma was unimportant. Unconvivial, serious to the point of early remoteness from his fellow men, Madison had resorted to digging into the interstices of government. F.D.R. in his bed and in his chair has relaxed with blueprints of the management of democratic society as if they were the architectural scale drawings of some building he has seen in a dream.

We are lucky people to have had a Benjamin Franklin-James Madison merger in F.D.R. And as for luck, I am sure no one credits more to that phantom than F.D.R. himself. I doubt if he ever forgets that in his first campaign for governor of New York in 1928, a now unknown Republican running against him would have been elected by a shift of 12,783 votes. That shift might have shifted history.

CHAPTER XLVIII

END OF VOLUME I

So far so good. At least good for me, good beyond my dreams or hopes. Early I learned that the area of misery is that barren aching gap between one's reach and one's dreams. Automatically I pull in my dreams—a far simpler trick for me than extending my capabilities. As a reflex I say, "That's not for me—but I have so much anyway." Only those who are thirsty cry over spilt milk. Good breaks have not, it seems to me, made me less passionate or intense than I was decades ago—maybe I'm more excited about more desires than in my phlegmatic youth. No one can hear with distinctive recognition his own voice, or describe for other minds a color, a taste or an odor. We human beings have egos which create a static interference with our own appraisal.

It's idle for me to list my benefactors—a father with enough vitality to flee, after the '48ers, from the outrages in Czechoslovakia. Immigrant stock is enriching influence in

[289]

the American folkway. A mother—one of the early graduates from a woman's college. A conscientious sister and a truly just brother. I think I like the attribute of "just" better than any other I know. Then also the president of my Twenty-Year Club—Paula Gross, the manager of my office life. My family, my friends, and my partners. These are my personal circumference. Varying in distance and time they have flattered, scolded, criticized and affected me in myriad ways—not always to their satisfaction or even my own. But touching the circumference as a moving cosine there was always luck.

If luck sloughs off, memory of episodes and human warmths may return some emotional investments I have made. But I doubt if I will ever be able to accept memory as a basic diet. That would seem somewhat like whistling in the dark, for I anticipate a new adventure every time I walk down the stoop of my home. I haven't learned how to live on life —rather do I live life. Maybe I will find a single ambition— a solitary emphasis. But that would be an odd circuit for one with my moods of easy excitability.

I've just planned to order a new kind of weather instrument to be made by a shaggy-haired worker at the Orange Street weather bureau. I want one single instrument to record temperature, barometric pressure, wind velocity, wind direction and humidity. Next year I hope to play with the inky paths of these simple phenomena scratched on finely ruled rolls of paper. Man's greatest master is weather. Correlations will ever be the guess and enigma of man. They are the jigsaw puzzle of our universe. Brashly I still believe that not all questions and answers are ineluctably written in calculus. Increasingly I find my greatest joy in search for odd flashes of cause and effect—flashes which make little sense to those fully informed, but give me satisfying insights into my own dark corners.

Society is at last accumulating a few scant statistics depicting the impact of law on our daily lives, charting the effect of ideas on the behavior of man, depicting the suicidal effects of personal greed and excess power in industry and government. With such new tools, the practice of the law should take on fresh meaning.

I find myself increasingly interested in man's frustrating fears of the mind's product. Why are most lives bent more by fear than by hope? What greater force for mental standstill exists than the tremble of the timid? Are not more errors committed in the name of deliberation than under the banner of impulse?

The law is on the march. It is growing up. It is no longer solely a defender of status quo. The industrial revolution is being pursued by a spiritual rebellion. With the reduction of want and fortunes we will see that there is no inconsistency in defending personal liberty and individual property, for whenever property is taken from a people who are free from want a piece of freedom goes with the seizure, although property can be voted away without any loss of liberty. The game of law will become still more exciting just because it has lagged for a half century, playing the reckless tune of laissez-faire in a world too big to exist unorganized or un-planned. With planning for us all we preserve unscathed a greater area of personal movement. With taxes we buy our daily co-operative living.

In the new stream of jurisprudence we face the perils of a too-big government—a government taking on functions before it has been educated to cope with novel situations. If the government grows too vast for its own breeches it will resent critics and suppress objectors—ending in that sterility of the human mind known as totalitarianism.

I've never planned my life. Each fall I wonder what new thrills will come across my desk. Fortuity has an extra spice separate and apart from its rival reality. Whether life rides me along or I feel that I am the driver I know that if I slip off its back I have Margaret, Connie, Roger and Joan—my friends—who each in a distinctive way will help as in the past to set me straight. If not straight—at least straighter.

Set in Linotype Electra
Format by A. W. Rushmore
Manufactured by the Haddon Craftsmen
Published by HARPER & BROTHERS
New York and London